El Salvador

WORLD BIBLIOGRAPHICAL SERIES
General Editors:
Robert G. Neville (Executive Editor)
John J. Horton   Ian Wallace
Hans H. Wellisch   Ralph Lee Woodward, Jr.

John J. Horton is Deputy Librarian of the University of Bradford and currently Chairman of its Academic Board of Studies in Social Sciences. He has maintained a longstanding interest in the discipline of area studies and its associated bibliographical problems, with special reference to European Studies. In particular he has published in the field of Icelandic and of Yugoslav studies, including the two relevant volumes in the World Bibliographical Series.

Ian Wallace is Professor of Modern Languages at Loughborough University of Technology. A graduate of Oxford in French and German, he also studied in Tübingen, Heidelberg and Lausanne before taking teaching posts at universities in the USA, Scotland and England. He specializes in East German affairs, especially literature and culture, on which he has published numerous articles and books. In 1979 he founded the journal *GDR Monitor*, which he continues to edit.

Hans H. Wellisch is Professor emeritus at the College of Library and Information Services, University of Maryland. He was President of the American Society of Indexers and was a member of the International Federation for Documentation. He is the author of numerous articles and several books on indexing and abstracting, and has published *The Conversion of Scripts* and *Indexing and Abstracting: an International Bibliography*. He also contributes frequently to *Journal of the American Society for Information Science, The Indexer* and other professional journals.

Ralph Lee Woodward, Jr. is Chairman of the Department of History at Tulane University, New Orleans, where he has been Professor of History since 1970. He is the author of *Central America, a Nation Divided*, 2nd ed. (1985), as well as several monographs and more than sixty scholarly articles on modern Latin America. He has also compiled volumes in the World Bibliographical Series on *Belize* (1980), *Nicaragua* (1983), and *El Salvador*. Dr. Woodward edited the Central American section of the *Research Guide to Central America and the Caribbean* (1985) and is currently editor of the Central American history section of the *Handbook of Latin American Studies*.

VOLUME 98

El Salvador

Ralph Lee Woodward, Jr.
Compiler

CLIO PRESS
OXFORD, ENGLAND · SANTA BARBARA, CALIFORNIA
DENVER, COLORADO

British Library Cataloguing in Publication Data

Woodward, Ralph Lee
El Salvador.—(World bibliographical
series : 98)
1.El Salvador. Bibliographies
I.Title
96.97284

ISBN 1–85109–073–8

Clio Press Ltd.,
55 St. Thomas' Street,
Oxford OX1 1JG, England.

ABC-Clio Information Services,
Riviera Campus, 2040 Alameda Padre Serra,
Santa Barbara, CA 93103, USA.

Designed by Bernard Crossland
Typeset by Columns Design and Production Services, Reading, England.
Printed and bound in Great Britain by
Billing and Sons Ltd., Worcester

THE WORLD BIBLIOGRAPHICAL SERIES

This series, which is principally designed for the English speaker, will
eventually cover every country in the world, each in a separate volume
comprising annotated entries on works dealing with its history,
geography, economy and politics; and with its people, their culture,
customs, religion and social organization. Attention will also be paid to
current living conditions – housing, education, newspapers, clothing,
etc. – that are all too often ignored in standard bibliographies; and to
those particular aspects relevant to individual countries. Each volume
seeks to achieve, by use of careful selectivity and critical assessment of
the literature, an expression of the country and an appreciation of its
nature and national aspirations, to guide the reader towards an
understanding of its importance. The keynote of the series is to provide,
in a uniform format, an interpretation of each country that will express
its culture, its place in the world, and the qualities and background that
make it unique. The views expressed in individual volumes are not
necessarily those of the publishers.

VOLUMES IN THE SERIES

1 *Yugoslavia*, John J. Horton
2 *Lebanon*, Shereen Khairallah
3 *Lesotho*, Shelagh M. Willet and
David Ambrose
4 *Rhodesia/Zimbabwe*, Oliver B.
Pollack and Karen Pollack
5 *Saudi Arabia*, Frank A. Clements
6 *USSR*, Anthony Thompson
7 *South Africa*, Reuben Musiker
8 *Malawi*, Robert B. Boeder
9 *Guatemala*, Woodman B. Franklin
11 *Uganda*, Robert L. Collison
12 *Malaysia*, Ian Brown and
Rajeswary Ampalavanar
13 *France*, Frances Chambers
14 *Panama*, Eleanor DeSelms
Langstaff
15 *Hungary*, Thomas Kabdebo
16 *USA*, Sheila R. Herstein and
Naomi Robbins
17 *Greece*, Richard Clogg and Mary
Jo Clogg
18 *New Zealand*, R. F. Grover
19 *Algeria*, Richard I. Lawless
20 *Sri Lanka*, Vijaya Samaraweera
21 *Belize*, Ralph Lee Woodward, Jr.
23 *Luxembourg*, Carlo Hury and Jul
Christophory

24 *Swaziland*, Balam Nyeko
25 *Kenya*, Robert L. Collison
26 *India*, Brijen K. Gupta and Datta
S. Kharbas
27 *Turkey*, Merel Güçlü
28 *Cyprus*, P. M. Kiromilides and
M. L. Evriviades
29 *Oman*, Frank A. Clements
31 *Finland*, J. E. O. Screen
32 *Poland*, Richard C. Lewański
33 *Tunisia*, Allan M. Findlay, Anne
M. Findlay and Richard
I. Lawless
34 *Scotland*, Eric G. Grant
35 *China*, Peter Cheng
36 *Qatar*, P. T. H. Unwin
37 *Iceland*, John J. Horton
39 *Haiti*, Frances Chambers
40 *Sudan*, M. W. Daly
41 *Vatican City State*, Michael
J. Walsh
42 *Iraq*, A. J. Abdulrahman
43 *United Arab Emirates*, Frank
A. Clements
44 *Nicaragua*, Ralph Lee
Woodward, Jr.
45 *Jamaica*, K. E. Ingram
46 *Australia*, I. Kepars

47 *Morocco*, Anne M. Findlay, Allan M. Findlay and Richard I. Lawless

48 *Mexico*, Naomi Robbins

49 *Bahrain*, P. T. H. Unwin

50 *The Yemens*, G. Rex Smith

51 *Zambia*, Anne M. Bliss and J. A. Rigg

52 *Puerto Rico*, Elena E. Cevallos

53 *Namibia*, Stanley Schoeman and Elna Schoeman

54 *Tanzania*, Colin Darch

55 *Jordan*, Ian J. Seccombe

56 *Kuwait*, Frank A. Clements

57 *Brazil*, Solena V. Bryant

58 *Israel*, Esther M. Snyder (preliminary compilation E. Kreiner)

59 *Romania*, Andrea Deletant and Dennis Deletant

60 *Spain*, Graham J. Shields

61 *Atlantic Ocean*, H. G. R. King

63 *Cameroon*, Mark W. DeLancey and Peter J. Schraeder

64 *Malta*, John Richard Thackrah

65 *Thailand*, Michael Watts

66 *Austria*, Denys Salt with the assistance of Arthur Farrand Radley

67 *Norway*, Leland B. Sather

68 *Czechoslovakia*, David Short

69 *Irish Republic*, Michael Owen Shannon

70 *Pacific Basin and Oceania*, Gerald W. Fry and Rufino Mauricio

71 *Portugal*, P. T. H. Unwin

72 *West Germany*, Donald S. Detwiler and Ilse E. Detwiler

73 *Syria*, Ian J. Seccombe

74 *Trinidad and Tobago*, Frances Chambers

76 *Barbados*, Robert B. Potter and Graham M. S. Dann

77 *East Germany*, Ian Wallace

78 *Mozambique*, Colin Darch with the assistance of Calisto Pachelete

79 *Libya*, Richard I. Lawless

80 *Sweden*, Leland B. Sather and Alan Swanson

81 *Iran*, Reza Navabpour

82 *Dominica*, Robert A. Myers

83 *Denmark*, Kenneth E. Miller

84 *Paraguay*, R. Andrew Nickson

85 *Indian Ocean*, Julia J. Gotthold with the assistance of Donald W. Gotthold

86 *Egypt*, Ragai N. Makar

87 *Gibraltar*, Graham J. Shields

88 *The Netherlands*, Peter King and Michael Wintle

89 *Bolivia*, Gertrude M. Yeager

90 *Papua New Guinea*, Fraiser McConnell

91 *The Gambia*, David P. Gamble

92 *Somalia*, Mark W. DeLancey, Sheila Elliott, December Green, Kenneth J. Menkhaus, Mohammed Haji Moqtar, Peter J. Schraeder

93 *Brunei*, Sylvia C. Engelen Krausse, Gerald H. Krausse

94 *Albania*, William B. Bland

95 *Singapore*, Stella R. Quah, and Jon S. T. Quah

96 *Guyana*, Frances Chambers

97 *Chile*, Harold Blakemore

98 *El Salvador*, Ralph Lee Woodward, Jr.

For Sue

Contents

INTRODUCTION xiii

THE COUNTRY AND ITS PEOPLE 1
    General 1
    Current events 5

GEOGRAPHY 7
    General surveys 7
    Regional geography 9
    Geology and natural resources 10
    Maps, atlases, and gazetteers 11
    Tourism and travel guides 12
    Sailing directions and cruising guides 13

TRAVELLERS' ACCOUNTS 14

FLORA AND FAUNA 22
    General 22
    Flora 23
    Fauna 24

PREHISTORY AND ARCHAEOLOGY 26

HISTORY 31
    Central America: general 31
    El Salvador: general 34
    Local, urban, regional, and departmental 37
    Hispanic El Salvador (1524–1821) 39
    19th-century El Salvador (1821–1900) 43
    20th-century El Salvador (1900–88) 48

POPULATION 54

NATIONALITIES AND MINORITIES 58

Contents

LANGUAGE 62

FOLKLORE 63

RELIGION 65

SOCIAL CONDITIONS 70
    General   70
    Social structure   71
    Social problems   74

SOCIAL SERVICES, HEALTH, AND WELFARE 76

HUMAN RIGHTS 78
    General   78
    Refugees   81

POLITICS 83
    General Central American political characteristics   83
    Salvadoran political characteristics   84
    The military   93

CONSTITUTION, LAWS, AND JUDICIAL SYSTEM 96

ADMINISTRATION AND LOCAL GOVERNMENT 100

FOREIGN RELATIONS 101
    General   101
    With other Central American states   102
    With the United States   105
    With the United Nations   113

ECONOMICS 114

INVESTMENT, FINANCE, BANKING, AND CURRENCY 123

TRADE 127

INDUSTRY 131

AGRICULTURE 133

TRANSPORT AND COMMUNICATIONS 141

EMPLOYMENT AND MANPOWER 143

LABOUR MOVEMENT AND TRADE UNIONS 145

Contents

STATISTICS 148

ENVIRONMENT 153

EDUCATION 155

SCIENCE AND TECHNOLOGY 159

LITERATURE 160

THE ARTS 164

ARCHITECTURE 166

SPORTS AND RECREATION 167

LIBRARIES, MUSEUMS, AND ARCHIVES 168

JOURNALISM AND PUBLISHING 170

MASS MEDIA 171

PROFESSIONAL PERIODICALS 174

ENCYCLOPAEDIAS AND DIRECTORIES 176

BIBLIOGRAPHIES 178
    General   178
    Topical   180

INDEX OF AUTHORS, TITLES AND SUBJECTS 185

MAP OF EL SALVADOR 215

Introduction

Today the Republic of El Salvador is at one of the most critical points in its history. Torn by civil war and political dissension, with appalling poverty and social injustice, and recuperating from the devastation of a major earthquake in its capital city, it faces the twenty-first century with uncertainty and bitter controversy as to the best way out of its difficulties. This bibliography presents an introduction to the study of this beautiful but unfortunate land which is in many ways a microcosm of the problems of the Third World in general.

El Salvador, named for the Saviour, Jesus of Nazareth, is a city-state that developed around its capital, San Salvador. It is the smallest of the Central American republics in area, but with a population of nearly 6,000,000 it is the most densely populated country on the mainland of the Western hemisphere. The only Central American state without a Caribbean coastline, El Salvador is about 50 miles wide and less than 200 miles in length along a volcanic chain on the Pacific coast between Guatemala, Honduras, and Nicaragua. Active volcanoes dominate the landscape, and earthquakes are frequent in this violent land. Most of the population lives in the valleys of this volcanic chain, at altitudes of 2,000 to 3,000 feet above sea level. The mountain elevation provides a year-round spring-like climate for much of the country, although the coastal plain is normally very hot. As with most of the Pacific coast of North and Central America, relative humidity is usually low. A rainy season from May to October brings most of El Salvador's annual average rainfall of about 80 inches, with dry and often dusty conditions prevailing during the intervening months. The mountains slope to a fertile, alluvial coastal plain along the Pacific, before dropping steeply into the ocean. El Salvador's fertile valleys and coastal plain have determined much of its modern history, as agroexports have been responsible for both the enrichment of a small oligarchy and the impoverishment of the rural masses.

Native American peoples inhabited the area now called El Salvador long before the sixteenth-century Spanish conquest. Some were Mayans, belonging to the dominant civilization of Meso-america during the millennium before the conquest. Ruins of their cities and ceremonial centres remain as evidence of advanced social and economic organization. Among other pre-Columbian peoples there, the Lenca were apparently of early South American origin, while a number of different Nahuat peoples migrated from central Mexico. Among the latter, the most important were the Pipil, who had arrived closer to the time of the Spanish conquest and after the Mayan civilization was already in decline. The Pipil developed dominance in the western part of the region. Although less advanced than the Maya in scientific or artistic ability, the Pipil were more aggressive and warlike, characteristics upon which Salvadorans later built a 'noble savage' mythology of their own superiority over other Central Americans, a development more related to the élite's desire to emphasize Salvadoran difference from the strong Maya heritage of neighbouring Guatemala and Honduras than to any real appreciation for Indian ethnic heritage in El Salvador.

The archaeological record of these pre-Columbian peoples is much less extensive than in neighbouring Guatemala, and survival of Indian culture has also been less notable in El Salvador. Nevertheless, Indian communities were important segments of the population until the 20th century. The vast majority of the modern Salvadoran population, however, are mestizos, descended from both Indian and European forebears.

Spanish rule began in 1524, under the command of the *conquistador* Pedro de Alvarado. Following the conquest of Aztec Mexico (1519-22), Fernán Cortés had sent Alvarado southward. Alvarado and his Indian allies had quickly overrun Guatemala, where he established his capital, and then marched into what is today El Salvador, encountering heavy resistance near the present-day port of Acajutla. As he advanced on Cuscatlán, a Pipil city of perhaps 10,000 at that time, most of the inhabitants fled rather than submit to Alvarado's rule. Subsequent Indian resistance delayed Spanish control of the region for several years. Several times the Spanish abandoned San Salvador, which they first established near Cuscatlán in 1525, but by 1540 Alvarado's forces had secured the region from both Indian rebellion and rival Spanish *conquistadores* in Nicaragua.

War, disease, and the slavery that accompanied the conquest

nearly annihilated the large native population. Although the Spaniards were few in number, their superior technology and organizational skill enabled them to subjugate the natives into a servile work-force. The Indians were parcelled out to the conquerors through the institution known as the *encomienda*, which, although formally abolished along with slavery in 1542, survived in varying forms throughout the colonial period. The Spaniards developed self-sufficient *haciendas*, in feudal style, and developed a relatively decentralized society in which the control of land and labour was the key to social and economic power. A small export trade in cacao, balsam, and, later, in indigo developed around Sonsonate.

Administratively, throughout most of the colonial period El Salvador was part of Guatemala, the principal province in the kingdom of the same name, within the Viceroyalty of New Spain. It was subdivided into *alcaldías mayores* (roughly equivalent to counties) around the major towns, which, in addition to San Salvador, were San Miguel, San Vicente, Santa Ana, and Sonsonate.

In the eighteenth century, the rise of indigo production and the succession of the Spanish monarchy from Habsburg to Bourbon rule brought changes to El Salvador that would greatly affect its subsequent development. The Bourbon kings sought to rejuvenate and modernize the Spanish empire through centralization of authority, stimulation of economic activity, military revitalization, and anticlerical measures designed to decrease the political and economic power of the Roman Catholic Church. Spanish encouragement of trade stimulated increased indigo production and made El Salvador the leading export region of the Kingdom of Guatemala. The rising economic importance of the region's indigo exports contributed to its establishment as an Intendancy in 1786, separate from the province of Guatemala, although it remained within the kingdom under the jurisdiction of the Guatemalan Captain-General. The establishment of the Intendancy of San Salvador marks the emergence of its legal territorial status and may be seen as the beginning of Salvadoran nationalism, a sentiment encouraged by several Spanish Intendants who defended and promoted Salvadoran economic interests. But Salvadoran planters chafed under the economic dominance of Guatemalan merchant capitalists, while the Salvadoran clergy objected on the one hand to the anticlericalism of the Bourbon rule and on the other hand to the conservative ecclesiastical hierarchy in Guatemala. They demanded a separate diocese for San Salvador, which remained under the jurisdiction of the Bishop of Guatemala.

In Guatemala, a major earthquake in 1773 had destroyed the capital city, resulting in a decision to move to a new site (the present Guatemala City). The disruption of the kingdom's capital coinciding with the rise of San Salvador as the major economic producer of the kingdom caused some Salvadoran creoles to favour, unsuccessfully, moving the capital to San Salvador, thus further heightening their rivalry with the Guatemalan élite.

These issues became more acute at the close of the colonial period when a severe economic recession troubled the kingdom. Regional separatism and resentment toward conservative Guatemala made San Salvador a centre for independence sentiment and the stronghold of liberalism in the 19th century. Abortive independence attempts in 1811 and 1814, led by Father Matías Delgado, reflected that sentiment, but were crushed by Guatemalan military force under the command of a new Intendant, José de Aycinena, scion of the most powerful Guatemalan merchant family; this defeat caused further Salvadoran resentment toward its larger neighbour.

Independence from Spain came fairly suddenly on 15 September 1821, when a junta in Guatemala City agreed to endorse the declaration of independence of the Mexican creole Agustín de Iturbide (Plan of Iguala). On 29 September, Salvadoran creoles agreed to independence from Spain, but they resisted incorporation into Iturbide's Mexican Empire and they sought a way out of continued domination from Guatemala City. The resulting military conflict forced the surrender of San Salvador after a long siege by a Mexican-Guatemalan force in 1823, but in the meantime the Mexican Empire itself collapsed. Salvadorans now successfully led the movement to declare Central America independent, and El Salvador became an autonomous state in the United Provinces of Central America on 1 July 1823.

The deep animosities mentioned above and strong differences between conservatives and liberals, however, plagued the administration of the new federal president, a Salvadoran military officer, Manuel José Arce. Eventually, Guatemalan conservatives took over the government of both the federal government and the state government of Guatemala, leading to a bloody civil war from 1826 to 1829. Liberal victory, under the leadership of the Honduran General Francisco Morazán restored Salvadoran importance, and San Salvador became the capital of the federation in 1834.

The Pipil Indian area of El Salvador, however, resisted the liberal development efforts, taxes, and reforms that threatened their land and traditional way of life. Under the leadership of Anastasio Aquino, a major Indian rebellion threatened the stability of the government. Although Morazán's forces were able to suppress this uprising, it weakened the liberals considerably. On the heels of that revolt came a similar and more successful peasant uprising in adjacent Guatemala, which toppled the liberal government there and led to the collapse of the federation when the Guatemalan caudillo Rafael Carrera routed Morazán at Guatemala City in 1840. Conservative strength in Nicaragua and Costa Rica sealed the doom of the federation as each of the individual states began to go their separate ways. Carrera's conservative Guatemalan regime (1839-65) dominated El Salvador through much of the mid-19th century, curtailing the liberal and unionist strength there, but El Salvador was the last of the Central American states, in 1856, to formally declare itself a separate republic.

The rise of General Gerardo Barrios after 1858 marked liberal resurgence. Barrios had commanded the Salvadoran forces in the Central American allied effort to drive the US filibuster William Walker out of Nicaragua (1856-57). Upon his return to El Salvador from that campaign, he became chief-of-state and began a programme of anticlerical and other liberal reforms. While this resulted in an invasion by Guatemala that ended his rule in 1863, the process of liberalization had begun and continued, especially under the rule of Santiago González (1871-76) and Rafael Zaldívar (1876-85).

Liberal dominance, 1871-1944, brought remarkable changes to El Salvador. Independence from Guatemalan intervention was achieved with the defeat and death of the invading Guatemalan dictator, Justo Rufino Barrios, in 1885. The governments that followed concentrated on economic development, as they facilitated the expansion of coffee exports by the planter élite at the expense of peasant land and labour. Indigo exports had continued to be important for El Salvador, but the development of aniline coal-tar dyes diminished its importance after 1860. The loose, volcanic soil and sub-tropical climate was ideal for the production of high-quality coffee, enabling a few planters to become dominant in economic and political affairs. Under their leadership, El Salvador became highly dependent on international markets for coffee. They modernized its transportation system and capital city and gained control over more rural land for coffee production. This 'coffee prosperity' gained El Salvador in the early 20th century the reputation of the most progressive of the Central American states. With new ports and railways, it also became the first in Central America to have paved highways, and the city of San Salvador grew impressively in appearance and economic activity. A stronger military force maintained the liberal oligarchy of 'fourteen families', which presided over governments that were generally more stable than those in the neighbouring states.

Spanish colonialism had left a heritage of a small élite ruling a servile mass, and feudal traditions have persisted well into the present century. The principal features of the Salvadoran social structure, however, are especially related to the rise of coffee cultivation and the emergence of the 'fourteen families' as a dominant oligarchy in the late 19th and early 20th centuries. Economic expansion into other agroexports and industry, and the military, especially since 1950, have expanded and diversified this élite which was recently counted at 254 families. Moreover, the modernization of the economy has contributed to the growth of a significant middle class in the capital, which has played a growing role in intellectual, political, and cultural development of the country. The vast majority of the population, however, remains poor, uneducated, and lacking in economic opportunity. The widening gulf between urban modernization and rural backwardness, and between rich and poor, is perhaps nowhere in Latin America so obvious as in El Salvador. These serious social and economic inequities have appeared to worsen in the late 20th century as rapid population growth has exceeded economic growth.

Modernization obscured the growing social inequities in El Salvador, aggravated by rapid population growth. While San Salvador became a modern, progressive city, rural poverty and malnutrition soared. Challenges to the liberal oligarchy began to appear in the 1920s, especially as articulated by the Salvadoran intellectual leader, Alberto Masferrer, who founded the Labour Party in 1930. Also founded in 1930 was the Communist Party of El Salvador, reflecting more radical opposition, among whom the most outspoken representative was Farabundo Martí. The economic hardships occasioned by the international depression following 1929 intensified the problems and encouraged significant labour organization and agitation. The surprise victory in the 1930 election of the Labour Party candidate, Arturo Araujo, a progressive member of the planter élite, brought unexpected moves toward social democracy, land reform, and improved health and education along the lines Masferrer had advocated. Following nearly a year of chaotic government and massive labour demonstrations, the military intervened and ousted Araujo in favour of the Vice-President, General Maximiliano Hernández Martínez, a Liberal. The Communists led a rural revolt in January 1932, but in a struggle that essentially pitted peasant machetes against army machine-guns, the result was a massacre of at least 10,000 peasants, followed by repression and the establishment of a military régime that would last until 1944.

The 1932 massacre was a watershed in Salvadoran history, for it marked the end of the relatively tolerant political structure with civilian rule and the growth of labour organizations. The élite, frightened by the 1932 revolt, became reactionary and relied on a repressive military to defend it from the masses, whose economic situation steadily deteriorated. Even after the end of Hernández Martínez' fascist-like dictatorship in 1944, the military continued to rule the country until the present day. The 1932 revolt also marked the end of identifiable Indian communities and culture in most of El Salvador, as the massacre had especially concentrated on Indians. Culturally, the remaining Indians quickly adopted mestizo dress and life-styles.

While coffee continued to be the primary export of the country, after World War II there was considerable expansion of other agroexports – cotton, sugar, rice, and beef – as the planter class expanded its holdings along the Pacific coastal plain. This expansion of agroexports enriched the élite, but in a period when the population was also expanding rapidly, caused impoverishment of rural peasants who were forced off their land and into unemployment or very low wages. Production of corn, beans, and other staples, forced on to the poorer land, could not keep up with the expanding population and in the latter half of the 20th century El Salvador became one of the most poorly nourished countries in the world.

Profits in agroexports and a growing awareness of the limitations of El Salvador's small area with its rapid population growth encouraged investment in manufacturing and service industries in San Salvador from the 1950s onward. The establishment of the Central American Common Market in 1960 contributed notably to industrial expansion as trade among the Central American states rose through the 1960s and 1970s. While much of this development came from the same families who had developed the agroexports, foreign investment was also important and multinational corporations became important to the Salvadoran economy.

Following the overthrow of Hernández Martínez by a combination of students, labour, and progressive military officers, a more open political climate had returned to El Salvador. Although military men continued to head the government, there was a more tolerant attitude toward political parties and trade unions, and the urban middle class became politically active. New parties replaced the long monopoly of the Liberal Party, which now disappeared, having been discredited by its association with the Hernández Martínez dictatorship. Yet the military-dominated Party of Democratic Revolutionary Unification (PRUD), with the support of the coffee élite, maintained power up till 1961. Then a new, but similar, Party of National Conciliation (PCN), dominated by General Julio Rivera, replaced it and ruled until 1979. Also notable during the period, however, was the growth of broader-based popular parties, especially the Christian Democrats (PDC) and the Social Democrats (MNR). Under the dynamic leadership of a US-trained civil engineer, José Napoleón Duarte, the Christian Democrats in the 1960s were effective in organizing students and workers and in gaining support from Catholic clergy and lay people. Duarte won election as Mayor of San Salvador in 1964, but the 1969 war with Honduras interrupted the Christian Democratic surge.

The 'Soccer War', so called because rioting between rival Honduran and Salvadoran fans at a World Cup playoff soccer game touched it off, had much more fundamental causes. Border disputes had occurred between the two states since colonial times, but more serious were the trade imbalances that the Common Market had occasioned: Honduran imports exceeded exports and Salvadoran manufactured goods destroyed or damaged Honduran infant industries. Most serious, however, was the basic social inequity and overpopulation in El Salvador, causing massive emigration into Honduras. The Salvadoran immigrants threatened Honduran jobs, wages, land, and businesses. Large Honduran landholders led a campaign against the Salvadoran immigrants. The war itself was brief but costly. It was a setback to the Central American economic integration movement, but in El Salvador it led to a resurgence of the military, which placed patriotism in support of the war effort ahead of the grim socio-economic realities of the country.

Returning refugees from Honduras put an even greater strain on El Salvador's land-poor population, and there was widespread opposition to the government by 1972. An opposition coalition, with Duarte at the head of the ticket and Guillermo Ungo of the MNR as the vice-presidential candidate, appeared to win a majority of the votes in the 1972 national election. Yet the government declared the PCN candidate victorious and drove Duarte and Ungo into exile. Repressive, reactionary rule followed. El Salvador became notorious for the military's violations of human rights, as the tide of civil disorder and dissent continued to rise.

The success of the Sandinistas in overthrowing the Somoza dynasty in neighbouring Nicaragua in July 1979 and the rising popular opposition to the PCN government of Carlos Humberto Romero prompted a military coup in October 1979 that sought conciliation with the opposition, but which was primarily concerned with preserving the power and prestige of the military institutions. Resignation of nearly all the civilians on the junta, including Guillermo Ungo, over continued military repression, precipitated a crisis in January 1980. The Christian Democrats now collaborated with the military to form a new junta, and Duarte became its chief later in the year. Under Duarte's leadership the government made some efforts at both restraining military repression and socio-economic reform, including an agrarian reform programme. But Duarte appeared impotent as the real power rested with the military. Political assassinations by the right, including those of the outspoken Archbishop Oscar Romero, several Christian Democratic leaders, and four US churchwomen, were common in 1980, while on the left guerrilla organizations, headed by the Farabundo Martí National Liberation Front (FMLN) launched a civil war against government forces. A new political party, the National Republican Alliance (ARENA) consolidated right-wing opposition behind the leadership of the charismatic Major Roberto D'Aubisson, who had been linked to death squad assassinations, including that of Archbishop Romero. United States military aid to the government became an element of rising importance in the escalating civil war.

With US assistance, the junta held a free election for a constitutional convention in 1982. Leftist parties did not participate, and the Christian Democrats won a plurality, but together the right-wing ARENA and the PCN held a commanding majority. The Convention elected D'Aubisson as its head, but US pressure prevented his selection as provisional president of the country, and under the Constitution which was drafted in 1983, Duarte won a decisive victory in the presidential election of 1984 and began a five-year term.

By 1988, amid recurring reports of a military coup, Duarte had been unable to revive the sagging economy. As a signatory to the Central American Peace Accord (The Arias Plan) of 1987, he had agreed to seek a peace agreement with the guerrilla forces, but had made little progress and his country continued to be torn by violence and civil war. In June 1988 he entered a hospital in the United States, reportedly dying of stomach cancer, and the future of his country remained uncertain.

The Salvadoran civil war and United States involvement in it has attracted considerable attention in the English-speaking world and there is a growing volume of publications on various aspects of recent Salvadoran history. In general, however, with some notable exceptions, serious writing on El Salvador in English has been limited to those areas of active US involvement.

This bibliography seeks to identify and comment on the principal works in each field, emphasizing works in English when available, but necessarily including many works in Spanish. The volume is primarily concerned with published books, but a considerable number of periodical articles have also been cited either because of their quality or because of the absence or rarity of books on the subject. In addition, several doctoral dissertations and a few masters theses have been listed, since they often represent the most penetrating research on specific subjects and in most cases are readily available through University Microfilms International in Ann Arbor, Michigan, USA. The bibliography is not intended as a comprehensive list of all publications on El Salvador, but rather as a guide to the most significant publications in each field, with annotations that should help the reader to identify both the scope and utility of individual items. In a very few instances entries are not annotated, either because the title is sufficiently explanatory as to the contents of the work, or because, although it appeared to be a title appropriate for inclusion, it was unavailable to the compiler in time to prepare an annotation.

Within each section, entries are arranged alphabetically by author, the only exception being in the section on travel accounts where they are listed in chronological order to facilitate the finding of works dealing with specific periods. Following the main entries in each section are cross-references to related works in other sections of the volume. An index enables easy location of specific authors, titles, and subjects.

The initial section, 'The Country and its People', is concerned with general works that introduce the reader to the country as a whole. No single volume does this adequately, especially since the political turmoil and economic crises of the 1980s, as well as the devastating earthquake of October 1986, have changed the country so greatly. Several recent overviews are useful, but not fully comprehensive, while earlier works such as White's *El Salvador*, or Parker's *Central American Republics* have lost much of their value as contemporary guides. Blutstein's useful US Army handbook series volume for El Salvador, for example, appeared just before the 1979 coup and therefore does not reflect the recent political changes. Most of the contemporary writing on El Salvador is strongly biased in favour of one political view or another, but among the most useful works as an introduction to the country is

Russell's *El Salvador in crisis*. Several general works on Central America have been included in this section as well. A subsection on current events lists a number of specialized newsletters that do provide up-to-date coverage of events in El Salvador. More general news publications, notably the *Economist* (London) and the *New York Times*, have also provided considerable coverage of El Salvador during the 1980s.

Except for David Browning's brilliant historical geography of El Salvador, there is not a great deal available in English on Salvadoran geography, although West and Augelli's *Middle America* provides an adequate introductory description of the country. The quality of Salvadoran geographical publications has improved notably in recent years, and a number of these have been included in the geography section, with special attention called to the volume edited by Luis Escamilla. The political violence in the country has seriously damaged its attractiveness to tourists, a fact reflected in the dearth of up-to-date tourist guides. The *South American Handbook* remains the most useful guide for the traveller.

The accounts of earlier travellers to the country are numerous and rich in their descriptive insights into Salvadoran history and customs. Most of them include El Salvador only as part of travels throughout Central America, but they are especially useful for their perceptions of contemporary events and practices. The representative selections in this section are mostly in English and date mostly from the 19th and 20th centuries. Although each of those selected has its own peculiar value, special attention is called to the accounts of Cockburn, Stephens, Dunlop, Tempsky, Squier, Scherzer, Foote, Martin, Carpenter, Krehm, Osborne, and Clements.

Although many of the travellers' accounts comment on El Salvador's varied and exotic flora and fauna, scientific writing in this area has not been very extensive. Several early general works on the region, however, provide excellent coverage of species found in El Salvador, notably the classic *Biologia centrali-americana*, and Choussy's *Flora salvadoreña*.

Although the archaeology of El Salvador is considerably less spectacular than that of neighbouring Guatemala or Honduras, there are some Maya and other pre-Columbian sites of note. There is no definitive work on Salvadoran prehistory, but there are a number of individual site studies, many of them in English. Doris Stone's *Pre-columbian man finds Central America* is a useful introduction to the field.

The history of El Salvador has been more fully developed by both native and foreign scholars, although there are many periods of the country's history that have yet to be fully explained, and for some periods there is little in English. A major obstacle to the scientific writing of Salvadoran history has been the periodic destruction of historical records in that country by natural disaster and civil disorder. The most serious losses occurred as a result of the earthquake and accompanying fires in 1889, when most of the Salvadoran government's records, as well as those of the Archivo General de la Federación Centroamericana (1821-40) and the Archivo de los Protocolos were destroyed. Fortunately, many records for colonial El Salvador are preserved in the Archivo General de Centroamérica in Guatemala City or in Spanish archives in Seville and elsewhere. The Archivo Nacional de El Salvador has made some effort to gather materials, but subsequent natural disasters have not been kind to this effort, most recently causing massive destruction in the October 1986 earthquake. Notwithstanding these limitations, some fine historical writing on the country does exist, among which the historical geography of David Browning, *El Salvador: landscape and society*, is an especially good example. Woodward's general history of Central America is a useful introduction to the region's history and El Salvador's position in it. For the first two centuries of Spanish rule, MacLeod's *Spanish Central America* is superb. The work of Wortman and Rodríguez is useful for understanding the 18th century and the roots of the turmoil in the 19th century. For those who read Spanish, Rodolfo Barón Castro's major work on the demographic history of the country is especially valuable. The modern history of El Salvador has been dealt with largely in monographs dealing with individual actors or events, and many of them reflect the lack of adequate documentation referred to above. Especially notable, however, among these works is Anderson's account of the 1932 *Matanza*. The civil war in El Salvador since 1979 has attracted increasing attention and a number of surveys of Salvadoran history have recently appeared that put their primary focus on the 20th century. Among these, clearly the best is Dunkerley's *Long war*. Salvadoran historians have tended to concentrate on recent history, also, reflecting strong social science methodological approaches in analysing El Salvador's contemporary difficulties.

El Salvador's dense population has prompted some considerable study of its demography. In addition to the major study of Barón Castro already mentioned, the superb interdisciplinary work of Durham, *Scarcity and survival*, is listed in the 'Population' section, although a number of other categories would have been equally appropriate. In any case, it is a work that makes a major contribution to understanding modern El Salvador and its problems.

A number of important anthropological works are reflected in the section entitled 'Nationalities and Minorities'. The Salvadoran government in the mid-20th century began to support considerable research and publication on the country's ethnic heritage and some of these works are also reflected here. Special note should be made of the *Handbook of Middle American Indians*. The standard work on the peculiarities of Salvadoran Spanish is that of Geoffroy Rivas, which has gone through many editions. Salvadoran folklore is diverse and interesting, but has not been highly developed. Traditionally, the élite has looked abroad for culture rather than to the native culture of the El Salvador, and this is reflected in the small number of publications in this category.

Strong religious overtones in the contemporary political struggle have elicited considerable publication. Although Protestant evangelical missionaries have been remarkably successful in gaining converts in El Salvador in recent years, as suggested in the work by Drost, the majority of Salvadorans are Roman Catholics. The Catholic clergy was traditionally conservative, but during the last two decades the theology of liberation has become a major force in El Salvador and both foreign and native clergy have taken a major role in emphasizing the role of the church in politicizing the rural and urban poor. Thus the Catholic clergy, from parish priest to archbishop, has once more become a major force in the political struggles, especially in the formation of Christian basic units in peasant communities that have raised the consciousness of the people and encouraged them to take a more active role in determining their political and economic destiny. The works of Berrigan, Berryman, the Bretts, Carrigan, and Montgomery reflect both the emotion and the depth of involvement of religion in the political struggle, while a number of works focus on the assassinated Archbishop Oscar Romero. The significance of the basic Christian communities, which have been especially important in El Salvador, is dealt with by the Salvadoran theologians Sobrino and Hernández, as well as by Galdámez and by Montgomery.

A number of studies by members of staff at the Universidad Centroamericana have advanced Salvadoran sociology, among which the work of Segundo Montes is especially significant. There is little in English in this category, however.

The notorious behaviour of the Salvadoran military in the area of human rights has drawn worldwide attention since the 1970s, reflected in a number of publications in this category. The Americas Watch Committee has published many books and pamphlets on the

Introduction

problem, and it is a topic that has been closely related to United States involvement in the country, especially since the US Congress began to require improvement in respect for human rights as a condition for US military aid. A related question involves the large number of refugees that have fled the country, especially to the neighbouring states and to the United States. Several works dealing with that problem have been included in this category.

The political turmoil in El Salvador since the 1960s has elicited a considerable amount of publication, especially from North Americans, and thus accounts for one of the largest sections in this bibliography. Thomas Anderson's *Politics in Central America* is an excellent introduction to the area, and is free of the strong political biases that characterize much of the writing on modern El Salvadoran politics. Focusing more specifically on El Salvador, Webre's work on the rise of José Napoleón Duarte and the Christian Democrats provides excellent analysis of the period to 1972, while Baloyra's fine work explains the developments in the 1970s and early 1980s. Montgomery's work, listed in the history section is also excellent, especially for its description of leftist organization and action. The article on 'Enemy Colleagues' by Gabriel Zaid is notable for its examination of the members of the leading political groups in the country. A subsection under 'Politics' deals specifically with 'the military', which has been so powerful an influence in the country's government since 1932.

A section on 'Constitution, Laws, and the Judicial System' lists the principal compilations of the many constitutions the country has had as well as its laws. For the most part this section is limited to Spanish titles, as is the following section on 'Administration and Local Government'.

The 'Foreign Relations' section is one of the larger sections, reflecting the greater amount of publication in English, especially as regards recent relations between the United States and El Salvador. The work of Gettleman *et al.* is a useful compilation of documents relative to El Salvador's foreign relations, as well as to the political struggle there in general. Also of note in the general section of this category is Jamail and Gutiérrez' exposé of Israeli involvement in the region. El Salvador's role in the Central American economic integration movement (the Central American Common Market) and the 'Soccer War' of 1969 with Honduras occupies much of the section dealing with El Salvador's relations with other states. Work on the Common Market is extensive in English, for it attracted a great deal of attention in the United States from a number of different perspectives and disciplines. It should be noted, however, that a number of the works dealing with economic and trade aspects of the Common Market are listed primarily in the 'Economics' and 'Trade' sections. On the 'Soccer War', the work of Anderson is especially noteworthy, as is that of Durham, mentioned earlier. The section on relations with the US is characterized by many works bitterly opposed to US military assistance to the Salvadoran government in its struggle against the FMLN guerrillas, as well as by some works defending the Reagan administration's policy. Especially influential among the works in this section have been the Kissinger Commission report and the works of LaFeber, Falcoff, Blachman, Leogrande, White, and Wiarda.

The 'Economics' section reflects considerable study of the Salvadoran economy by both native and foreign scholars, and widely differing views on how to deal with the present economic crisis. An especially useful introduction to the subject is Weeks's *Economies of Central America*. Additional works on aspects of the economy are found in the subsequent sections on 'Investment, Finance, Banking, and Currency', 'Trade', 'Industry', 'Agriculture', 'Transportation and Communications', 'Employment', and 'Labour'. It should be noted that agrarian reform has been an especially important issue in Salvadoran politics and works dealing with that topic are found in the section on 'Agriculture'. The section on 'Statistics' includes statistical compilations on all topics.

The political turmoil and socio-economic inequities have been reflected in the cultural development of El Salvador. Better public education was a stated goal of the Liberal Party and with the rise of the coffee prosperity more resources were committed to it, especially in the cities. Under Spanish rule education at all levels was under the administration of the Roman Catholic Church, which was supposed to establish a school in each parish, but compliance had been lax and rural areas often had no education. After independence, with the strong anti-clericalism of the Liberals, the quality of this system suffered. But in the latter part of the century, at least in urban areas, there was considerable improvement. A national university was established in 1841, but did not become a major institution until the early 20th century. Educational reform has been a topic of considerable writing in El Salvador, but the literature on Salvadoran education in English is quite limited. Development of literature and the arts in early 20th-century El Salvador, led by the work of Alberto Masferrer, Francisco Gavidia, and Jorge Lardé, has diminished in recent years under repressive military governments and civil war conditions. Many earlier scholarly and artistic journals are no longer published, although there continues to be innovative work done in the social sciences and humanities, especially at the Catholic Universidad Centro-americana, where the work of the historian Italo López Vallecillos and the sociologist Segundo Montes has been especially noteworthy.

Libraries, museums, and archives have suffered greatly in El Salvador because of both natural disasters and political and economic crises. The 1986 earthquake did major damage to the National Library and the Archives as well as to most other public structures in downtown San Salvador, and made research on this volume especially difficult. The *Research Guide to Central America and the Caribbean* contains a section on El Salvador, providing a brief description of the principal depositories for historical research, but it should be useful to other disciplines as well.

Although illiteracy remains very high in rural El Salvador, most urban Salvadorans are literate and there are a remarkable number of daily newspapers in San Salvador which are briefly described in the section on 'Mass Media'. For so many newspapers, however, the political spectrum they represent is remarkably narrow, nearly all reflecting strong right-wing views. There are also numerous television and radio stations, including a clandestine radio service, Radio Venceremos, representing the guerrilla opposition.

A final section deals with bibliographies, another area where there has been little systematic attention specifically to El Salvador. Notable exceptions are the recent work of Grieb, *Central America in the nineteenth and twentieth centuries*, which includes a large section on El Salvador, and the CAMINO, *El Salvador: bibliography and research guide*, which focuses especially on the contemporary scene and is thus rapidly becoming out of date.

Acknowledgements

A number of people provided valuable assistance to the compiler in the preparation of this volume. I am especially grateful to my graduate assistants, Pamela Murray, Michael F. Fry, and Regina Wagner, who were of great assistance in locating and evaluating potential entries. For their assistance in helping me identify and locate works to include, I am also greatly indebted to Dr Thomas Niehaus and his staff at the Latin American Library of Tulane University, especially Cecilia Montenegro-Teague and Martha Robertson; to Philip Leinbach and his staff at Tulane's Howard-Tilton Library, especially Barbara Everet; to John Hébert and Georgette Dorn at the Hispanic Division of the Library of Congress; to Laura Gutiérrez and Ann Hartness-Kane at the Nettie

Introduction

Lee Benson Latin American Collection at the University of Texas; and in San Salvador to the staffs of the Biblioteca Nacional de El Salvador, the Biblioteca of the Universidad Centroamericana, the Museo Nacional 'David J. Guzmán', and the Archivo Nacional de El Salvador. In San Salvador, too, I am especially indebted to the hospitality of Xavier Simán and his family, and to the staff at the United States Information Service in San Salvador. I also wish to thank Richard Greenleaf and his staff of the Roger Thayer Stone Center for Latin American Studies at Tulane, especially Gene Yeager, Bridget M. Johnson, and Martha Peters-Hernández, for their support in assisting me carry on the research for this project both in San Salvador and New Orleans, and in the preparation of the final manuscript. I also wish to thank Dr James F. Kilroy, Dean of Liberal Arts and Sciences at Tulane, for his support in the preparation of this work. Finally, I am eternally grateful for the patience and encouragement of my wife, Sue McGrady Woodward. The assistance, advice, and support of all of these people contributed enormously to the completion of this bibliography, but the compiler must bear full responsibility for any omissions or errors which it may contain.

Ralph Lee Woodward, Jr
New Orleans
June 1988

The Country and Its People

General

1 **El Salvador: beauty among the ashes.**
Faith Adams.   Minneapolis, Minnesota: Dillon Press, 1986. 135p.
bibliog.
A brief survey of Salvadoran history and sights, emphasizing the intrinsic beauty of
the country despite the terrible civil war there.

2 **The Central America fact book.**
Tom Barry, Deb Preusch.   New York: Grove, 1986. 357p.
A sequel to the following item, this is a handy reference book for background and
facts on each of the contemporary Central American states. It includes a list of US
corporate investments and information about land tenure, poverty, economic aid,
labour organization, and the military.

3 **Dollars and dictators, a guide to Central America.**
Tom Barry, Beth Wood, Deb Preusch.   Albuquerque, New Mexico:
The Resource Center, 1982. 272p.
A profile of each Central American country, with a thorough examination of US
foreign aid there and a detailed account of US business and military activity. El
Salvador is dealt with especially on pages 180-97.

4 **Inside Central America: the essential facts past and present on El
Salvador, Nicaragua, Honduras, Guatemala, and Costa Rica.**
Phillip Berryman.   New York: Pantheon, 1985. 166p.
A readable and intelligent analysis from a leftist perspective of US policy in Central
America since the Sandinista revolution in Nicaragua. An ex-Catholic priest,

1

Berryman proposes negotiations as the best way to end the country's violent struggles and to remove them from the arena of 'Cold War confrontation'. He discusses the major issues involved in attempts to bring peace and a better standard of living for Central Americans, claiming to represent a non-partisan approach grounded in humanitarian concern.

5 **El Salvador, a country study.**
   Howard I. Blutstein.   Washington, DC: Foreign Area Studies,
   American University, 1979. 260p. map. bibliog.

A volume in the 'US Army handbook' series, this work contains a great many basic data on El Salvador up to the revolt of 1979. The tumultuous political developments since that date, however, make much of the political commentary in this work obsolete.

6 **El Salvador**
   Allan Carpenter, Eloise Baker.   Chicago: Children's Press, 1971. 95p.
   maps.

An illustrated introduction to El Salvador for children, presenting the geography, history, economy, culture and people in simple English.

7 **El Salvador: background to the crisis.**
   Central America Information Office.   Cambridge, Massachusetts:
   CAMINO, 1982. 144p.

This passionate, documented analysis of the repressive political situation in El Salvador is intended to alert the American public to the nature of US policy there. It portrays El Salvador as 'another Vietnam' that the US should avoid getting involved in. CAMINO is an organization dedicated to disseminating information about Central America.

8 **El Salvador.**
   Roque Dalton.   Havana: Casa de las Américas, 1963. 91p. 2 maps.
   bibliog.

A brief, Marxist overview of El Salvador, with frequent comparisons to Cuba.

9 **El Salvador: work of thirty photographers.**
   Carolyn Forche.   New York: Writers and Readers Publishing
   Cooperative, 1983. 120p.

Presents photographs of the civil war, street killings, etc., depicting the grim reality of life in El Salvador in the 1980s.

10 **El Salvador in pictures.**
    Nathan A. Haverstock.   Minneapolis, Minnesota: Lerner Publications,
    1987. 64p. map.

A geographical guide to El Salvador for children, providing brief textual comment together with many photographs.

2

11 **Centro América 19--, análisis económico y político sobre la región.**
(Central America 19--, economic and political analyses of the region.)
Inforpress Centroamericana. Guatemala: División de Estudios
Económicos, Inforpress Centroamericana, 1982-. annual. maps.
An annual publication prepared by the publishers of *Central America Report* (q.v.)
and *Inforpress Centroamericana* (q.v.), this statistical and analytical survey of Central
America provides a great deal of information on the region as a whole and on each
state. It focuses especially on economic information and is also useful for details on
the political structure and personnel of each state. Although expensive, its objective
and comprehensive coverage make it a most valuable reference volume and an
essential acquisition for libraries with a serious interest in covering Central America.

12 **Central America: the real stakes.**
Lester D. Langley. New York: Crown, 1985. 288p. map. bibliog.
Langley, a leading diplomatic historian of US-Central American relations, provides a
strongly impressionistic view of Central America's problems and attitudes, based
especially on a trip through the isthmus in which he interviewed many ordinary
people. A view from 'the bottom up', it reflects many of the fundamental economic
and social problems of the region and the dilemmas of US policy in the region. There
is considerable attention to El Salvador in this work.

13 **Latin American perspectives.**
Riverside, California, 1974-.
This quarterly review contains frequent and perceptive coverage of El Salvador by
distinguished Latin American authors. The journal focuses on the struggle between
capitalism and socialism in Latin America. Of particular interest are nos. 25-26 (vol.
7) (spring-summer 1980) dedicated to 'Central America: The strong men are
shaking', particularly Norma Stoltz Chinchilla: 'Class struggle in Central America:
Background and Overview' (p. 2-23); and Ernesto Richter: 'Social Classes,
Accumulation, and the crisis of "Overpopulation" in El Salvador' (p. 114-37); No. 34
(vol. 9) (summer 1982) is also dedicated to 'Crisis in Central America' (p. 111-28).

14 **El Salvador – Le Salvador.**
Andre Lefebvre, René Moser, Xavier Richer. Paris: Delroisse,
1976. 163p.
A collection of coloured photographs with an accompanying text in Spanish, French,
English, and German.

15 **The Central American republics.**
Franklin D. Parker. New York: Oxford University Press, 1964. 348p.
Although now somewhat dated, this general reference work is still a valuable basic
source of information on each of the Central American republics. It includes a
perceptive history of the region and useful data on a broad range of topics for the
individual states.

3

16   **El Salvador.**
Renfield Sanders.   New York: Chelsea House, 1988. 124p.
Designed for children, this work surveys the history, geography, people, and culture
of El Salvador, with emphasis on its current economy, industry, and place in the
political world.

17   **El Salvador in crisis.**
Philip L. Russell.   Austin, Texas: Colorado River Press, 1984. 168p.
maps. bibliog.
An excellent introduction to El Salvador, with a competent history of the country
followed by a series of informative and perceptive chapters on the economy and
society. It concludes with a detailed analysis of various aspects of El Salvador in the
1980s, including the civil war and relations with the United States.

18   **South American handbook.**
London: Rand McNally, 1987. 63rd ed. 1350p. maps.
Despite its title (which varies slightly), the *South American Handbook* covers all of
Latin America and the Caribbean and is one of the best compact guides to basic data
available on the entire region. First published in 1921, and annually since 1924, it
devotes only 20 pages exclusively to El Salvador, but is a handy reference item for
historical, geographical, economic, and statistical data as well as a practical guide to
hotels, currency exchange, and other introductory information. It is especially
recommended to travellers who may be going through several Latin American
countries.

19   **El Salvador.**
Alastair White.   New York: Praeger, 1973. 288p. maps. bibliog.
This work provided an excellent introduction to El Salvador at a time when there was
little else in English. Although it has subsequently been eclipsed by more recent
works and is not exhaustive in its sources, it still offers a useful historical overview
and is particularly valuable for its description of the 1960s.

20   **Image of El Salvador.**
Guillermo de Zendegui.   *Americas*, vol. 25 (1973), p. 1-24.
A survey of Salvadoran demography, geography, history, politics, society, and the
economy prior to 1973.

Centro América, subdesarrollo y dependencia. (Central America, underdevelopment and dependency.) *See* item no. 277.

Current events

21 **Central America report.**
Guatemala: Inforpress Centroamericana, 1974-. weekly.
A very informative and objective weekly review of economics and politics. Normally 8 pages in length, it has substantial coverage of El Salvador.

22 **Inforpress centroamericana.** (Central American Information Press.)
Guatemala: Inforpress Centroamericana, 1972-.
A 16-page weekly report on political and economic events in all the Central American countries, with frequent in-depth special economic reports. More detailed than *Central American report* (q.v.) which is also published by Inforpress. *Inforpress Centroamericana* is published in Spanish only.

23 **Latin America, 19-.**
New York: Facts on File, 1973-79.
Issued annually for the years 1972-78, these volumes, organized by country, provide a summary of the principal news stories of the year. Useful for reviewing recent events or for updating. Unfortunately, this series was not continued after the 1978 edition, but see the next item (the Cozean series).

24 **Latin America 19-.**
Edited by Jon D. Cozean. Washington, D.C. and Harpers Ferry, West Virginia: Stryker-Post Publications, 1967-. annual. (World Today Series).
Although the review of the past year's events is less complete in this series than in the Facts on File series of the same title (q.v.), this series includes basic data on each Latin American country, making it a useful reference. It is organized by country.

25 **Latin America Regional Reports: Caribbean.**
London: Latin American Newsletters, 1979-.
Succeeds earlier publications by the same publisher: *Latin America* (1967-77); *Latin America Economic Report* (1973-79); and *Latin America Political Report* (1977-79). Published about ten times per year, this newsletter provides excellent summary news coverage of El Salvador and the region. See also by the same publisher, *Latin America Weekly Report* (1979-00), which also has frequent coverage on El Salvador. To a substantial degree, it duplicates the coverage of *Latin America Regional Reports*, but in a different format.

26 **Mesoamerica.** (Costa Rica.)
Fred B. Morris, Director. San José, Costa Rica: Institute for Central American Studies, 1982-. monthly.
A competent and fairly objective monthly review of events in Central America, with both commentary and factual reporting. It includes both political and economic coverage.

27   **La nación internacional, edición centroamericana.** (The nation international, Central American edition.)
Edited by Marcel Angulo de Castro.   San José, Costa Rica, 1982-.
weekly.

A weekly review of Central American news, published by one of the leading Costa Rican dailies.

28   **Update Latin America.**
Washington: Washington Office on Latin America, 1976-. bi-monthly.

A newsletter with particularly extensive coverage of Central America. The Washington Office on Latin America is a non-governmental human rights organization supported by religious organizations and private foundations.

29   **Venceremos.**
New York: Venceremos Publications, 1987-. bi-monthly.

Published in Spanish for nearly a decade, *Venceremos* is now published bi-monthly in an English edition, providing news of El Salvador from the perspective of the revolutionary Farabundo Martí National Liberation Front (FMLN).

Geography

General surveys

30 **Descripción geográfica y estadística de la República de El Salvador.**
(Geographical and statistical description of El Salvador.)
Santiago I. Barberena.   San Salvador: Imprenta Nacional, 1892. 114p.
maps.
A careful statistical description of El Salvador at the end of the last century by one of
the country's leading historian-geographers. Barberena later published a somewhat
similar, but briefer collection of data, *Estudios estadísticos respecto a las riquezas
naturales, industriales, y comercio de la República de El Salvador* (San Salvador:
Imprenta Nacional, 1907-08).

31 **El Salvador: landscape and society**.
David G. Browning.   London: Oxford University Press, 1971. 482p.
maps. bibliog.
An extremely thorough study of the relationship between man and land in El
Salvador since pre-Columbian times. The author's ability to show changing patterns
of land tenure and settlement through time, in conjunction with cultural and political
changes, throws much light on the development of present ecological problems. This
work is one of the most significant studies in Salvadoran historical geography and
helps to explain the basic social and economic structure of the country better than
any other single volume.

32 **Monografía de la República de El Salvador**. (Monograph of the Republic of El Salvador.)
Godofredo Calderón Chacón. San Salvador: Impresos Prisma, 1986. 132p. maps. bibliog.

An outline geographical description of El Salvador, providing basic data on each department and major physical features, along with a discussion of natural resources, economic activities, history, communications and transport, and a guide to the country's commerce, financial institutions, social development, and political structure. This brief guidebook does not provide much depth, but it is a handy compilation of basic facts about the country.

33 **Diccionario geográfico de El Salvador**. (Geographical dictionary of El Salvador.)
El Salvador. Ministerio de Obras Públicas. San Salvador: Instituto Geográfico Nacional, 1985-86. 2 vols.

Issued periodically, this is the basic guide to geographical names in El Salvador. See also the *Indice del Diccionario geográfico de El Salvador*, 2 vols. (San Salvador: Instituto Geográfico Nacional, 1978). Now dated, but still possibly useful is Rafael González Sol, *Indice geográfico de la República de El Salvador* (San Salvador: Editorial Ahora, 1948).

34 **Guía para investigadores, República de El Salvador**. (Guide for researchers, Republic of El Salvador.)
El Salvador. Ministerio de Obras Públicas. San Salvador: Pan American Institute of Geography and History, 1977. 81p. bibliog.

Primarily a bibliography for geographical research, this volume may be useful in connection with other disciplines as well.

35 **Geografía de El Salvador**. (Geography of El Salvador.)
Edited by Manuel Luis Escamilla. San Salvador: Ministerio de Cultura y Comunicaciones, 1986. 256p. maps. bibliog.

A collaborative volume with many maps and charts in colour. Each chapter is written by a specialist. The work is divided into four parts: geography; geology; soils; and territorial waters and coastal changes. This useful volume represents a major advance in Salvadoran geographical publications.

36 **Middle America, its lands and peoples**.
Robert C. West, John P. Augelli. Englewood Cliffs, New Jersey: Prentice Hall, 1976. 2nd ed. 512p. maps. bibliog.

The standard geography of Central America, Mexico, and the West Indies. Three of the 16 chapters deal with Central America. With a strong cultural and historical perspective, it serves as an excellent introduction to the Middle American region.

El Salvador in pictures.
See item no. 10.

Central American jungles.
See item no. 99.

Scarcity and survival in Central America: ecological origins of the Soccer War.
See item no. 222.

Handbook of Middle American Indians.
See item no. 241.

Indigenous tropical agriculture in Central America: land use, systems, and problems.
See item no. 513.

Man, crops and pests in Central America.
See item no. 522.

Export agriculture and the crisis in Central America.
See item no. 530.

Regional geography

37 **Monografías departamentales.** (Departmental monographs.)
Santiago I. Barberena, Pedro S. Fonseca. San Salvador: Imprenta Nacional, 1909-14. 14 vols. maps.

A collection of brief volumes, principally written by Barberena, describing each of El Salvador's 14 departments. They include brief historical sketches and current data on each department, indicating major towns, institutions, and leading personages. Highly useful for a view of the country in the early twentieth century.

38 **Monografías departamentales.** (Departmental monographs.)
Antonio Cardona Lazo. San Salvador: Imprenta Nacional, 1938.
3 vols.

Similar, if somewhat less detailed, to Barberena and Fonseca's earlier descriptions under the same title, with brief descriptions of each department and statistical information on population, resources, economic activity, etc., and historical sketches.

39 **Some factors in urbanism in a quasi-rural setting: San Salvador and San José.**
R. C. Williamson. *Sociology and Social Research* vol. 47 (January 1963), p. 187-200.

A scholarly study comparing urban life with rural life, is based on 507 interviews in El Salvador and Costa Rica. It identifies 'urbanism' as a middle-class phenomenon.

Geology and natural resources

40 **Contribución a la mineralogía y geología de El Salvador.** (Contribution to the mineralogy and geology of El Salvador.)
Daniel Basauri. San Salvador: Tipografía La Unión, 1945. 207p. maps. bibliog.
This volume reprints several articles originally published between 1943 and 1945 on Salvadoran mineralogy and geology. It is extensively illustrated.

41 **La costa de El Salvador.** (The Salvadoran coast.)
H. G. Gierloff-Emden. El Salvador: Ministerio de Educación, 1976. 273p. maps. bibliog. (Monografía morfológica-oceonográfica).
A detailed survey of the Salvadoran coastline, originally published in German in 1959.

42 **Obras completas.** (Complete works.)
Jorge Lardé. San Salvador: Ministerio de Cultura, 1960. 597p.
The published work of a leading Salvadoran geologist of the early twentieth century, including his *Geología general de Centroamérica y especial de El Salvador* (General geology of Central America and especially of El Salvador) (San Salvador: Imprenta Nacional, 1924), and *El volcán de Izalco* (Izalco volcano) (San Salvador: Imprenta Nacional, 1923).

43 **Los estudios sobre los recursos naturales en las Américas. Tomo 1. Estudio preliminar en Guatemala, El Salvador, Honduras, Nicaragua, Costa Rica, Panamá y Zona del Canal sobre la situación actual de la investigación y de la organización relativa al estudio de los recursos naturales.** (Studies on natural resources in the Americas. Volume 1. Preliminary study on Guatemala, El Salvador, Honduras, Nicaragua, Costa Rica, Panama and the Canal Zone on the present situation in research and relative organization of the study of natural resources.)
México: Instituto Panamericano de Geografía e Historia, 1953. 446p. maps. (Proyecto 29 del Programa de Cooperación Técnica de la Organización de Estados Americanos, Centro de Entrenamiento para la Evaluación de Recursos Naturales).
A very thorough survey of the cartography, geology, hydrology, soils, vegetation, fishing, hunting, and organization of each state. El Salvador is dealt with especially on pages 97-168.

44 **Development of geological resources in El Salvador.**
Solco Walle Tromp. New York: United Nations, 1952. 100p.
This is a report by a US technical assistant on El Salvador's geological resources. It

includes an evaluation of its unique geological problems (such as the presence of active volcanoes), water shortage, the need to establish a deep-sea fishing industry, and recommendations for establishing a geological institute to address these problems. Tromp was part of a US technical mission of the United Nations in El Salvador.

El terremoto de octubre de 1986 en San Salvador y la situación habitacional de los sectores populares. (The October 1986 earthquake in San Salvador and the housing situation in the populous sectors.)
See item no. 290.

Las perspectivas del desarrollo agropecuario y la tenencia de la tierra. (Perspectives on agricultural development and land tenure.)
See item no. 503.

Maps, atlases, and gazetteers

45 **Atlas of Central America.**
Stanley A. Arbingast (et al.). Austin, Texas: University of Texas Press, 1979. 65p. maps.
Good colour maps of each Central American state show basic geographical features while topical maps show topographical characteristics, population, agricultural, transportation, and other economic data for each state. This atlas does not include maps of internal divisions within each state.

46 **Atlas económico de El Salvador, 1974.** (Economic atlas of El Salvador, 1974.)
San Salvador: Editorial Itzcalco, 1974. 181p. bibliog.
A useful collection of maps, tables, and charts that reflect the Salvadoran economy in the mid-1970s.

47 **Atlas de El Salvador.** (Atlas of El Salvador.)
San Salvador: Ministerio de Obras Públicas, Instituto Geográfico Nacional Ing. Pablo Arnoldo Guzmán, 1979. 87p. maps.
A basic atlas, with physical, geological, mineral, hydrological, climatic, ecological, and economic maps.

48 **Central America early maps up to 1860.**
Capt. K. S. Kapp. North Bend, Ohio: K. S. Kapp Productions, 1974. 64p.
An annotated list of 277 maps of Central America from 1548 to 1860. Annotations indicate location of original maps and distinguishing characteristics as well as later

reproductions. Twenty-eight of the maps are reproduced in black and white plates. The list is arranged chronologically, with an alphabetical index appended.

49 **A catalogue of Latin American flat maps, 1926-1964.**
    Palmyra V. M. Montiero.   Austin: University of Texas Press, 1967. 311p.

A descriptive catalogue of maps published within the dates indicated. It is organized by countries and the entries describe the size and content of each map. Geological and urban maps are not included.

50 **Annotated index of aerial photographic coverage and mapping of topography and natural resources: El Salvador.**
    Organization of American States, Department of Economic Affairs. Washington: OAS, 1964. 11p. maps.

A description, in English and Spanish, of the available aerial photographic maps. It indicates for what sectors of El Salvador topographical and planimetric maps, soil and land capability maps, geological maps, and vegetation, land use, forest inventory, and ecological maps are available.

Planos urbanos. (Urban maps.)
See item no. 567.

Tourism and travel guides

51 **Fodor's Central America.**
    Edited by Michael Hutchinson, (et al.).   New York: David McKay, 1982. 453p. map.
    In this otherwise competent tourist guide to Central America coverage on El Salvador is very limited, but it does provide basic data on the country, including an ample listing of hotels and useful city maps.

52 **Your El Salvador guide.**
    Henry Godfrey.   New York: Funk and Wagnalls, 1968. 168p. map.

This travel guide is divided into two parts: an introduction to El Salvador and a description of the sights. Although out of date now, it is still useful as a guide to historic and scenic points of interest in the country.

South American Handbook.
See item no. 18.

Another world: Central America.
See item no. 90.

12

Sailing directions and cruising guides

53 **Catalogue of admiralty charts and other hydrographic publications 1982.**
   Taunton, England: Hydrographer of the Navy, 1982. 156p. maps.
   (Publication No. NP131).
This catalogue of British charts and other publications useful to mariners in Salvadoran waters was corrected up to November 1981. A new edition was published in 1983. Salvadoran charts are found in Index T, p. 119. See also *The mariner's handbook*, 5th ed. (Taunton: Hydrographer of the Navy, 1979), containing information on admiralty charts and navigation publications, general navigation, general meteorology, etc.

54 **Catalog of nautical charts, region 2. USA. Defense Mapping Agency.**
   Defense Mapping Agency catalog of maps, charts and related products, Part 2 – Hydrographic products, vol. 2 Central and South America and Antarctica.
   Washington, DC: Defense Mapping Agency Office of Distribution Services, 1981. 60p.
A catalogue of available charts on the Salvadoran region. For other publications of the Defense Mapping Agency, see Part 2 – Hydrographic products, vol. 10, Miscellaneous and special purpose navigational charts, sheets, and tables. (Publication 1NA), and Part 3 – Topographic products, vol. 5, Western hemisphere, large-scale and city maps.

55 **Pacific coasts of Central America and United States pilot.**
   Great Britain. Hydrographer of the Navy. Taunton, England:
   Hydrographic Department, 1975. 8th ed. (with supplements). (Publication 8).
Sailing directions covering the Pacific coasts of Panama northward through the United States, including off-lying islands between latitudes 4°N. and 48°2525'N.

56 **Sailing directions (enroute) for the west coasts of Mexico and Central America.**
   Defense Mapping Agency Hydrographic/Topographic Center.
   Washington: GPO, 1980 (with subsequent changes). 2nd ed. 171p.
   maps. (Publication 153).
The standard US guide to the Pacific coast of El Salvador with information on signals, cautions, regulations, climate, etc. Specific sailing instructions for the coast of El Salvador are found in Sector 7, p. 109-15. Corrections are issued periodically.

Travellers' Accounts

57 **Relación breve y verdadera de algunas cosas de las muchas que
    sucedieron al Padre Fray Alonso Ponce en las provincias de la Nueva
    España, siendo comisario general de aquellas partes. . .**
    (Brief and true account of some things among the many that happened
    to Friar Alonso Ponce in the provinces of New Spain, he being
    Comisar General of those parts. . .)
    Alonso Ponce [Alonso de San Juan].   Madrid: Viuda de Calero, 1873.
    2 vols.

A fascinating 16th-century description of Central America. Observations on El
Salvador are found only in vol. 1, p. 321, 325-29, 384, 398-400, 403. There is a
separate, published index of this rare edition by Raul Guerrero, *Indice clasificado de
la Relación breve y verdadera de algunas cosas de las muchas que sucedieron al padre
fray Alonso Ponce en las provincias de Nueva España* (México: Vargas Bea [Rea],
1949 [Biblioteca Aportación Histórica], 86p.). Only 100 copies of this index were
printed, but it appeared previously in the *Boletín Bibliográfico de Antropología
Americana*, vol. 7 (1943), p. 56-84.

58 **The English-American, his travail by sea and land; or a new survey of
    the West India's, containing a journall of three thousand and three
    hundred miles within the mainland of America.**
    Thomas Gage.   London: R. Cotes, 1648. 220p. (many subsequent
    editions).

This is one of the classics of Central American travel literature. Gage was an English
friar who had migrated to Spain and then made a journey through Central America,
before returning to England and publishing this highly critical work on the Spanish
Empire in 1648. His descriptions are fascinating and revealing of the social and
economic conditions as well as the physical realities of 17th-century Central America.
The account includes considerable comment on El Salvador. A modern biographical

14

recounting of Gage's tale is Norman Newton's *Thomas Gage in Spanish America* (London: Faber and Faber; New York: Barnes & Noble, 1969). 214p.

59 The unfortunate Englishman. . . . A journey over land from the gulph [sic] of Honduras to the great South Sea.

John Cockburn. London: C. Rivington, 1735. 349p. (several subsequent editions were published).

Vivid travel account of Cockburn's escape from a jail in San Pedro Sula and his journey across the isthmus to San Salvador. First published in 1735, this is one of the few foreign accounts of the first half of the eighteenth century.

60 Travels in Central America, 1821-1840.

Franklin D. Parker. Gainesville, Florida: University of Florida Press, 1970. 340p. map. bibliog.

Using excerpts from the major travellers' accounts during the period, Parker provides a fascinating description of Central American customs, politics, economy and society, with considerable discussion of El Salvador included. Featured in the volume are the works of Orlando Roberts, James Wilson, George Alexander Thompson, Jacob Haefkens, Henry Dunn, James Jackson Jarves, George Washington Montgomery, George Byam, Thomas Young, and John Lloyd Stephens.

61 Incidents of travel in Central America, Chiapas and Yucatan.

John Lloyd Stephens. New York: Dover, 1969. 2 vols.

A facsimile reprint of the first edition (New York: Harper, 1841), 2 vols. There were many subsequent editions. The US government sent John Lloyd Stephens as its envoy to find the disintegrating Central American government in 1839. He failed in that task, but succeeded in producing one of the most delightful and informative descriptions ever written about Central America. He travelled widely and commented on the politics, society, geography, inhabitants, archaeology, and economy.

62 Travels in Central America; being a journal of nearly three years' residence in the country. Together with a sketch of the history of the republic, and an account of its climate, productions, commerce, etc.

Robert G. Dunlop. London: Longman, Brown, Green & Longman, 1847. 358p.

One of the most informative accounts of the 1840s. El Salvador is dealt with especially on pages 60-73.

63 Central America.

John Baily. London: T. Saunders, 1850. 164p. map.

John Baily, a British naval officer, engineer, and canal agent, spent many years in Central America during the first half of the 19th century, and his guide is one of the most useful on the period. It has descriptive chapters on the state of El Salvador as well as a general chapter on Central American characteristics and physical conditions. It is an important historical source for the mid-19th century and also has an excellent map of the period.

64 **Mitla. A narrative of incidents and personal adventures on a journey in Mexico, Guatemala, and Salvador, 1853-55.**
G. F. Von Tempsky.   London: Longman, Brown, Green, Longmans & Roberts, 1858. 436p.

A highly descriptive account of travels in the region, with perceptive comments on the local population. Chapter 11 deals with El Salvador, describing visits to the Izalco region, Sonsonate, Cojutepec, San Vicente, San Miguel, and the Bay of Fonseca. It includes some interesting observations on the Indian balsam producers of Sonsonate.

65 **Notes on Central America, particularly the States of Honduras and San Salvador: their geography, topography, climate, population, resources, production, commerce, political organization, aborigines, etc., and the proposed Honduras Inter-oceanic Railway.**
Ephraim George Squier.   New York: Praeger, 1969. 397p. bibliog.

This account was originally published in 1855, following the author's service as US minister in Central America. El Salvador is especially dealt with on pages 295-352.

66 **Repúblicas de Centro America o idea de su historia i de su estado actual.** (The republics of Central America, or an idea of their history and present state.)
Francisco Solano Astaburuaga y Cienfuegos.   Santiago, Chile: Imprenta del Ferrocarril, 1857. 116p.

Astaburuaga was the Chilean chargé d'affaires in Central America. He spent most of his time in Costa Rica, but he makes some very perceptive comments on politics and life in El Salvador on pages 73-77.

67 **Travels in the free states of Central America: Nicaragua, Honduras and San Salvador.**
Carl Scherzer.   London: Longman, Brown, Green, Longmans & Roberts, 1857. 2 vols. maps.

One of the most careful and detailed 19th-century descriptions of El Salvador is found in volume 2, pages 120-251. Scherzer describes both the physical and human characteristics, with substantial attention to geography, geology, flora and fauna, political events, social customs, agriculture, trade, religion, etc. The author visited remote areas usually not seen by foreign visitors. Scherzer published a number of other volumes and articles dealing with more specialized scientific data on the region.

68 **The states of Central America: their geography, topography, climate, population, resources, production, commerce, political organization, aborigines, etc., etc., comprising chapters on Honduras, San Salvador, Nicaragua, Costa Rica, Guatemala, Belize, the Bay Islands, the Mosquito Shore, and the Honduras Inter-Oceanic Railway.**
Ephraim George Squier.   New York: Harper & Brothers, 1858. 782p.
A detailed and often strongly opinionated description of El Salvador by the US envoy to Central America in the middle of the 19th century, this work reflects Squier's ambitious hopes for US development of the region and his compilation of a wide variety of informative data. El Salvador is especially dealt with on pages 279-345.

69 **La république de Salvador.** (The republic of El Salvador.)
Gustave de Belot.   Paris: Dentu, 1865. 90p.
An important French impression of the country in the 1860s. The Lost Cause Press, Louisville, Kentucky, published a microfiche reprint of this work in 1968.

70 **Recollections of Central America and the west coast of Africa.**
Mrs Henry G. Foote.   London: T. C. Newby, 1869. 221p.
These detailed and perceptive observations on social and economic conditions in mid-19th-century El Salvador by the wife of a British diplomat are based on her residence in San Salvador and travels in the country. The author includes a description of the 1854 earthquake.

71 **Salvador.**
Marie Robinson Wright.   New York: L'Artiste, 1893. 46p.
An enthusiastic description of El Salvador with many illustrations.

72 **Central America and its problems: an account of a journey from the Rio Grande to Panama.**
Frederick Palmer.   New York: Moffat, Yard; London: T. W. Laurie, 1910. 347p.
Travel description and personal impressions during a 1909 trip through Central America. Palmer comments on political leaders and the people's life-styles, and includes a little history from standard sources. Considerable attention is given to El Salvador, especially on pages 102-13, but with other references scattered throughout the book.

73 **Salvador of the twentieth century.**
Percy F. Martin.   London: Edward Arnold, New York: Longman's Green, 1911. 344p.
The most important visitor's account of El Salvador in the early twentieth century, containing a great deal of information on the country. The author, an Englishman, provides detailed economic data along with his impressions of the people and culture. A Spanish translation, *El Salvador del siglo veinte* (San Salvador: UCA Editores, 1985) has appeared recently.

17

74   **A student in Central America, 1914-1916.**
Dana Gardner Munro.   New Orleans: Middle American Research
Institute, Tulane University, 1983. 75p. (Publication No. 51).

Perceptive observations by a University of Pennsylvania doctoral student who later
became a top State Department official involved with Central America and a leading
historian of the region. Munro's observations on El Salvador are brief but revealing;
they are to be found in the final chapter, pp. 63-68.

75   **Central America: Guatemala, Nicaragua, Costa Rica, Honduras,
Panama and Salvador.**
William H. Koebel.   London: Fisher Unwin, 1917. 375p. map.

Following a lengthy historical narrative through the mid-19th-century, Koebel
devotes several chapters to specific contemporary topics and states. These include El
Salvador on pages 273-79.

76   **The land beyond Mexico.**
Rhys Carpenter.   Boston: R. G. Badger, 1920. 181p.

The account of a muleback trip through Guatemala, El Salvador, and Honduras. The
author was an archaeologist, but this account focuses less on archaeological sites than
on the country in general. Carpenter's careful observations and photographs makes
this account one of the more valuable windows on early 20th-century Salvadoran
conditions.

77   **Gypsying through Central America.**
Eugene Cunningham.   London: Fisher Unwin; New York:
E. P. Dutton, 1922. 259p.

An interesting travel account, emphasizing physical backwardness and transportation
difficulties in Central America, but also providing considerable information on the
customs and situation of the period. The book reflects an attitude of cultural
superiority found in much of the travel literature of the period.

78   **Central American Indians and the Bible.**
William F. Jordan.   New York: Fleming H. Revell, 1926. 91p.

A memoir of Jordan's experiences as a missionary for the American Bible Society in
El Salvador, Guatemala, and Panama. The work focuses on Indian populations, and
on the effort to recruit missionaries for this area.

79   **Rainbow countries of Central America.**
Wallace Thompson.   New York: E. P. Dutton, 1926. 284p. map.

A highly descriptive travel account by an experienced travel writer, this book
contains many illustrations. The discussion of El Salvador, on pages 87-109, pays
considerable attention to the conditions and life-styles of the people.

80 **The Central Americans: adventures and impressions between Mexico and Panama.**
Arthur J. Ruhl. New York and London: Scribner's, 1928. 284p.

This chatty, illustrated travel account contains descriptions of social conditions in Central America, and provides a vast amount of information in the course of an impressionistic narrative. It reveals the nature of the countries and the peoples. Chapter 6 (pages 171-206) is concerned with El Salvador.

81 **The Pan American highway from the Río Grande to the Canal Zone.**
Harry A. Franck, Herbert C. Lanks. New York: Appleton-Century, 1940. 249p. maps.

Two experienced travellers describe their trip along the Pan American highway through Mexico and Central America. The treatment of El Salvador is not extensive, but it is descriptive of the condition of the highway in that country about 1940, and of the people and scenes on that route. Photographs supplement the text.

82 **Democracies and tyrannies of the Caribbean.**
William Krehm. Westport, Connecticut: Lawrence Hill, 1984. 244p.

Krehm was a *Time* magazine reporter who reported on a number of revolutions in the mid-1940s. This memoir contains his eloquent observations of life in El Salvador under the rule of Maximiliano Hernández Martínez and sheds light on the US policy of supporting Central American dictatorships during World War II. This account is excellent for gaining a sense of the country's political atmosphere during these years.

83 **The rainbow republics, Central America.**
Ralph Hancock. New York: Coward-McCann, 1947. 317p. maps.

Detailed description of many aspects of Central American life in the mid-1940s. Organization of the volume is topical, with sections on each country within topical chapters. The book is not very profound, but it offers considerable descriptive detail.

84 **El Salvador: país de lagos y volcanos.** (El Salvador: land of lakes and volcanoes.)
Alberto de Mestas. Madrid: Ediciones de Cultura Hispánica, 1950. 684p. maps. bibliog.

A perceptive and informative descriptive survey by a Spanish diplomat in El Salvador. Most of the work is divided between an economic history of the period from about 1930 to 1950 and a review of pre-Columbian and colonial history. The remainder is devoted to descriptions of contemporary politics, society, cultural and literary characteristics, transportation, communications, etc.

85 **Wayfarer in Central America.**
Tord K. E. Wallström, translated by M. A. Michel. London: Arthur Barker; New York: Roy Publishers, 1955. 192p.

This travel account is by a Swedish journalist. Wallström talked to a lot of ordinary people, but he also provides considerable description of the physical geography, and the flora and fauna.

86 **Four keys to El Salvador**.
Lilly de Jongh Osborne. New York, 1956.
A light and varied descriptive introduction to the history, traditions, and everyday life of El Salvador written by a well-informed foreigner.

87 **The lands and peoples of Central America: Guatemala, El Salvador, Costa Rica, Honduras, Nicaragua, Panama, British Honduras**.
Gerard Colvin. London: Adam & Charles Black; New York: Macmillan, 1961. 96p.
In this descriptive, illustrated view of contemporary Central America by an English observer coverage of El Salvador, pages 38-47, is brief and candid. It provides a sympathetic impression of the country about 1960, but avoids any discussion of the politics of the country or of the serious socio-economic inequities.

88 **Red rumba: a journey through the Caribbean and Central America**.
Nicholas Wollaston. London: Hodder and Stoughton, 1962. 231p.
Useful for the author's interviews with ordinary people on a trip through Cuba, Guatemala, Honduras, Nicaragua, Costa Rica, El Salvador, Panama, Puerto Rico, Haiti, and the Dominican Republic. El Salvador is covered on pages 107-21.

89 **The middle beat: a correspondent's view of Mexico, Guatemala, and El Salvador**.
Paul P. Kennedy. New York: Teachers College Press, 1971. 244p.
maps.
The memoir of an experienced journalist who covered these countries from 1954 to 1965. The greater part of this account deals with Mexico, but there are some revealing comments and episodes reported on El Salvador. The account consists of excerpts from his reports, interviews, and descriptive impressions.

90 **Another world: Central America.**
Hilda C. Espy, Lex Creamer. New York: Viking, 1970. 310p.
An impressionistic travel guide that still has much value as a description of the country's principal points of interest. Chatty and unscientific, it is nevertheless interesting. El Salvador is dealt with especially on pages 165-97.

91 **Central America: how to get there and back in one piece with a minimum of hassle**.
Doug Richmond. Tucson, Arizona: H. P. Books, 1974. 176p.
A travel guide emphasizing procedures to follow to avoid or at least minimize difficulties in the Central American states. Although much of the information contained in it is no longer accurate, it still contains much useful advice, and its many photographs make it an important window on Central America in the mid-1970s. There is a chapter on each state, and El Salvador, covered on pages 72-108, receives more attention in this volume than in most other travel guides.

92 **El Salvador: embassy under attack**.
Frank J. Devine. New York: Vantage, 1981. 209p.

This is a straightforward memoir of events in El Salvador during the author's tenure as United States ambassador to that country during the period 1977-80. Devine is reluctant to draw conclusions or take sides in the conflict. Rather, the work is a first-hand chronicle of the fast-moving events as he saw them from the Embassy. As such it is a useful historical source for the period. Unfortunately, the work does not have an index and for the most part no documentation is provided for the events mentioned.

93 **Salvador**.
Joan Didion. New York: Simon and Schuster, 1983. 108p.

Didion emphasizes the horrible cruelty of the right wing in the Salvadoran civil war. Although not altogether coherent, the book is quite graphic in its description of the deadliness of the conflict.

94 **Violent neighbors: El Salvador, Central America, and the United States**.
Tom Buckley. New York: Times Books, 1984. 358p. map.

A rambling, journalistic impression of Central America in the early 1980s. It gives considerable attention to El Salvador and its political difficulties, but it also deals with all of the other Central American states as well and is highly critical of Ronald Reagan's policy on the isthmus.

95 **Witness to war: an American doctor in El Salvador**.
Charles Clements. Toronto: Bantam, 1984. 268p.

A gripping account of a physician's year-long experience among Salvadoran peasants in a guerrilla-controlled war zone. An excellent 'grass-roots' view of the conflict.

Central America: the real stakes.
See item no. 12.

Descripción geográfico-moral de la diócesis de Goathemala. (Geographical and moral description of the Diocese of Guatemala.)
See item no. 166.

Latin America in the nineteenth century: a selected bibliography of books of travel and description published in English.
See item no. 659.

Flora and Fauna

General

96 **Flora y Fauna.** (Flora and fauna.)
San Salvador: Facultad de Ciencias y Humanidades, Universidad de El Salvador, 1975-. irregular.

This very irregular university publication is dedicated to the study of flora and fauna in El Salvador.

97 **Biologia centrali-americana, zoology, botany and archaeology**.
Edited by Frederick Ducane Goodman, Osbert Salvin. London: R. H. Porter and Dulau for the editors, 1879-1915. 63 vols. maps. bibliog.

This is a massive study of the flora and fauna of the region from Mexico through Panama, containing much information on El Salvador. Volume 1, published in 1915, contains an introduction to the work and outlines its contents. Vols. 2-52, prepared by a large number of distinguished scholars and published between 1879 and 1915, identify 38,637 different species of the fauna of the Middle American region, of which 19,067 are described for the first time and 18,051 are illustrated. These volumes contain 1,173 plates, including maps. Vols. 53-57, prepared by W. B. Hemsley, on the botany of the region, describe 11,626 species, 196 for the first time, with 44 illustrations and 111 plates, including maps. Vols. 58-63, prepared by Alfred P. Maudslay, deal with the archaeology of the region, but include nothing on El Salvador. This remarkable collection, with its magnificent plates, provides a solid base for the study of the flora and fauna of El Salvador, although the volumes, for the most part, are not organized geographically.

98   **Aquatic biota of Mexico, Central America and the West Indies, being a
     compilation of taxonomic bibliographies for the fauna and flora of
     inland waters of Mesoamerica and the Caribbean region.**
     Edited by Stuart H. Hurlbert, Alejandro Villalobos-Figueroa.   San
     Diego: San Diego State University, 1982. 529p.
One volume of a series called *Aquatic biota of Latin America.* Seventy-eight
bibliographical lists deal with the various orders of flora and fauna, each prepared by
a specialist. Each section begins with a brief summary, in both English and Spanish,
of the existing information on the taxonomy, biogeography, and the natural history
of the group. Some of the bibliographical entries are annotated.

99   **Central American jungles.**
     Don Moser.   New York: Time-Life Books, 1975. 184p. The American
     Wilderness).
A lavishly illustrated odyssey of Central American flora, fauna, and landscape, with
many full-colour photos.

Flora

100   **Flora salvadoreña.** (Salvadoran flora.)
      Felix Choussy.   San Salvador: Editorial Universitaria, 1975. 2nd ed.
      4 vols.
Originally published in 1926, this is a well-illustrated dictionary of Salvadoran plants
with short descriptions and comments on their medicinal and culinary properties.

101   **Especies útiles de la flora salvadoreña médico-industrial con aplicación
      a la medicina, farmacia, agricultura, artes, industria y comercio.**
      (Useful species of Salvadoran medical-industrial flora with application
      to medicine, pharmacy, agriculture, arts, industry and commerce.)
      David Joaquín Guzmán.   San Salvador: Ministerio de Educación,
      1975-76. 3rd ed. 2 vols. (Colección Biblioteca del Maestro, no. 6).
An important 19th-century work.

102   **Las orquídeas de El Salvador – The orchids of El Salvador – Die
      Orchideen El Salvador.**
      Fritz Hamer.   San Salvador: Ministerio de Educación, 1974. 2 vols.
      bibliog.
A multilingual guide to Salvadoran orchids, with many illustrations, some in colour.

23

103 **Lista preliminar de las plantas de El Salvador**. (Preliminary list of the
plants of El Salvador.)
Paul C. Standley, with the collaboration of W. A. Murrill, Salvador
Calderón. San Salvador: Tipografía la Unión, Dutriz Hermanos,
1925. 277p.

A non-illustrated list of plant species in El Salvador based on collections made by the
author and his collaborators. Most of the plants collected went to the United States
National Herbarium in Washington or to the Herbarium in the New York Botanical
Garden.

Fauna

104 **Noteworthy records of bats from El Salvador, Honduras, and
Nicaragua.**
Ira F. Greenbaum. Lubbock: Museum, Texas Tech University,
1978. 7p.

105 **Notes on amphibians and reptiles from El Salvador.**
Stanley Rand. *Fieldiana: Zoology* (Chicago Natural History
Museum), vol. 34, no. 42 (18 April 1957), p. 504-34.

Describes 43 species investigated from February to June 1951, in various parts of the
country.

106 **Birds of tropical America.**
Alexander F. Skutch. Austin: University of Texas Press, 1983. 320p.

This volume describes, with beautiful drawings by Dana Gardner and photographs by
the author, 34 species of tropical Central and South American birds. Painstaking
detail is included on the lives and daily habits of these birds.

107 **An annotated list of the hesperiidae of El Salvador.**
Stephen R. Steinhauser. Sarasota, Florida: Allyn Museum of
Entomology, 1975. 34p. map. bibliog. (Bulletin of the Allyn Museum,
no. 29).

See also by the same author, *Notes on neotropical nymphalidae and hesperiidae, with
description of new species and sub species of a new genus* (Sarasota, Florida: Allyn
Museum of Entomology, 1974) (Bulletin of the Allyn Museum, no. 22).

108 **Fauna of Middle America.**
L. C. Stuart. In: *Handbook of Middle American Indians*, vol. 1.
Austin, Texas: University of Texas Press, 1964, p. 316-62.

An excellent introduction to the fauna of the region.

109   **Zoo-noticias.** (Zoo-news.)
      San Salvador: Universidad Nacional de El Salvador, Facultad de
      Ciencias Agronómicas, Departamento de Zootécnica, 1979-80.
A periodical publication on zoology, published for only a brief period.

Prehistory and
Archaeology

110 **The archaeology of Quelapa, El Salvador.**
    E. Wyllys Andrews.   Tulane University, New Orleans: Middle
    American Research Institute, 1976. 199p. bibliog. (Publication 42).
Based on excavations conducted at the site of Quelapa in eastern El Salvador,
1967-69, this monograph provides illumination on late preclassical and classical
Mesoamerican civilization in El Salvador.

111 **La cultura pipil de Centro América.** (The Pipil culture of Central
    America.)
    Miguel Armas Molina.   San Salvador: Ministerio de Educación,
    1974. 60p. map. bibliog.
The author surveys the origins, immigrations, language, religion, social, economic,
and political organization of the Pipil Indians who settled in El Salvador.

112 **Central America.**
    Claude F. Baudez, translated by James Hogarth.   Geneva: Nagel,
    1970. 255p. maps. bibliog.
A richly illustrated guide to the archaeology of Central America by a leading French
archaeologist. Baudez defines Central America as that area between Guatemala and
Colombia, thus excluding Guatemala from this study.

113 **Figurillas con ruedas de Cihuatán y el oriente de El Salvador.)** (Small,
    wheeled figurines from Cihuatán and eastern El Salvador.)
    Stanley H. Boggs.   San Salvador: Ministerio de Educación, 1973.
    74p. (Colección Antropología no. 3).
Study of miniature clay figurines with wheels which resemble those found earlier in
Mexico and which constitute the only evidence that Indian cultures of Central

26

America knew of the wheel. It is published in Spanish and English, the latter being on pages 37-74.

114 **Pre-Maya costumes and coiffures.**
   Stanley H. Boggs. *Americas*, vol. 25, no. 2 (Feb. 1973), p. 19-24.
Analysis of the Bolinas style of Olmec figurines from El Salvador, suggesting several possible uses that were made of them by the pre-Columbian inhabitants.

115 **Archaeology of Cihuatán in El Salvador: preliminary report.**
   Karen O. Bruhns. *Calgary Archaeologist*, vol. 5 (1977), p. 7-10.
A survey and mapping project of the Cihuatán site in the Department of San Salvador was carried out as a feasibility study for a complete examination of the ancient urban site.

116 **The archaeology of Santa Leticia and the rise of Maya civilization.**
   Arthur A. Demarest.   New Orleans: Middle American Research Institute, Tulane University, 1986. 285p.
An important study of preclassical Mayan culture in western El Salvador based on excavations at Santa Leticia.

117 **The dating and cultural associations of the 'potbellied' sculptural style: new evidence from western El Salvador.**
   Arthur Demarest, Roy Switsur, Rainer Berger.   *American Antiquity*, vol. 47 (1982), p. 557-71.
In southern Mesoamerica, one of the major archaeological controversies has revolved around the 'potbellied' monuments of the preclassical period. An old view held that they were contemporary with, or even ancestral to, the Olmec style. The evidence presented here from a site at Santa Leticia, El Salvador, indicates that they are not as old as that, and probably date from the late classical period.

118 **Marihua rojo sobre beige y el problema pipil.** (Red on beige marihua and the Pipil question.)
   Wolfgang Haberland.   San Salvador: Administración de Patrimonio Cultural, 1978. 34p. bibliog. (Colección Antropología e Historia no. 13).
Originally published in English in *Ethnos* (Stockholm, 1964), this study of clay pots is based on research conducted in western and central El Salvador (1954-58). It sheds considerable light on the Pipil immigration from Mexico.

119 **Un complejo preclásico del occidente salvadoreño.** (A preclassic site in the Salvadoran west.)
   Wolfgang Haberland.   San Salvador: Ministerio de Educación, 1977. 9p. bibliog. (Colección Antropología e Historia, no. 12).
Originally published in English under the title: 'A pre-classic complex of western El Salvador, Central America', in *Proceedings of the XXXII International Congress of*

27

Americanists (Copenhagen, 1956), p. 485-90, this brief work provides a description of an important site in western El Salvador.

120 **The Maya and their neighbors.**
   C. L. Hay (et al.).   New York: Appleton-Century, 1940. 606p.

This Festschrift in honour of A. M. Tozzer included several articles which deal with El Salvador. These include chapter 6, 'The linguistic map of Mexico and Central America', by Frederick Johnson, p. 88-114; chapter 28, 'Anthropological problems in Central America', by Duncan Strong, p. 377-85; and chapter 30, 'Non-Maya monumental sculpture of Central America', by Francis B. Richardson, pp. 395-416.

121 **A guide to ancient Maya ruins.**
   C. Bruce Hunter.   Norman: University of Oklahoma Press, 1986.
   rev. ed. 342p. maps. bibliog.

A richly illustrated guide to Maya ruins. Since few of the notable Mayan sites are in El Salvador, this guide does not include extensive attention to ruins in El Salvador as such, but they are mentioned. As a general guide to the Maya area, however, this is the standard guidebook.

122 **What is lower Central American archaeology?**
   Olga F. Linares.   *Annual Review of Anthropology*, vol. 8 (1979),
   p. 21-43.

This survey of recent archaeology in Lower Central America includes El Salvador. Most of the work outlined is descriptive and, the author laments, lacking in analysis.

123 **Mesoamerican archaeology, a guide to the literature and other information sources.**
   Susan Fortson Magee.   Austin, Texas: Institute of Latin American
   Studies, University of Texas, 1981. 71p. bibliog.

A basic guide to archaeological sources for the region whose southern boundary 'extends from the mouth of the Ulua River in Honduras to the Nicoya Peninsula in Costa Rica'. This includes all of El Salvador. Magee reviews the principal general works on the region, guides to the literature, bibliographies, periodicals, and indexes to abstracts, reviews, theses and dissertations, associations and societies, grants and research centres, international agencies, government agencies, special library collections, Human Relations Area Files, museums, atlases and maps, specialists, academic institutions and field schools, biographical dictionaries, non-print materials and search techniques.

124 **Facts and artifacts of ancient Middle America: a glossary of terms and words used in the archaeology and art history of pre-columbian Mexico and Central America.**
   Compiled by Curt Muuser.   New York: E. R. Dutton, 1978.

This glossary of terms is designed to facilitate the study of ancient Middle America with 2,000 entries in the fields of geography, archaeology, linguistics, art, ethnography, and literature.

125 **Interaction on the southeast Mesoamerican frontier.**
Edited by Eugenia J. Robinson. Oxford: British Archaeological
Reports, 1987. 2 vols.

A group of scholarly archaeological papers dealing with prehistoric El Salvador and
Honduras.

126 **The prehistory of Chalchuapa, El Salvador.**
Edited by Robert J. Sharer. Philadelphia: University of
Pennsylvania Press, 1978. 3 vols. (Museum Monographs, University
Museum, University of Pennsylvania).

Volume 1 contains a series of reports on archaeological research (surveys and
excavations) conducted at the Chalchuapa archaeological site, with diagrams and
photographs. Volume 2 covers ceramics and figurines, and volume 3 discusses
pottery and presents conclusions.

127 **Archaeology and volcanism in Central America: the Zapotitán Valley
of El Salvador.**
Edited by Payson D. Sheets. Austin: University of Texas Press,
1983. 307p. maps. bibliog. (The Texas Pan American Series).

A series of articles by scholars involved in the University of Colorado's 'Postclassic
Project' in El Salvador's Zapotitán Valley, evaluating the diverse effects of the third-
century Ilopango eruption on valley inhabitants.

128 **Behavioral analysis and the structure of a prehistoric industry.**
Payson D. Sheets. *Current Anthropology*, vol. 16, no. 3 (Sep. 1975),
p. 369-91.

The author uses scientific analysis of obsidian blades found in Chalcuapa, El
Salvador, to suggest a model for understanding the nature of the stone-cutting
industry in the southeastern Mayan highlands of Central America.

129 **The prehistory of El Salvador: an interpretive summary.**
Payson D. Sheets. In: *Archaeology of Lower Central America*,
edited by Frederick W. Lange, Doris Z. Stone. Albuquerque:
University of New Mexico Press, 1984, p. 85-112. maps. bibliog.

A review of the prehistory of El Salvador, paying particular attention to external
relationships, ecology and adaptation, volcanism, and regional economics. This
chapter is also a useful guide to the current state of archaeological research on El
Salvador.

130 **Pre-columbian man finds Central America: the archaeological bridge**.
Doris Stone. Cambridge, Massachusetts: Peabody Museum Press,
Harvard University, 1972. 248p. map. bibliog.

An excellent introduction to the archaeology of Central America, this much
illustrated volume does a good job of placing the archaeology of El Salvador in its
regional context.

131 **A classic period Maya agricultural field in western El Salvador.**
Christian J. Zier. *Journal of Field Archaeology*, vol. 7, no. 1 (1980),
p. 65-74.

The author describes a prehistoric Mayan cornfield in the Zapotitán Valley of
western El Salvador.

132 **A functional analysis of late classic period Maya settlements in the
Zapotitán Valley, El Salvador.**
Christian John Zier. PhD Dissertation, University of Colorado at
Boulder, 1981. (University Microfilms order no. 8209869).

Part of a larger project seeking the manner in which reoccupation of the Zapotitán
Valley occurred after the eruption of Ilopango volcano in the third century AD. The
study stresses population growth, agricultural intensification, political consolidation,
and economic exchange.

El poblamiento nahuat de El Salvador y otros paises de Centroamérica. (The
Nahuat population of El Salvador and other countries of Central America.)
See item no. 240.

Handbook of Middle American Indians.
See item no. 241.

**The art and archaeology of pre-Columbian Middle America: annotated
bibliography of works in English.**
See item no. 654.

History

Central America: general

133 **History of Central America.**
Hubert Howe Bancroft. San Francisco: History Co., 1886-87. 3 vols.
Although heavily influenced by the Liberal historians of his time and certainly out of date in many respects, Bancroft's compendious work is still one of the best sources for colonial and 19th-century Central American history.

134 **La América Central ante la historia.** (A history of Central America.)
Antonio Batres Jáuregui. Guatemala: Marroquín Hermanos, Sánchez y De Guise, and Tipografía Nacional, 1916-1949. 3 vols.
A good general survey of Central American political history. Tends to favour the Conservatives more than most of the histories written by Central Americans in the late 19th or early 20th centuries. The first two volumes treat the colonial period; the third volume covers the period 1821-1921.

135 **Centroamérica y la economía occidental (1520-1930).** (Central America and the western economy (1520-1930).)
Ciro Cardoso, Hector Pérez Brignoli. San José: Editorial Universidad de Costa Rica, 1977. 395p. bibliog.
An outline history of Central America in the broader context of Western economic history. A very useful volume for seeing the highlights of Central American economic history and for understanding the growing dependency of Central America on the industrialized nations.

31

History. Central America: general

136 **Dependency and development in Latin America**.
Fernando Henrique Cardoso, Enzo Faletto. Berkeley: University of
California Press, 1979. 227p.

One of the classic expositions of dependency theory as an explanation for Latin
American development, this work has considerable relevance for Central American
history. This work offers many definitions of dependency, some of which appear
contradictory, but it is one of the better introductory works on the subject. For a
critical evaluation of dependency theory, see Robert A. Packenham, 'Holistic
dependency'. *New World, A Journal of Latin American Studies*, vol. 2, nos 1-2
(1987), p. 12-48.

137 **Central America and the Caribbean**.
New York: Arno Press, 1980. 412p. bibliog. (The Great
Contemporary Issues).

Facsimile reprints of articles from the *New York Times* tell the history of the
Caribbean region from 1868 to 1980, providing insight into the relationship of the
region to the United States and the place of El Salvador within the region.

138 **Class struggle in Central America: background and overview.**
Norma Stoltz Chinchilla. *Latin American Perspectives*, vol. 3,
nos. 2-3 (1980), p. 2-23.

A convenient overview of Central American history from a Marxist perspective.

139 **Historia de Centroamérica.** (History of Central America.)
Ernesto Chinchilla Aguílar. Guatemala: Ministerio de Educación
Pública, 1974-77. 3 vols. bibliog.

A major history of Central America by a distinguished Guatemalan historian. The
work is a detailed narrative, but focuses heavily on the pre-Columbian (vol. 1) and
colonial (vol. 2 and half of vol. 3) periods, with only cursory coverage of the
nineteenth and twentieth centuries since independence. Understandably, this work is
Guatemalan oriented, but nevertheless an important contribution to the history of El
Salvador.

140 **The historiography of Central America since 1830.**
William J. Griffith. *Hispanic American Historical Review*, vol. 40,
no. 4 (1960), p. 548-69.

A masterful description of the literature of 19th and 20th century Central American
history, providing scholarly evaluation of the quality and quantity of historical writing
on the region to 1960.

141 **The failure of union: Central America, 1824-1960.**
Thomas L. Karnes. Tempe, Arizona: Center for Latin American
Studies, Arizona State University, 1976. 2nd ed. 283p. map. bibliog.

Karnes surveys the frequent attempts at Central American union from the
establishment of the United Provinces in 1824 to the present. This is a scholarly and
readable volume, a standard work in Central American history.

142   **Spanish Central America: a socioeconomic history, 1520-1720.**
      Murdo J. MacLeod.   Berkeley, California: University of California
      Press, 1973. 554p. maps. bibliog.
MacLeod's monumental study of Central America under Habsburg rule is essential to
any study of the colonial period. He documents thoroughly the development of the
population and economy during the first two centuries of Spanish rule in Central
America, providing perceptive analysis and description. Although he is primarily
concerned with social and economic development, he tells us a great deal about the
political structure as well.

143   **Breve historia de Centroamérica.** (Brief history of Central America.)
      Hector Pérez Brignoli.   Madrid: Alianza Editorial, 1985. 169p.
      maps. bibliog.
A brief synthesis of Central American history, written by one of the leading
historians at the University of Costa Rica. He covers major themes from 1520 to
1984, but with particular emphasis on the 20th century.

144   **Middle American governors.**
      Compiled by Glen W. Taplin.   Metuchen, New Jersey: Scarecrow
      Press, 1972. 196p. bibliog.
This volume includes a chronological listing of the chief executives of El Salvador,
from the sixteenth to the twentieth century. The principal events of their
administrations are noted.

145   **Central America, a nation divided.**
      Ralph Lee Woodward, Jr.   New York: Oxford University Press,
      1985. 2nd ed. 390p. map. bibliog. (Latin American Histories series).
A general, socio-economic survey of Central American history from pre-Columbian
times to 1985. The author considers the five Central American states as a single unit,
but substantial coverage is given to El Salvador and its role within Central America.
The volume includes an extensive bibliographical essay. See also Woodward's essay
on modern Central American political development, 'The rise and decline of
liberalism in Central America: historical perspectives on the contemporary crises',
Journal of Inter-American Studies and World Affairs, vol. 26, no. 3 (1984), p. 291-
312.

146   **The historiography of modern Central America since 1960.**
      Ralph Lee Woodward, Jr.   *Hispanic American Historical Review*,
      vol. 67, no. 3 (1987), p. 461-96.
Discusses historical works on 19th- and 20th-century Central America published since
1960, thus updating Griffith's earlier historiographical article (q.v.).

147   **Government and society in Central America, 1680-1840.**
      Miles Wortman.   New York: Columbia University Press, 1982. 373p.
      bibliog.
Although the focus of this important study of colonial and early independent Central

America is on Guatemala, it refers frequently to El Salvador, and provides a useful synthesis of the important changes that occurred there in the eighteenth century.

148 **Vida militar de Centro América.** (The military life of Central America.)
Pedro Zamora Castellanos.   Guatemala: Tipografía Nacional, 1924. 562p.

A traditional military history of Central America, principally dealing with the 19th century, although there is a brief colonial section. It includes detailed descriptions of battles, especially for the nineteenth century and the federation period. Written by a Guatemalan army officer, coverage is heavily weighted toward his own state, but there is nevertheless considerable coverage of Salvadoran military history also.

The Central American republics.
See item no. 15.

Central America early maps up to 1860.
See item no. 48.

Handbook of Middle American Indians.
See item no. 241.

Interpretación del desarrollo social centroamericano, procesos y estructuras de una sociedad dependiente. (Interpretation of Central American social development, processes and structures of a dependent society.)
See item no. 284.

Economía agraria y movimiento obrero en Centroamérica (1850-1933). (The agrarian economy and the labour movement in Central America (1850-1933).)
See item no. 551.

Central America in the nineteenth and twentieth centuries: an annotated bibliography.
See item no. 641.

El Salvador: general

149 **Historia militar de El Salvador.** (Military history of El Salvador.)
Gregorio Bustamante Maceo.   San Salvador: Imprenta Nacional, 1951. 2nd ed. 211p.

A summary of Salvadoran military history to 1931, containing brief accounts of major battles and sketches of leading military figures. This work is a convenient index to key battles and military figures, but it offers little in the way of substantial detail or analysis.

150 **Recordatorio histórico de la República de El Salvador**. (Historical journal of the Republic of El Salvador.)
José F. Figeac.   San Salvador: Talleres Gráficos Cisneros, 1938. rev. ed. 500p.

A narrative overview of Salvadoran history through the nineteenth century, heavily weighted toward the colonial period, this volume includes lengthy quotations from documents from government archives in San Salvador and Guatemala. It lacks analysis, but provides a chronicle of the political history El Salvador to about 1900. It also includes brief essays on the histories of the capitals of each of the departments of El Salvador.

151 **Historical dictionary of El Salvador**.
Philip F. Flemion.   Metuchen, New Jersey: Scarecrow Press, 1972. 157p. bibliog.

A handy, but scarcely comprehensive, reference work, with cross-referenced entries dealing with various subjects. Useful for quickly identifying major figures, events, and places in Salvadoran history.

152 **Origen, desarrollo y crisis de las formas de dominación en El Salvador.** (The origins, development and crisis of the forms of domination in El Salvador.)
Mario Flores Macal.   San José: Servicios Editoriales Centroamericanos, 1983. 144p. bibliog.

A careful and painstaking dependency analysis of the historical evolution of the socio-economic structure of El Salvador. A basic work for research in Salvadoran history.

153 **El Salvador: background to the struggle.**
Richard Lapper, Hazel Johnson.   *Race and Class*, vol. 22 (1980), p. 63-76.

The authors maintain that since the decline of indigo and the rise of coffee in the late 19th century, the Salvadoran élite, represented by the '14 families', has dominated the economy. Since 1932 it has ruled through the military, crushing all movements for popular reform. This article is a useful review of the various long-term analyses of Salvadoran history.

154 **Gobernantes de El Salvador (biografías).** (Governors of El Salvador (biographies).)
María Leistenschneider, Freddy Leistenschneider.   San Salvador: Ministerio del Interior, 1980. 280p.

Brief biographical sketches with photographs of the chiefs of state of El Salvador from 1821 to 1980, including interim and provisional chief executives and members of ruling juntas. A useful reference volume for biographical data, but this work makes no attempt at detailed evaluations of individual administrations.

155 **Manual de historia económica de El Salvador.** (Manual for the economic history of El Salvador.)
David A. Luna. El Salvador: Editorial Universitaria, 1986. 2d ed. 230p.

A traditional textbook of Salvadoran economic history, providing a useful reference volume with considerable detail on the principal events and changes, but less analytical than Flores Macal's work (q.v.). Most of the work concentrates on the colonial history and the nineteenth century, with only very cursory treatment of the twentieth century.

156 **Historia del Ministerio del Interior.** (History of the Ministry of the Interior.)
José María Melgar Callejas, J. Armando Dueñas C. San Salvador: Ministerio del Interior, 1976. 135p.

Official history of the ministry charged with the internal government of the country. The volume includes pertinent legislation and bibliographical references.

El Salvador in crisis.
See item no. 17.

El Salvador: landscape and society.
See item no. 31.

La población de El Salvador. (The population of El Salvador.)
See item no. 220.

Mitras salvadoreñas. (Salvadoran mitres.)
See item no. 262.

Períodos presidenciales y constituciones federales y políticas de El Salvador. (Presidential terms and political and federal constitutions of El Salvador.)
See item no. 377.

Historia de las instituciones jurídicas salvadoreñas. (History of Salvadoran juridical institutions.) *See* item no. 380.

Codificación de leyes patrias de la República de El Salvador, desde la independencia hasta el año de 1875. (Codification of the national laws of the Republic of El Salvador from independence to the year 1875.)
See item no. 381.

Historia de la Universidad de El Salvador, 1841-1930. (History of the University of El Salvador, 1841-1930.)
See item no. 570.

Historia de la Universidad de El Salvador. (History of the University of El Salvador.)
See item no. 575.

El periodismo en El Salvador. . . (Journalism in El Salvador. . .)
See item no. 617.

La libertad de imprenta en El Salvador. (Freedom of the press in El Salvador.)
See item no. 623.

Diccionario histórico enciclopédico de la República de El Salvador.
(Encyclopaedic historical dictionary of the Republic of El Salvador.)
See item no. 636.

Local, urban, regional, and departmental

157 **Biografía de vicentinos ilustres: homenaje al tercer centenario de la fundación de la ciudad de San Vicente.** (Biography of illustrious Vincentines: tribute to the tricentennial of the foundation of the city of San Vicente.)
Academia Salvadoreña de la Historia. San Salvador: Imprenta Nacional, 1962. 2nd ed. 178p.

Brief biographical sketches are included of 27 individuals from San Vicente who have distinguished themselves in a variety of endeavours. Most are nineteenth-century figures. Many of the sketches are accompanied by photographs.

158 **San Salvador y sus hombres.** (San Salvador and its men.)
Academia Salvadoreña de la Historia. San Salvador: Ministerio de Educación, 1967. 2nd ed. 424p. map.

This collaborative effort of many authors in the Salvadoran Academy of History, originally published in 1938, provides biographical sketches of historic residents of San Salvador. The bulk of the volume, p. 13-308, is taken up with sketches of from one to ten pages each on men from the sixteenth through to the early twentieth century. These are arranged in chronological order by birth dates. A second part, p. 311-37, arranged alphabetically, contains many more paragraph-length biographical sketches. The third part, p. 341-424, contains a history of the Spanish conquest and the founding of San Salvador, written by José Lardé and followed by some documents related to the founding of the city. For a more complete study of the early history of San Salvador, see Rodolfo Barón Castro, *Reseña histórica de la villa de San Salvador, desde sus fundación en 1525 hasta que recibe el título de ciudad en 1546* (Historical survey of the town of El Salvador, from its founding in 1525 until it received the title of city in 1546), 323p. bibliog. (Madrid: Ediciones Cultura Hispánica, 1950).

159 **San Miguel y sus hombres: apuntes biográficos e históricos.** (San
Miguel and its men: biographical and historical notes.)
Joaquín E. Cárdenas. San Salvador: Editorial Ahora, 1962. 271p.

This volume contains brief biographical sketches of important men in the history of
the Department of San Miguel. They mostly date from the 19th century.

160 **The early days of San Miguel de la Frontera.**
Robert Chamberlain. *Hispanic American Historical Review*, vol. 27
(Nov. 1947), p. 623-46.

This interesting account of the tumultuous early years (ca. 1530-43) of the province of
San Miguel, in eastern El Salvador, is based on archival and published sources.
During this period San Miguel evolved from a rough frontier province to a settled
and moderately prosperous colony.

161 **Hombres y cosas de Santa Ana: crónicas históricas documentadas de
hechos y obras notables de la ciudad y rasgos de la vida de sus hijos
más ilustres.** (Men and things of Santa Ana: documented historical
chronicles of notable events and works of the city and sketches of the
lives of its most illustrious sons.)
Edited by Juan Galdames Armas. Santa Ana: Imprenta Gutenberg,
1943. 245p.

A disparate collection of episodic chronicles and documents on Santa Ana, with brief
sketches on major individuals, plus a list of all the mayors and members of the city
council since the establishment of independence.

162 **Cojutepeque Cushutepec: biografía de un pueblo.** (Cojutepeque
Cushutepec: biography of a people).
Jorge B. Laínez. San Salvador: Ministerio del Interior, 1984. 3 vols
in 1. 444p.

A compilation of local history, legend, folklore, and promotion, designed to give
little more than a bit of Cojutepeque's flavour. Separate chapters deal with the
town's various landmarks, fiestas, education, sports, institutions, products, and
chronology of notable events from 1520 to 1983, followed by some brief biographical
sketches of distinguished Cojutepecans.

163 **El Salvador: historia de sus pueblos, villas y ciudades.** (El Salvador:
history of its villages, towns and cities.)
Jorge Lardé y Larín. San Salvador: Ministerio de Cultura, 1957.
571p.

The author gives brief, descriptive sketches, arranged alphabetically, on each
municipality in the republic.

Monografías departamentales. (Departmental monographs.)
See items no. 37, 38.

Exploración etnográfica en el Departamento de Santa Ana. (Ethnographic exploration in the Department of Santa Ana.)
See item no. 232.

Exploración etnográfica: Departamento de Sonsonate. (Ethnographic exploration: Department of Sonsonate.)
See item no. 233.

The decision-making process in El Salvador.
See item no. 331.

Recopilación de leyes relativas a la historia de los municipios de El Salvador. (Compilation of laws relating to the history of the municipalities of El Salvador.)
See item no. 384.

Hispanic El Salvador (1524-1821)

164 **An account of the conquest of Guatemala in 1524.**
Pedro de Alvarado, edited by Sedley J. Mackie.   Boston: Longwood Press, 1978. 146p.
A reprint of the translation of a vivid account of the conquest of El Salvador by its conqueror, Pedro de Alvarado. The first edition was published in New York by the Cortés Society in 1924. The work includes a facsimile of the original 1524 manuscript, sent by Alvarado to Fernán Cortés.

165 **Historia de El Salvador**. (History of El Salvador.)
Santiago I. Barberena.   San Salvador: Ministerio de Educación, 1966-69. 2 vols.
A narrative history by a leading 19th-century historian, who was born and educated in Guatemala but who spent much of his adult life in El Salvador. The work was first published in 1914, and covers only the pre-Columbian, conquest, and colonial periods, the main emphasis being on the pre-Columbian and conquest periods.

166 **Descripción geográfico-moral de la diócesis de Goathemala.**
(Geographical and moral description of the Diocese of Guatemala.)
Pedro Cortés y Larraz.   Guatemala: Sociedad de Geografía e Historia de Guatemala, 1958. 2 vols. (Biblioteca 'Goathemala' de la Sociedad de Geografía e Historia de Guatemala, vol. 20).
One of the most complete descriptions of El Salvador in the late colonial period, this work is based on an extensive survey conducted by the Archbishop of Guatemala. It is very useful for specific details on individual communities, for he describes each

parish's population, public works and roads, customs, indigenous languages, religious activities, and taxable wealth.

167 **La hacienda colonial en El Salvador: sus orígenes.** (The colonial hacienda in El Salvador: its origins.)
Mario Flores Macal. *Estudios Sociales Centroamericanos*, vol. 9 (1980), p. 355-80.

The author has studied the decline of cacao production and the subsequent turn to the production of indigo, and the effects of those changes on the labouring classes.

168 **The Guatemalan merchants, the government, and the 'provincianos', 1750-1800.**
Troy Floyd. *Hispanic American Historical Review*, vol. 41, no. 1 (Jan. 1961), p. 90-110.

Floyd demonstrates the economic and political relationships between the several provinces of colonial Central America, and the obstacles that would contribute to the disruption of Central American union following independence. For more detail, see Floyd's PhD. dissertation, *Salvadorean indigo and the Guatemalan merchants* (University of California, Berkeley, 1959).

169 **Estado general de la provincia de San Salvador (año de 1807).**
(General state of the province of San Salvador (in the year 1807).)
Antonio Gutiérrez y Ulloa. San Salvador: Ministerio de Educación, 1962. 2nd ed. 145p. (Colección Historia, 9).

This is a very useful contemporary statistical report on the population and production of El Salvador near the close of the colonial era.

170 **A statistical and commercial history of the Kingdom of Guatemala, in Spanish America. (Containing important particulars relative to its productions, manufactures, customs, &c, an account of its conquest by the Spaniards, and a narrative of the principal events down to the present time: from original records in the archives; actual observation; and other authentic sources).**
Domingo Juarros, translated by John Baily. London: J. Hearne, 1823. Reprinted, New York: AMS Press, 1971. 520p.

Although much less informative about El Salvador than Guatemala, this is still one of the basic source works for the end of the colonial period. Baily's translation is not complete, and the serious student will want to consult the original, *Compendio de la historia de la ciudad de Guatemala*, 2 vols. (Guatemala: Beteta, 1808-10). This work includes statistical data on population and economic affairs and is a useful source for understanding the changes that occurred in the kingdom near the close of the Hispanic era. It was, in fact, one of the principal sources for most histories of the late colonial period written in the 19th century.

171   **Estudios del Reino de Guatemala: homenaje al Profesor**
      S. D. Markman. (Studies of the Kingdom of Guatemala: tribute to
      Professor S. D. Markman)
      Edited by Duncan Kinkead.   Sevilla: Escuela de Estudios
      Hispanoamericanos, 1985. 201p.

This *Festschrift* for the Duke University art historian, Sidney Markman, contains a
number of articles relating to the colonial history of El Salvador, most notably 'La
conquista urbana de América Central (1509-1579)', by Francisco de Solano, p. 5-16;
'Apuntes para una historia de la cartografía urbana en América Central durante el
período colonial', by Jorge E. Hardoy, p. 17-48; 'Disasters, natural and otherwise,
and their effects upon population centers in the Reino de Guatemala', by Lawrence
Feldman, p. 49-60; and 'The economy of Central America at the close of the colonial
period', by Ralph Lee Woodward, Jr., p. 117-34. As indicated by their titles, the
articles are published in the language in which they were written.

172   **La patria del criollo: ensayo de interpretación de la realidad**
      guatemalteca. (The fatherland of the creole: an interpretive essay on
      the Guatemalan reality.)
      Severo Martínez Peláez.   Guatemala: Editorial Universitaria, 1971.
      786p. bibliog. (Colección Realidad Nuestra, vol. 1).

This is one of the major interpretive works in the recent historiography of colonial
Central America, and is especially useful for understanding the mentality of the
creole class. While its focus is on the creoles of Guatemala City, it has great
relevance for colonial El Salvador. The ideas developed by Martínez in this work are
based rather heavily on the 17th-century chronicle of Francisco Antonio de Fuentes y
Guzmán, *Recordación Florida* (3 vols. Guatemala: Sociedad de Geografía e Historia
de Guatemala, 1932).

173   **El añil en El Salvador.** (Indigo in El Salvador.)
      Jaime Mirando Flamenco.   *Anales del Museo Nacional David J.*
      Guzmán, vol. 50 (1977), p. 43-63.

In this brief account of the role of indigo production in Salvadoran history, the
author touches on some points overlooked by Robert Smith's 1959 article (q.v.).

174   **Raíces históricas del estado en Centroamérica**. (Historical roots of the
      state in Central America.)
      Julio C. Pinto Soria.   Guatemala: Editorial Universitaria, 1983. 2nd
      ed. 171p. (Colección Realidad Nuestra, vol. 10).

A solid synthesis is presented of the colonial factors that led to formation of the
Central American states. Based primarily on secondary sources, this work offers a
fine overview of political, economic, and social aspects of colonial Central America
and the foundations of the administrative and power structure of the independent
republics that followed.

175 **Alcaldes mayores: historia de los alcaldes mayores, justicias mayores, gobernadores, intendentes, corregidores, y jefes políticos de las provincias de San Salvador, San Miguel, y San Vicente.** (*Alcaldes mayores*: history of the *alcaldes mayores*, chief justices, governors, intendents, corregidors, and political chiefs of the provinces of San Salvador, San Miguel, and San Vicente.)
Manuel Rubio Sánchez.   San Salvador: Ministerio de Educación, 1979. 2 vols.

Following a brief survey of the founding and early development of San Salvador, this work sketches the careers of the *alcaldes mayores* and other governing officials of El Salvador from the sixteenth to the nineteenth century. These sketches range from a few paragraphs to 20 pages or more, and often include extensive quotations from documents of the period.

176 **Comercio terrestre de y entre las provincias de Centroamérica.** (Trade from and among the provinces of Central America.)
Manuel Rubio Sánchez.   Guatemala: Editorial del Ejército, 1973. 366p.

Based on extensive study of colonial documents, Rubio traces trade and trade policy from the Spanish conquest to the middle of the 18th century. As with most of Rubio's works, there is little analysis, but an enormous amount of information and liberal quotation from the documents. A projected future volume will continue this story to 1821.

177 **Forced native labor in sixteenth-century Central America.**
William L. Sherman.   Lincoln: University of Nebraska Press, 1979. 469p. bibliog.

One of the major works on 16th-century Central America, this thoroughly researched history contains much more detail than its title implies. The work also includes an extensive bibliography. See also Sherman's 'Indian slavery and the Cerrato reforms', *Hispanic American Historical Review*, vol. 51 (1971), p. 25-50.

178 **Indigo production and trade in colonial Guatemala.**
Robert S. Smith.   *Hispanic American Historical Review*, vol. 39 (1959), p. 181-211.

In a carefully researched article on the late 18th-century indigo trade, the author focuses on production in El Salvador and the relation between planters there and the Guatemalan merchants.

179 **Bourbon reforms in Central America: 1750-1786.**
Miles Wortman.   *The Americas*, vol. 32 (Oct. 1975), p. 222-38.

A useful overview of the Bourbon efforts to rejuvenate the Central American economy in the late 18th century. Wortman pays considerable attention to El Salvador in assessing the effects of the reforms in terms of economic development and increasing provincial autonomy within the kingdom.

Spanish Central America: a socioeconomic history, 1520-1720.
See item no. 142.

Government and society in Central America, 1680-1840.
See item no. 147.

The early days of San Miguel de la Frontera.
See item no. 160.

National origins in Central America.
See item no. 236.

19th-century El Salvador (1821-1900)

180 **El liberalismo en el Salvador a finales del siglo XIX.** (Liberalism in El Salvador at the end of the 19th century.)
Patricia A. Andrews. *Revista del Pensamiento Centroamericano*, vol. 36, no. 172/173 (1981), p. 89-93.

The article focuses on the administration of President Tomás Regalado (1898-1902), who restored constitutional government to El Salvador and initiated many liberal programmes, including expanded public education, health, and communications systems, promotion of new export crops and industry, and modernization of the army. Despite these efforts, Andrews points out that political instability, low government revenue, and the continued influence of the wealthy planters limited significant change.

181 **José Matías Delgado y el movimiento insurgente de 1811.** (José Matías Delgado and the insurgent movement of 1811.)
Rodolfo Barón Castro. San Salvador: Ministerio de Educación, 1962. 239p. (Biblioteca José Matías Delgado, 3).

This is the best work among many on the priest who led the movement for Salvadoran independence and separation from Guatemala. It is based on research in Spanish archives.

182 **The intellectual infrastructure of modernization in El Salvador, 1870-1900.**
E. Bradford Burns. *The Americas*, vol. 41, no. 3 (1985), p. 57-82.

An excellent survey of intellectual influence on the Salvadoran élite in the late 19th century in support of rapid economic development following North Atlantic models. Burns reviews literary, political, and social attitudes regarding economic development, the Indian, and the world, as he explains how an intellectual élite developed to support an institutional framework of modernization based on rapid agro-export expansion at the expense of rural masses.

183 **The modernization of underdevelopment: El Salvador, 1858-1831.**
E. Bradford Burns. *The Journal of Developing Areas*, vol. 18 (April 1984), p. 293-316.

A provocative article, following the themes laid down in his *Poverty of progress* (Berkeley: University of California Press, 1980), in which Burns illustrates, especially using travellers' accounts, how 'modernization' has expanded poverty, developed class antagonisms, and generally created results very different from those promised by the Liberal 'modernizers' of the 19th century.

184 **Historia de la Federación de la América Central, 1823-1840.** (History of the Central American Federation, 1823-1840.)
Pedro Joaquín Chamorro Zelaya. Madrid: Ediciones Cultura Hispánica, 1951. 644p.

This extensive history of the Central American federation, written by a leading Nicaraguan historian, is based largely on published documents, from which the author quotes extensively.

185 **Ensayo histórico sobre las tribus Nonualcas y su caudillo Anastacio Aquino.** (Historical essay on the Nonualca tribes and their great leader Anastasio Aquino.)
Julio Alberto Domínguez Sosa. San Salvador: Ministerio de Educación, 1964. 202p. bibliog.

A narrative history of one of the most important native uprisings in 19th-century Central America, which occurred in western El Salvador in the 1830s.

186 **El obispado de San Salvador: foco de desavenencia político-religiosa.** (The bishopric question in San Salvador: political and religious focus of discord.)
Mauricio Domínguez T. *Anuario de Estudios Centroamericanos*, vol. 1 (1974), p. 87-133.

A separate diocese for El Salvador was one of the major political issues in early 19th-century Central America, as the Salvadorans sought ecclesiastical as well as political independence from Guatemala. Domínguez traces this major controversy in this translation of his 1965 MA thesis at Tulane University, New Orleans; the original was presented in English.

187 **States' rights and partisan politics: Manuel José Arce and the struggle for Central American union.**
Philip Flemion. *Hispanic American Historical Review*, vol. 53, no. 4 (1973), p. 600-18.

Flemion's article is a scholarly treatment of the first president of the Central American federation, the Salvadoran Manuel José Arce, and the relationship between politics in El Salvador and the federal government during those years (1824-26).

188 **Documentos para la historia de la guerra nacional contra los**
filibusteros en Nicaragua. (Documents for the history of the National
War against the filibusters in Nicaragua.)
Angelita García Paz. San Salvador: Editorial Ahora, 1958. 233p.

This interesting collection of 113 documents on the Walker episode from a wide
range of published and archival sources includes several documents regarding El
Salvador's participation in the war against Walker.

189 **Historia moderna de El Salvador**. (Modern history of El Salvador.)
Francisco A. Gavidia. San Salvador: Ministerio de Cultura, 1958.
2nd ed. 497p.

Written in the early twentieth century, this was the first of a projected 2 volumes.
The second was never completed, but this volume is a detailed, traditional narrative,
focusing entirely on the attempted independence coups of 1811 and 1814. The work
includes a number of historical documents, and emphasizes the conflict between
Spanish *peninsulares* and creoles.

190 **The role of the coffee industry in the history of El Salvador, 1840-1906.**
Derek N. Kerr. MA thesis, University of Calgary, 1977. 182p.

Analyses the switch from indigo to coffee in the mid-nineteenth century under a
Liberal leadership influenced by positivist doctrines, and examines how the
consequent change in infrastructure destroyed traditional systems of the indigenous
agricultural sector.

191 **El positivismo de Gerardo Barrios**. (The positivism of Gerardo
Barrios).
Gary G. Kuhn. *Revista del Pensamiento Centroamericano*, vol. 36,
no. 172/173 (1981), p. 87-88.

Kuhn notes the elements of positivism in the policies of the Salvadoran liberal
president of El Salvador, 1858-63.

192 **Gerardo Barrios y su tiempo**. (Gerardo Barrios and his time.)
Italo López Vallecillos. San Salvador: Ministerio de Educación,
1965. 2 vols. bibliog.

This is the most complete and perceptive biography of the Salvadoran liberal leader
of the 1850s and 1860s. Volume 1 deals with his early career, before becoming
president, and volume 2 deals with his years as chief of state (1858-65). The earlier
biography by José D. Gámez, *Gerardo Barrios ante la posteridad* (San Salvador:
Ministerio de Educación, 1965), originally published in 1901, is also useful for its
extensive publication of documents.

193 **Guión histórico del poder legislativo de El Salvador: constituyentes-legislaturas: síntesis biográficas de sus presidentes**. (Historical guide to the legislative power of El Salvador: constituent assemblies – legislatures: biographical synopses of its presidents.)
Roberto Molina y Molina. San Salvador: Asamblea Legislativa, 1966-69. 2 vols.
The guide comprises brief biographical sketches of both the presidents and the representatives in Salvadoran legislatures and constitutional assemblies from 1822 to 1900. Volume 1 includes assemblies from 1822 to 1870 and volume 2 has those of 1870 to 1900. Photographs of many of the legislators are included.

194 **Los ministros de hacienda, 1838-1871**. (The ministers of finance, 1838-1871.)
Roberto Molina y Morales. San Salvador: Ministerio de Hacienda, 1970. 290p.
A volume of biographical sketches and photographs of the Salvadoran finance ministers during the years indicated. The sketches say little or nothing about their policies in office, but provide data on their backgrounds and careers and their relations with the presidents they served.

195 **Historia de El Salvador, anotaciones cronológicas**. (History of El Salvador, chronological annotations.)
Francisco J. Monterrey. San Salvador: Editorial Universitaria, 1978. 2 vols.
Organized chronologically, this is a collection of brief notes on events as they occurred, day by day. Volume 1 covers 17 March 1810 to 5 December 1842, and volume 2 covers 4 January 1843 to December 1871. Its utility as a reference work is greatly enhanced by the inclusion of a general index to names at the conclusion of volume 2.

196 **Reseña histórica de Centro-América**. (Historical review of Central America.)
Lorenzo Montúfar y Rivera Maestre. Guatemala: Tipografía El Progreso, 1877-87. 7 vols.
This is the classic Liberal account of their struggle with the Conservatives from the 1820s through 1871. Massively detailed, although not always accurate, this work deals primarily with Guatemala, but includes much on Salvadoran history as well. Montúfar was an active Liberal political leader during the period, and this work was as much designed to influence history as to record it. It was a major source for subsequent histories of the period.

197 **The Cádiz experiment in Central America, 1808 to 1826**.
Mario Rodríguez. Berkeley: University of California Press, 1978. 316p. bibliog.
A detailed and persuasive account of the emergence of liberalism in Central America

as a result of the ideology that dominated the Córtes of Cádiz, 1808-14. An impressive and highly significant scholarly work which contributes to a better understanding of the philosophy, goals, and methods of the Central American Liberals of the 19th and 20th centuries.

198   **A Palmerstonian diplomat in Central America: Frederick Chatfield, Esq.**
       Mario Rodríguez.   Tucson, Arizona: University of Arizona Press, 1964. map. bibliog.

A major monograph based on extensive research in diplomatic correspondence, detailing the career of the British envoy in Central America from 1833 to 1852. Reading this volume is absolutely essential to any understanding of mid-nineteenth century Central America and the British role there.

199   **Central American commerce and maritime activity in the 19th century: sources for a quantitative approach.**
       Thomas Schoonover.   *Latin American Research Review*, vol. 13 (1978), p. 157-69.

Identifies sources for the study of commercial activity in 19th-century El Salvador and, although it is not altogether comprehensive, it is definitely a contribution to improved research in Salvadoran economic history.

200   **La formación del estado en El Salvador.** (The formation of the state in El Salvador.)
       Horacio Trujillo.   *Estudios Sociales Centroamericanos*, vol. 10 (1981), p. 117-31. bibliog.

A useful survey, tracing most of the internal contradictions of the Salvadoran state to the development of coffee production and the Liberal Revolution in the 19th century. The Liberals created a new system of political domination but left the social structure unchanged.

201   **Central America, 1821-c. 1870.**
       Ralph Lee Woodward, Jr.   *In: Cambridge History of Latin America*, vol. 3. Cambridge: Cambridge University Press, 1985, p. 471-506.

A detailed discussion and interpretation of the first half century of Central American independence, discussing the collapse of the Central American federation, the emergence of the independent republic of El Salvador, and the social and economic problems of the new republic. This study provides greater depth on the period indicated than the author's *Central America, a Nation Divided* (q.v.). It also contains a detailed bibliographical essay, p. 874-79.

Descripción geográfica y estadística de la República de El Salvador.
(Geographical and statistical description of El Salvador.)
See item no. 30.

Travels in Central America, 1821-1840.
See item no. 60.

El poder eclesiástico en El Salvador, 1871-1931. (Ecclesiastical power in El Salvador, 1871-1931.)
See item no. 255.

La compañía de Jesús en El Salvador, C. A., desde 1864 a 1872. (The Society of Jesus in El Salvador, C. A., from 1864 to 1872.)
See item no. 263.

Recopilación de las leyes del Salvador en Centroamérica. (Compilation of the laws of El Salvador in Central America.)
See item no. 378.

La unión de Centroamérica. (The Central American union.)
See item no. 399.

Historia de las relaciones interestatuales de Centro América. (History of Central American interstate relations.)
See item no. 401.

20th-century El Salvador (1900-88)

202 **Matanza: El Salvador's communist revolt of 1932.**
Thomas P. Anderson. Lincoln: University of Nebraska Press, 1971. 175p. map. bibliog.

A well-researched and vigorously written account of the origins of the peasant uprising of 1932 and of the brutal suppression of it by the Salvadoran army. From a different perspective, Rodolfo Cerdas, *La hoz y el machete: la internacional comunista en América Latina* (The sickle and the machete: the communist international in Latin America) (San José: Editorial Universitaria Estatal a Distancia, 1986. 445p.), explains the Communist International's failed efforts in this revolt.

203 **Esbozo biográfico: Farabundo Martí.** (Biographical sketch: Farabundo Martí.)
Jorge Arias Gómez. San José: EDUCA, 1980. 2nd ed. 162p.

Gómez has written a fairly objective, albeit sympathetic, biography of the leader of the 1932 communist peasant uprising in El Salvador.

204 **Consideraciones sobre el discurso político de la revolución de 1948 en El Salvador.** (Thoughts on the political meaning of the revolution of 1948 in El Salvador.)
Jorge Rafael Cáceres Prendes. *Anuario de Estudios Centroamericanos*, vol. 5 (1979), p. 33–52. bibliog.

An informative and thoughtful article suggesting an approach to 20th-century Salvadoran history in which the 1948 revolution is a key watershed. He periodizes Salvadoran development in this century as follows: (1) dependent capitalism and liberal authoritarianism, 1900-30; (2) paternalistic militarism, 1930-44; (3) democracy with socialist undertones, 1944-48; (4) since 1950, a period in which moderates have hindered true democracy and socio-economic reform.

205 **Paseo de recuerdo: San Salvador, 1900-1925.** (Memory lane: San Salvador, 1900-1925).
Casas y Bolsas, SA. San Salvador: Casas y Bolsas, 1985. 103p.

A collection of 172 photographs, some in colour, taken in San Salvador and other locations in El Salvador during the first quarter of the 20th century. Includes public buildings, churches, hotels, street scenes, economic activity, markets, historic monuments, natural scenery, and damage scenes from the 1917 earthquake.

206 **Miguel Marmol: los sucesos de 1932 en El Salvador.** (Miguel Marmol: the events of 1932 in El Salvador.)
Roque Dalton. San José: EDUCA, 1972. 566p. bibliog.

This biography of one of the leaders in the 1932 peasant uprising is actually a valuable autobiographical memoir of the period and helps the reader to understand the early development of the Salvadoran Communist party.

207 **The long war: dictatorship and revolution in El Salvador.**
James Dunkerley. London: Verso, 1982, 1985. 318p. map. bibliog.

An excellent review of twentieth-century Salvadoran history, the development of the class conflict and the present civil war. The work emphasizes the ongoing, underlying conflicts in Salvadoran society and politics, and contains considerable data on the oligarchies. See also his *Power in the Isthmus* (London: Verso, 1988).

208 **The Japanese and Central America.**
C. Harvey Gardiner. *Journal of Inter-American Studies and World Affairs*, vol. 14 (May 1972), p. 15-47.

The author examines Japanese interest in the isthmus from 1908 to about 1970, noting especially early Japanese interest in El Salvador.

209 **La hegemonía del pueblo y la lucha centroamericana.** (The hegemony of the people and the Central American struggle.)
Pablo González Casanova. Ciudad Universitaria Rodrigo Facio, Costa Rica: EDUCA, 1984. 126p. (Colección Debate)

Three essays by a leading Mexican historian which provide a thoughtful, sympathetic

interpretation of the revolutionary struggles in Central America. A theoretical
discussion argues that hegemony is a concept that must be adapted to the complex
reality of Central American society. The author reviews popular struggles in El
Salvador, Nicaragua, and Guatemala over the past thirty years and is critical of the
'limited democracy' proposed by North Americans as being merely a veil for the old
imperialism. González views Mexico's proper role as that of defending self-
determination for Central America.

210 **Trayectoria y crisis del estado salvadoreño, 1918-1981.** (Trajectory and
crisis of the Salvadoran state, 1918-1981.)
Italo López Vallecillos. *Estudios Centroamericanos*, vol. 36, no. 392
(1981), p. 499-528.

A superb overview of the political difficulties of government of El Salvador in this
century, in which the author analyses the economic system of the country and how
the élite managed various crises until the present breakdown. His central
hypothesis – that the ruling class had two leading sectors: the traditional agro-
exporters and a more modern industrial and financial group – is sound and helps to
explain the division within the élite along economic lines.

211 **Revolution in El Salvador, origins and evolution.**
Tommie Sue Montgomery. Boulder, Colorado: Westview Press,
1982. 252p. bibliog.

The author examines the historical and economic roots of the current crisis in El
Salvador, especially since about 1932, and with particular attention to events since
1979. It is argued that no lasting solution to problems in El Salvador is possible
without the participation of the Democratic Revolutionary Front and the Martí Front
for National Liberation (FDR/FMLN). This is a major contribution to understanding
the civil war in El Salvador.

212 **The five republics of Central America, their political and economic
development and their relations with the United States.**
Dana G. Munro, edited by David Kinley. New York: Russell &
Russell, 1967 (Reprint of original publication by the Carnegie
Endowment for International Peace, 1918). 348p.

Munro's survey of Central America is especially useful for its analysis and description
of the region during the first two decades of the twentieth century. Munro was an
official of the State Department present in Central America during much of the
period, and his astute observations provide excellent insights. His historical surveys
of earlier eras have less value today. He describes El Salvador on pages 99-118, but
El Salvador is also dealt with in a number of topical chapters. See also Munro's *A
Student in Central America.*

213 **Nonviolent insurrection in El Salvador: the fall of Maximiliano
Hernández Martínez.**
Patricia Parkman. Tucson: University of Arizona Press, 1988. 260p.

A careful, scholarly study of the use of the general strike to topple the Hernández
Martínez dictatorship in 1944.

214 **La Guardia Nacional Salvadoreña, desde su fundación, año 1912, al año 1927.** (The Salvadoran National Guard, from its foundation in the year 1912 to the year 1927.)
José T. Romeu. San Salvador: Imprenta Nacional, 1927. 208p. maps.

A descriptive and laudatory description of the founding and early years of the Salvadoran National Guard, written by its chief. This work is useful for its description of the organization and functioning of the Guard, its photographs, and for the listing of all officers as of 1927.

215 **El Salvador: crisis, dictadura, lucha, 1920-1980.** (El Salvador: crisis, dictatorship, struggle, 1920-1980.)
Mario Salazar Valiente. In: *América Latina: historia de medio siglo*, vol. 2, *Centroamérica, México y el Caribe*, edited by Pablo González Casanova. México: Siglo Veintiuno, 1981, p. 87-138.

An excellent overview, from a socialist perspective, of the mid-20th century in El Salvador.

216 **'Libro azul' de El Salvador/'Blue Book' of Salvador.**
Compiled and edited by L. A. Ward. San Salvador: Latin American Publicity Bureau, 1916. 393p.

This bilingual (English/Spanish) descriptive guide contains detailed accounts of the history, commerce, industry, and social life of El Salvador as of 1916, and is a useful source for the economic, political, and social history of the country, with numerous facts and statistics regarding government and private offices and personnel. Most of the data for the volume were collected by David J. Guzmán. The work includes a passable history of the country, as well as commentary on its geology, geography, communications, intellectual activity, flora and fauna, and society, including 'foreign colonies', and mini-biographies of principal officials and prominent citizens. It also includes sections on important national institutions, such as the National Guard and army, the church, and educational institutions. Finally, an appendix comprises a classified directory of businesses and professional people throughout El Salvador. It is, as such, an informative window on El Salvador in 1916 and an important source for historians. Unfortunately, this is the only year for which it was published.

217 **The crisis of national integration in El Salvador, 1919-1935.**
Everett A. Wilson. PhD dissertation, Stanford University, 1970. 295p. bibliog. (University Microfilms order No. 7018508).

A detailed study, based on published sources, of the transition of Salvadoran political and economic development from the apparently progressive Liberal élite of the early twentieth century to the military dictatorship of Maximiliano Hernández Martínez. Wilson argues that this shift following the Great Depression of 1929 represented the emergence of a national system within El Salvador, as opposed to the loosely organized society of the earlier period. As such, he believes it represented a step away from Central American union toward a stronger Salvadoran national state. The study contains considerable detail on the economic and political history of the period.

51

El Salvador.
See item no. 19.

Democracies and tyrannies of the Caribbean.
See item no. 82.

El Salvador: Background to the struggle.
See item no. 153.

El poder eclesiástico en El Salvador, 1871-1931. (Ecclesiastical power in El Salvador, 1871-1931.)
See item no. 255.

The Catholic Church in Central America.
See item no. 267.

El Salvador, acumulación de capital y proceso revolucionario (1932-1981). (Capital accumulation and the revolutionary process in El Salvador (1932-1981).)
See item no. 337.

Bitter grounds: roots of revolt in El Salvador.
See item no. 346.

José Napoleón Duarte and the Christian Democratic Party in Salvadoran politics, 1960-1972.
See item no. 354.

Función política del ejército salvadoreño en el presente siglo. (Political function of the Salvadoran army in the present century.)
See item no. 356.

Crisis política y organización popular en El Salvador. (Political crisis and peoples' organization in El Salvador.)
See item no. 360.

El ascenso del militarismo en El Salvador. (The rise of militarism in El Salvador.)
See item no. 361.

The war of the dispossessed: Honduras and El Salvador, 1969.
See item no. 391.

The Martínez era: Salvadoran-American relations, 1931-1944.
See item no. 404.

The U.S. and the rise of General Maximiliano Hernández Martínez.
See item no. 415.

The political economy of Central America since 1920.
See item no. 438.

Economic development of El Salvador, 1945-1965.
See item no. 455.

El Banco Central de Reserva en el desarrollo económico de El Salvador.
(The Central Reserve Bank in the economic development of El Salvador.)
See item no. 465.

Las perspectivas del desarrollo agropecuario y la tenencia de la tierra.
(Perspectives on agricultural development and land tenure.)
See item no. 503.

Export agriculture and the crisis in Central America.
See item no. 530.

Historia del movimiento obrero en América Latina. (History of the labour
movement in Latin America.)
See item no. 549.

**Art as a source for the study of Central America, 1945-1975: an exploratory
essay.**
See item no. 605.

Population

218   **La población de Centroamérica y sus perspectivas**. (The population of Central America and its perspectives.)
Jorge Arias de Blois.   Guatemala: Universidad de San Carlos de Guatemala, Facultad de Ingeniería, 1966. 59p.

The author surveys population and related statistics, including distribution characteristics, growth and its implications.

219   **ADS. Carta Informativa**. (ADS newsletter.)
San Salvador: Asociación Demográfica Salvadoreña, 1983-. irregular.

This is the newsletter of a Salvadoran organization formed to educate the public on questions of demography, birth control, and population problems.

220   **La población de El Salvador**. (The population of El Salvador.)
Rodolfo Barón Castro.   San Salvador: UCA Editores, 1978. 708p.

A reprint of the classic demographic history of El Salvador, originally published in 1942, this work is a careful compilation and analysis of the growth of the Salvadoran population. Much of the work deals with the colonial period and the author has rested heavily on the report of the Salvadoran Intendente, Antonio Gutiérrez y Ulloa, *Estado general de la provincia de San Salvador (año de 1807)* (General state of the Province of San Salvador (in the year 1807) (q.v.).

221   **Human resources of Central America, Panama, and Mexico, 1950-1980, in relation to some aspects of economic development**.
L. A. Ducoff.   New York: United Nations, 1960. 155p.

A thorough statistical study of population trends and the labour force and their relation to the economic development of the region.

54

222 **Scarcity and survival in Central America: ecological origins of the Soccer War.**
William H. Durham. Stanford: Stanford University Press, 1979. 226p. maps. bibliog.

A splendid analysis of the causes of the 1969 war between El Salvador and Honduras, stressing the relationship between population and the availability of land. It goes far beyond the root causes of the war and gets at the fundamental problems in Salvadoran society caused by the expansion of agro-exports. This is one of the most significant books ever written about El Salvador.

223 **Population and urban trends in Central America and Panama.**
Robert W. Fox, Jerrold W. Huguet. Washington: Inter-American Development Bank, 1977. 233p. bibliog.

Based on data from the mid-1970s and earlier census data, this study projects population trends on the isthmus through to the year 2000 with the purpose of facilitating economic planning.

224 **Plantations, population, and poverty: the roots of the demographic crisis in El Salvador.**
Gerald E. Karush. *Studies in Comparative International Development*, vol. 13 (1978), p. 59-75.

An explanation of poverty in El Salvador along dependency theory lines, which the author perceives to be the cause of a demographic crisis. He is critical of family planning programmes because they ignore the effects of social structure on reproductive behaviour. Until changes in that structure eliminate poverty, he argues that El Salvador cannot expect demographic changes such as those experienced by Cuba and many industrial nations.

225 **Population densities using a new approach: a preliminary report.**
Robert E. Nunley. *Revista Geográfica* (Instituto Panamericano de Geografía e Historia, Brazil), no. 66 (June 1967), p. 55-93. maps.

These are the preliminary findings of a research project designed to develop more effective approaches to studying the distribution of human populations. The article deals with Nicaragua, Guatemala, Honduras, El Salvador, Costa Rica, and Belize. It is useful for its information about and comparisons of population density in Central America.

226 **Ecología humana en Centroamérica: un ensayo sobre la regionalización como instrumento de desarrollo.** (Human ecology in Central America: an essay on regionalization as an instrument of development.)
Gabriel Pons. San Salvador: ODECA, 1970. 247p. maps.

An erudite discussion of population trends and problems in Central America, calling for a Central American regional plan to coordinate population and resource policy. It includes a great deal of data on population, resources, and infrastructure, as well as photographs and tables.

227 **Demographic Yearbook.**
United Nations, Department of Economic and Social Affairs,
Statistical Office. New York: United Nations, 1948-. annual.

Provides detailed statistics on population, including birth and mortality rates,
migration, marriages, annulment, divorce, and marital status and household
composition. Information for El Salvador is not complete for all categories, but this
yearbook will provide a great deal of information on the country's population. In
English and French.

228 **El Salvador, estudios de población.** (El Salvador, population studies.)
United Nations Fund for Population Activities. San Salvador:
Ministerio de Planificación y Coordinación del Desarrollo Económico
y Social, Unidad de Población y Recursos Humanos, Fondo de
Naciones Unidas para Actividades de Población, 1979. 3 vols in 2.

Extensive tables and charts showing demographic indicators in the 1970s and
projections to the year 2000. A major source for population study, these studies are
the result of intensive research conducted by a United Nations commission in
cooperation with the government of El Salvador. Among the studies published here
are several by Alex Alens on the country's principal demographic characteristics
(1950-70); projections of the principal demographic indicators by sex and age to the
year 2000; the population by sex, age, urban, and rural residence, 1950-2000; and the
economically active population, urban and rural, 1970-85; studies by Peter Jones on
the relations between economic, social, and demographic variables in El Salvador;
and a study by Joseph Van der Boomer on the socio-economic characteristics of
migrants to San Salvador in 1976.

229 **Legislative attitudes toward over-population: the case of El Salvador**.
Joel G. Verner. *Journal of Developing Areas*, vol. 10 (Oct. 1975),
p. 61-76.

Reviews El Salvador's serious population explosion in the 20th century, noting the
absence of serious family planning in the country. Describes and analyses attitudes
and opinions of Salvadoran legislators toward various aspects of the country's critical
population problem, based on data obtained in 1973 and 1974. Verner concluded that
legislators were aware of the problem and believed that something should be done
about it, but that none of the 50 legislators interviewed had actually done anything
themselves. This article offers considerable enlightenment on attitudes toward sex
among élite sectors in El Salvador.

**Scarcity and survival in Central America: ecological origins of the Soccer
War**.
See item no. 222.

**Social classes, accumulation, and the crisis of 'overpopulation' in El
Salvador**.
See item no. 283.

Salud pública y crecimiento demográfico en Centro América. (Public health and population growth in Central America.)
See item no. 296.

Situación demográfica, social, económica y educativa de El Salvador. (Demographic, social, economic and educational situation of El Salvador.)
See item no. 558.

Nationalities and Minorities

230 **Cultural components of Central America.**
Richard N. Adams. *American Anthropologist*, vol. 58 (1956),
p. 881-907.
This basic article classifies the various modifications of Indian and Spanish culture in
Central America.

231 **Cultural surveys of Panama – Nicaragua – Guatemala – El Salvador –
Honduras.**
Richard N. Adams. Washington: Pan American Union, 1957. 669p.
maps. bibliog.
A fairly comprehensive survey of the peoples of each of the Central American states.
Although now dated, it remains an important introduction to the anthropology of the
Central American states.

232 **Exploración etnográfica en el Departamento de Santa Ana.**
(Ethnographic exploration in the Department of Santa Ana.)
Concepción de Guevara. San Salvador: Ministerio de Educación,
Dirección de Cultura, 1973. 231p. maps. bibliog. (Etnografía
Salvadoreña, 1).
A detailed ethnographic survey of the Department of Santa Ana. A general
discussion of the characteristics of the department is followed by specific treatment of
the municipalities of Santa Ana, Coatepeque, El Congo, Texistepeque, Chalcuapa,
Candelaria de la Frontera, El Porvenir, San Sebastián, Salitrillo, Metapán, Masajuat,
Santa Rosa Guachipilín, Santiago de la Frontera, and San Antonio Pajonal. A
concluding section consists of tables identifying which of 100 ethnographic features
exist in each municipality.

233 **Exploración etnográfica: Departamento de Sonsonate**. (Ethnographic
exploration: Department of Sonsonate.)
Concepción Clara de Guevara.   San Salvador: Ministerio de
Educación, Dirección General de Cultura, 1975. 415p. maps. bibliog.
(Etnografía Salvadoreña, 2).

A detailed ethnographic survey of the Department of Sonsonate. A general
discussion of the characteristics of the department is followed by specific treatment of
the municipalities of Sonsonate, Nahuizalco, San Antonio del Monte, Santo
Domingo de Guzmán, Nahulingo, Sonzacate, Acajutla, Izalco, Armenia, Caluco,
San Julián, Santa Isabel Ishuatán, Cuisnahuat, Juayúa, Salcoatitán, and Santa
Catarina Masahuat. A concluding section consists of tables identifying which of 100
ethnographic features exist in each municipality.

234 **El problema indígena en El Salvador.** (The Indian problem in El
Salvador.)
Alejandro D. Marroquín.   *América Indígena*, vol. 35, no. 4 (1975),
p. 747-70.

In an attempt to refute those who believe that El Salvador has no Indian problem,
this general survey calls for cooperation of anthropologists and other social scientists
to deal with that small number of unintegrated Salvadoran Indians. This issue of
América Indígena, devoted entirely to the study and analysis of the indigenous
population of El Salvador, includes several other articles on the indigenous
population of the country.

235 **Etnografía de El Salvador.** (Ethnography of El Salvador.)
Gloria A. Mejía de Gutiérrez.   San Salvador: Departamento de
Etnografía, Dirección de Investigaciones, Dirección de Patrimonio
Cultural, Ministerio de Cultura y Comunicaciones, 1985. 200p. map.
bibliog.

Prepared as part of the reorganizational plan of the David J. Guzmán National
Museum, this outline survey indicates the principal areas of Salvadoran ethnography.
Separate sections deal with popular religion, social organization, rural life, traditional
cooking, entertainment, the oral tradition, humour, colloquialisms, popular traditional medicine, and popular art. An extensive bibliography is appended.

236 **National origins in Central America.**
Francis Merriman Stanger.   *Hispanic American Historical Review*,
vol. 12, no. 1 (1932), p. 18-45. bibliog.

A thoughtful article attributing the separate development of the Central American
states to their isolation and closer contact with outside powers than with one another.
They also eacl have a distinct ethnic development in terms of their origins from
indigenous populations.

237 **Etnohistoria de El Salvador: el guachival centroamericano.** (Ethnohistory of El Salvador: the Central American *guachival*.)
Santiago Montes.   San Salvador: Ministerio de Educación, 1977.
2 vols.
A major study of Salvadoran Indians, social organization, religion and mythology,
social life, and customs.

238 **Indiana.**
Leonhard Sigmund Schultze-Jena.   Jena: Gustav Fischer, 1933-38.
3 vols.
A major German anthropological study of Middle American Indians, with volume 2,
Mythen in der Muttersprache: der Pipil von Izalco in El Salvador (Myth in the native
language: the Pipil of Izalco in El Salvador), concentrating on the Pipil of El
Salvador. An initial section, p. 1-187, deals with history, pre-Columbian to the
twentieth century, with considerable attention given to contemporary living
conditions and customs, but the majority of the volume is concerned with the Pipil
language.

239 **Women of El Salvador: the price of freedom.**
Marilyn Thomson.   London: Zed; and Philadelphia: Institute for the
Study of Human Issues, 1986. 165p. bibliog.
A thorough survey of the role of women in El Salvador in the 1980s, including
discussion of their life-styles, health conditions, family relations, and family planning.
Several sections deal with women in organizations, including the church, trade
unions, marketplaces, and education. It also discusses the activities of several women
in the Salvadoran civil war and in areas controlled by guerrilla forces. Other works
on Salvadoran women in the civil war which may be of interest include Claribel
Alegría's *They won't take me alive* (q.v.) and a collection of articles, interviews,
comment, and poetry by women involved early in the conflict, emphasizing human
rights violations and oppression by Salvadoran government forces, published under
the title *Women and war – El Salvador* (New York: Women's International Resource
Exchange, 1981).

240 **El poblamiento nahuat de El Salvador y otros paises de Centroamérica.**
(The Nahuat population of El Salvador and other countries of Central
America.)
Jorge A. Vivó Escoto.   San Salvador: Ministerio de Educación,
1973. 27p. maps. (Colección Antropología, no. 2).
A well-documented and fundamental analysis of the question of Nahuat migration
from Mexico to Central America and especially to El Salvador. The pamphlet
discusses methodological questions and reviews what is known on the topic. It also
includes a discussion of place-names of Nahuat origin. It concludes that at the time of
the Spanish conquest, El Salvador was dominated by Nahuat peoples.

241 **Handbook of Middle American Indians.**
Edited by Robert Wauchope (et al.). Austin: University of Texas
Press, 1964-. 16 vols, plus supplement.

Edited at the Middle American Research Institute of Tulane University, this is a massive collaborative collection. The work in broad in scope and contains not only materials specifically relating to Indians, but also a great deal on the region's geography, archaeology, history, population, linguistics, flora and fauna, economic development and culture. Volume titles only begin to indicate the breadth and utility of this remarkable collection: 1. Natural environment and early cultures, edited by Robert C. West; 2. and 3. Archaeology of southern Mesoamerica, edited by Gordon R. Willey; 4. Archaeological frontiers and external connections, edited by Gordon Ekholm and Gordon R. Willey; 5. Linguistics, edited by Norman A. McQuown; 6. Social anthropology, edited by Manning Nash; 7. and 8. Ethnology, edited by Evon Z. Vogt; 9. Physical anthropology, edited T. Dale Stewart; 10. and 11. Archaeology of northern Mesoamerica, edited by Gordon Ekholm and Ignacio Bernal; 12. to 15. Guide to ethno-historical sources, edited by Howard Cline; 16. Sources cited and artifacts illustrated, edited by Margaret A. L. Harrison; Supplement, edited by Victoria Bricker: vol. 1, Archaeology, edited by Jeremy A. Sabloff; vol. 2, Linguistics, and vol. 3, Literatures, edited by Munro S. Edmonson, and vol. 4, Ethnohistory, edited by Ronald Spores.

242 **Sons of the shaking earth.**
Eric R. Wolf. Chicago: University of Chicago Press, 1959. 302p.
bibliog.

This classic anthropological interpretation of the people of Middle America puts great emphasis on the importance of the land to the Indians of the region. Wolf provides insight and understanding of the life of the peasants of Central America, especially of the Indian regions.

Ensayo histórico sobre las tribus Nonualcas y su caudillo Anastacio Aquino.
(Historical essay on the Nonualca tribes and their great leader Anastasio Aquino.)
See item no. 185.

Language

243 **La lengua salvadoreña.** (The Salvadoran language.)
Pedro Geoffroy Rivas. San Salvador: Ministerio de Cultura y
Comunicaciones, 1987. 131p. 2nd ed. bibliog. (Colección V
centenario).

The author describes and analyses the peculiarities of Salvadoran Spanish, including
a discussion of local provincialisms, foreign elements in the language, and Indian
words that have entered it. Several earlier editions of this work were published under
the title *El español que hablamos en El Salvador* (The Spanish we speak in El
Salvador).

244 **Fundación de la Academia Salvadoreña de la Lengua, correspondiente
de la Real Academia Española, 1876: documentos históricos: vida
académica.** (Foundation of the Salvadoran Academy of Language,
correspondent of the Royal Spanish Academy, 1876: historical
documents: academic life.)
Academia Salvadoreña de la Lengua. San Salvador: Ministerio del
Interior, 1981. 486p.

Documents published commemorating the centennial of the Academia Salvadoreña
de la Lengua, 1876-1976.

Indiana
See item no. 238.
Handbook of Middle American Indians.
See item no. 241.

Folklore

245 **Estampas y música folklórica**. (Folkloric impressions and music.)
María de los Angeles de Castillo.   San Salvador: Imprenta Nacional,
1968. 34p.
A small collection of poems, songs, dances, and little stories expressing contemporary Salvadoran folk culture.

246 **Recopilación de materiales folklóricos salvadoreños**. (Compilation of
Salvadoran folkloric materials.)
Concepción Clara de Guevara.   San Salvador: Comité de
Investigaciones del Folklore Nacional y Arte Típico Salvadoreño. San
Salvador: Imprenta Nacional, 1944. 412p.
This work was the result of a major collaborative effort by the nation's
schoolteachers who combined their efforts to produce a compilation of representative
examples of Salvadoran folklore, including poetry, songs, legends, stories, colloquialisms, games, proverbs, etc.

247 **Calendario de fiestas religiosas tradicionales de El Salvador**. (Calendar
of traditional religious festivals of El Salvador.)
Concepción Clara de Guevara.   San Salvador: Dirección de
Patrimonio Cultural, Departamento de Etnografía, Ministerio de
Educación, 1978. 258p.
Arranged chronologically, this is an excellent guide to traditional fiestas throughout
the country. Each entry indicates the annual dates and location of the fiesta, the
distance from San Salvador and the condition of the roads and means of
transportation available. In addition, there is a brief description of the festival,
indicating its special qualities, highlights, activities, and what crafts and other goods

Folklore

are sold there. The civil war has undoubtedly curtailed and limited the continuance of some of these festivals in recent years.

248 **Leyendas salvadoreñas**. (Salvadoran legends.)
Compiled by Adolfo de Jesús Márquez.   San Salvador: Imprenta La República, 1942. 130p.
A collection of short stories and poetry reflecting Salvadoran folklore tradition from pre-Columbian times to the mid-twentieth century.

249 **El folklore en la literatura de Centro América.** (Folklore in Central American literature.)
Rafael Heliodoro Valle. *Journal of American Folklore*, vol. 36 (April-June), p. 105-34. bibliog.
A brief overview of Central American folklore in literature, with an extensive bibliography, p. 110-34.

Exploración etnográfica en el Departamento de Santa Ana. (Ethnographic exploration in the Department of Santa Ana.)
See item no. 232.

Exploración etnográfica: Departamento de Sonsonate. (Ethnographic exploration: Department of Sonsonate.)
See item no. 233.

Religion

250 **La iglesia en América Central y el Caribe.** (The church in Central
America and the Caribbean.)
Isidoro Alonso, Gines Garrido. Bogotá: Oficina Internacional de
Investigaciones Sociales de FERES, 1962. 282p. maps. (Estudios
socio-religiosas latinoamericanos, no. 4).

A useful overview for the 1950s, but this is not a history of the church in the region.
A section on El Salvador, p. 149-64, describes the social structure of the country,
based on the 1950 census, as a background for a discussion of the ecclesiastical
structure, and includes chapters on the secular and regular clergy and its
characteristics. It documents a considerable growth in the clergy between 1944 and
1960, although at a rate slightly lower than the general population growth in the same
period. Statistical tables, p. 251-61, provide additional detail on the Catholic Church
and clergy by regions of the country.

251 **Steadfastness of the saints, a journey of peace and war in Central and
North America**.
Daniel Berrigan. Maryknoll, NY: Orbis; Melbourne: Dove
Communications, 1985. 140p.

This poignant, insightful, and beautifully written account of a well-known Catholic
peace activist's journey through Nicaragua and El Salvador links the violence there to
the contorted ethics of violence in the United States.

252 **The religious roots of rebellion: Christians in Central American
revolutions**.
Philip Berryman. Maryknoll, NY: Orbis Books, 1984. 464p. bibliog.

A systematic analysis of the role of liberation theology in Central America, relating it
closely to the revolutionary struggles there. Considerable attention to the Church's
role in El Salvador and the Basic Christian Community movement. A major work,

strongly approving liberation theology and the involvement of Christians in the struggle to improve the opportunities of the poor.

253 **Murdered in Central America: the stories of eleven U.S. missionaries.** Donna Whitson Brett, Edward T. Brett. Maryknoll, NY: Orbis, 1988. 300p.

The appalling and distressing account of US missionaries murdered in Central America, including Jean Donovan, Dorothy Kazel, Ita Ford, and Maura Clark in El Salvador. The authors argue that US policy adds to the violence in El Salvador rather than helping to end it.

254 **The world remains: a life of Oscar Romero.** James R. Brockman. Maryknoll, NY: Orbis, 1982. 256p. bibliog.

A well documented biography of San Salvador's martyred archbishop, a vicitim of the political violence in that country.

255 **El poder eclesiástico en El Salvador, 1871-1931.** (Ecclesiastical power in El Salvador, 1871-1931.) Rodolfo Cardenal. San Salvador: UCA Editores, 1980. 342p.

A balanced history of church-state relations in El Salvador from 1871 to 1931, emphasizing the anti-clericalism of the Salvadoran Liberals, followed by the alliance of the coffee élite with a servile clergy. For the earlier period, see the pro-church, narrative ecclesiastical history covering the colonial period and the nineteenth century by Santiago R. Vilanova, *Apuntamientos de historia patria eclesiástica* (Notes on the national ecclesiastical history) (San Salvador: Imprenta Diario de El Salvador, 1911).

256 **Salvador witness: the life and calling of Jean Donovan.** Ana Carrigan. New York: Simon & Schuster, 1984. 320p.

The tragic and inspiring story of a young American Catholic missionary who was murdered with three other American missionaries in December 1980. It offers a unique view of the savageness of the civil war in El Salvador, along with the story of a remarkable woman and her work in that country.

257 **El Salvador in revival.** T. Wynn Drost. Hazelwood, Missouri: Word Aflame Press (Pentecostal Publishing Co.), 1987. rev. ed. 141p.

First published in a private edition in 1983, this is a description of the experiences of a Pentecostal missionary in El Salvador in the early 1980s. It reflects both the political and religious situation there, explaining how the United Pentecostal Church grew from nothing to more than 10,000 members in only seven years. In part, the book is a practical handbook for conducting revivals in El Salvador.

258 **Archbishop Romero, martyr of Salvador.**
Plácido Erdozain. Maryknoll, NY: Orbis, 1980. 128p.

Erdozain focuses on the life of Oscar Romero from the time he became Archbishop of San Salvador through to his assassination in 1980. The author, an Augustinian priest who worked closely with Romero, eulogizes the martyred archbishop and tells of his conversion from conservative views to becoming an outspoken advocate of the poor.

259 **Faith of a people: the life of a basic Christian community in El Salvador.**
Pablo Galdámez. Maryknoll, NY: Orbis, 1986. 112p.

Recording the history of a basic Christian community in the outskirts of San Salvador from 1970-80, this is an important documentary example of the power of the theology of liberation in El Salvador. The book won the 1986 Christopher Award.

260 **Religion in Central America.**
Kenneth Grubb. London: World Dominion Press, 1937. 147p. maps.

Grubb describes Protestant missions in Central America a half century ago.

261 **Romero, El Salvador's martyr: a study of the tragedy of El Salvador.**
Dermot Keogh. Dublin: Dominican Publications, 1981. 160p. map. bibliog.

A sympathetic account by an Irish journalist and historian of Archbishop Oscar Romero's opposition to right-wing repression and of Romero's assassination in 1980. It also looks at the lives of some ordinary Salvadorans who have suffered serious human rights abuses.

262 **Mitras salvadoreñas.** (Salvadoran mitres.)
Ramón López Jiménez. San Salvador: Imprenta Nacional, 1960. 185p.

Biographical sketches are given of the seven bishops (or archbishops) of San Salvador from independence to 1960. The work includes discussion of church-state relations and the major accomplishments of each bishop's tenure, as well as excerpts from major pastorals and other writings of the prelates.

263 **La compañía de Jesús en El Salvador, C. A., desde 1864 a 1872.** (The Society of Jesus in El Salvador, C. A., from 1864 to 1872.)
Santiago Malaina. San Salvador: Imprenta Nacional, 1939. 125p.

A scholarly treatment by a Jesuit priest of the brief return of the Jesuit order to El Salvador in 1864 up to their expulsion by the Liberals in 1872. An important study for understanding the nature of the church-state conflict in 19th-century El Salvador. The work includes biographical sketches of the Jesuits.

Religion

264 **The church in the Salvadoran revolution.**
Tommie Sue Montgomery. *Latin American Perspectives*, vol. 10, no. 1 (winter 1983), p. 62-87. bibliog.

A detailed description of the role of the Catholic Church and clergy in the Salvadoran civil war. This thorough review examines the social doctrines of the church and the changes that occurred in the attitudes of the Salvadoran ecclesiastical hierarchy, clerical activism, Christian base communities, the Jesuit Universidad Centroamericana, the role of Archbishop Oscar Romero, and the ongoing role of the church and clergy in the struggle against oppression after his assassination. See also Montgomery's comparison of the church's role in El Salvador and Nicaragua in her 'Cross and rifle: revolution and the church in El Salvador and Nicaragua,' *Journal of International Affairs*, vol. 36 (winter 1982), p. 209-21.

265 **The same fate as the poor.**
Judith M. Noone. Maryknoll, NY: Orbis, 1984. 160p.

A description, with photographs, of the active role of the clergy in El Salvador in trying to improve the social condition of the poor.

266 **The voice of blood: five Christian martyrs of our time.**
William J. O'Malley. Maryknoll, NY: Orbis, 1980. 204p.

This book tells the stories of five martyrs in El Salvador, Rhodesia, and Brazil.

267 **The Catholic Church in Central America.**
Frederick D. Pike. *Review of Politics*, vol. 21 (Jan. 1959), p. 83-113.

A good historical overview of the Catholic Church's role in Central America throughout the 1960s, with considerable attention paid to El Salvador.

268 **Revista Latinoamericana de Teología** (Latin American Review of Theology.)
San Salvador: Centro de Reflexión Teológica, Universidad Centroamericana José Simeón Cañas, 1984-.

A major journal with a strong influence of liberation theology.

269 **Iglesias de los pobres y organizaciones populares.** (Churches of the poor and popular organizations.)
Monsignor Oscar A. Romero, Monsignor Arturo Rivera Damas, Ignacio Ellacuria, Jon Sobrino, Tomás R. Campos. San Salvador: UCA Editores, 1978. 249p.

A collection of documents and essays on the relation of the church to the poor and relations between the church and organizations representing the poor people of El Salvador. It includes both theoretical essays and documents relating to developments in these areas in El Salvador.

270 **Voice of the voiceless: the four pastoral letters and other statements.**
Oscar A. Romero. Maryknoll, NY: Orbis, 1985. 208p.

Romero's moving statements on behalf of the poor of El Salvador, including a pastoral message to the US Council of Churches, addresses at the universities of Georgetown and Louvain, a letter to President Jimmy Carter, and his last homily.

271   **Central America and politicized religion.**
       James V. Schall.   *World Affairs*, vol. 144 (1981), p. 126-49.
An analysis of the Roman Catholic clergy in El Salvador, particularly the Jesuit Order, and its relationship with the political left.

272   **Theology of Christian solidarity.**
       Jon Sobrino, Juan Hernández Pico.   Maryknoll, NY: Orbis, 1985.
       112p. bibliog.
Two Salvadoran Jesuit theologians reflect on the significance of the basic Christian communities among the poor in El Salvador and Latin America.

273   **The impact of Monsignor Romero on the churches of El Salvador and the United States.**
       José Jorge Simán.   Washington: The Wilson Center, 1983. 28p.
A leading Salvadoran political scientist cómments on the role and assassination of Archbishop Oscar Romero, on his country's developments, and on relations with the United States.

274   **La iglesia en El Salvador en 1970.** (The church in El Salvador in 1970.)
       Juan Ramón Vega.   *Estudios Centroamericanos,* vol. 26 (1971),
       p. 235-49.
An examination of the continuing importance of the Roman Catholic Church in El Salvador during the 1960s.

Calendario de fiestas religiosas tradicionales de El Salvador. (Calendar of traditional religious festivals of El Salvador.)
See item no. 247.

El Salvador entre el terror y la esperanza: los sucesos de 1979 y su impacto en el drama salvadoreño de los años siguientes. (El Salvador between terror and hope: the events of 1979 and their impact on the Salvadoran drama of the following years.)
See item no. 326.

Iglesias coloniales en El Salvador. (Colonial churches in El Salvador.)
See item no. 609.

Orientación. (Orientation.)
See item no. 626.

Proceso. Informativo Semanal del Centro de Documentación e Información. (Process. Weekly newsletter of the Centre for Documentation and Information.)
See item no. 633.

Social Conditions

General

275 **Boletín de Investigación** (Research bulletin.)
San Salvador: Facultad de Ciencias Sociales, Departamento de
Ciencias Políticas y Sociales, Universidad de El Salvador, 1979-.
irregular.

This journal is dedicated to the publication of research in the social sciences; it gives considerable attention to sociological studies and theoretical articles on social and political structure.

276 **La imagen de la mujer en El Salvador.** (The image of the woman in El
Salvador.)
Ignacio Martín-Baró. *Estudios Centroamericanos*, vol. 35 (1980),
p. 557-68.

The author analyses the attitudes towards women of 800 men and women in El Salvador between the ages of 14 and 40. Macho attitudes were most prevalent among the least educated and those unable to overcome the demands of the dominant culture.

277 **Centro América, subdesarrollo y dependencia.** (Central America,
underdevelopment and dependency.)
Mario Monteforte Toledo.   México: Universidad Nacional
Autónoma de México, 1972. 2 vols. maps. bibliog.

A major socio-economic study of Central America in which successive chapters survey geography, demography, health, agriculture, industry, integration movement, foreign domination and dependence, politics, labour, the military, the church, and the tradition of violence.

Steadfastness of the saints, a journey of peace and war in Central and North America.
See item no. 251.

Indicadores económicos y sociales CONAPLAN. (CONAPLAN economic and social indicators.)
See item no. 443.

Roots of rebellion: land and hunger in Central America.
See item no. 506.

Social structure

278   **Estructura y desarrollo social en El Salvador.** (Structure and social development in El Salvador.)
Victor Brodersohn.   *Desarrollo Económico* [Argentina], vol. 20 (1980), p. 121-34.

A brief and lucid survey of the recent development of the relationship between social and economic structures in El Salvador. The emphasis on production for export and on international trade has neglected the majority of the people by creating gross inequality in the distribution of income and permitting the concentration of economic power into the hands of local and foreign capital. The government has allowed this process to flourish with little intervention.

279   **Fundamentos económicos de la burguesía salvadoreña.** (Economic foundations of the Salvadoran bourgeoisie.)
Eduardo Colindres.   San Salvador: UCA Editores, 1977. 590p. bibliog.

Colindres describes the social structure of El Salvador in terms of the economic history of the country, focusing especially on the substantial economic change that occurred after 1950, with the rise of cotton and sugar exports in addition to coffee, and with the industrialization accompanying the Central American Common Market. Foreign capital played an important role in this development, but it also created a new bourgeoisie. This class, however, was too closely connected to the traditional landholding class to be progressive. The study, based on relatively few secondary works and government reports, includes extensive statistical tables. See also the author's *Approche d'une analyse des classes sociales au Salvador* (Approaching an analysis of social classes in El Salvador) (Louvain: Université Catholique de Louvain, 1973).

71

Social Conditions. Social structure

280 **El compadrazgo, una estructura de poder en El Salvador.** (The
     compadrazgo, a power structure in El Salvador.)
     Segundo Montes.   San Salvador: UCA Editores, c.1979. 386p.
     bibliog. (Colección Estructuras y procesos: Serie mayor, vol. 2).
Originally the author's thesis at the Universidad Complutense de Madrid, this wor
details the important godparent and kinship relationships that are highly important i
Salvadoran society.

281 **El Salvador: las fuerzas sociales en la presente coyuntura (enero 1980 i
     diciembre 1983).** (El Salvador: the social forces at the present junctur
     (January 1980 to December 1983.)
     Segundo Montes.   San Salvador: Universidad Centroamericana José
     Simeón Cañas, 1984. 221p. bibliog.
A detailed study of the various social forces, or factions, in El Salvador in thi
period, showing how they relate to the political struggle in the country and wher
they fit into the political structure. Extensive appendixes list all the social forces c
the right, centre, and left, as well as labour unions, political organization!
government institutions, and private organizations. This is an immensely valuabl
work for anyone interested in the social structure of El Salvador and its relation t
the present conflict.

282 **Estudio sobre estratificación social en El Salvador.** (Study on social
     stratification in El Salvador.)
     Segundo Montes.   San Salvador: Departamento de Sociología y
     Ciencias Políticas, Universidad Centroamericana José Simeón Cañas,
     1979. 534p. bibliog.
In this major work on Salvadoran social structure, one of El Salvador's leadin
sociologists has compiled a great deal of statistical data on the Salvadora
population. It concentrates on the period 1960-77.

283 **Social classes, accumulation, and the crisis of 'overpopulation' in El
     Salvador.**
     Ernesto Richter.   *Latin American Perspectives*, vol. 7 (1980),
     p. 114-35.
The 1969 Football War influenced the military later to take repressive measure
against the populance and caused much misunderstanding over the problem c
population growth.

284 **Interpretación del desarrollo social centroamericano, procesos y
     estructuras de una sociedad dependiente.** (Interpretation of Central
     American social development, processes and structures of a
     dependent society.)
     Edelberto Torres Rivas.   Ciudad Universitaria Rodrigo Facio, Costa
     Rica: EDUCA, 1971. 317p. bibliog.
A major contribution toward understanding the socio-economic dynamics of th

Central American countries, this has been a very influential work among Central American social scientists. It analyses the economy of Central America, especially from 1870 to 1970, in a dependency framework.

Origen, desarrollo y crisis de las formas de dominación en El Salvador. (The origins, development and crisis of the forms of domination in El Salvador.)
See item no. 152.

El Salvador: background to the struggle.
See item no. 153.

Scarcity and survival in Central America: ecological origins of the Soccer War.
See item no. 222.

Plantations, population, and poverty: the roots of the demographic crisis in El Salvador.
See item no. 224.

El Salvador: ¿por qué la insurrección? (El Salvador: why the insurrection?)
See item no. 298.

Rasgos sociales y tendencias políticas en El Salvador (1969-1979).(Social characteristics and political tendencies in El Salvador (1969-1979).)
See item no. 341.

Enemy colleagues: a reading of the Salvadoran tragedy.
See item no. 355.

Crisis política y organización popular en El Salvador. (Political crisis and peoples' organization in El Salvador.)
See item no. 360.

Análisis sobre el conflicto entre Honduras y El Salvador. (Analysis of the conflict between Honduras and El Salvador.)
See item no. 392.

Export agriculture and the crisis in Central America.
See item no. 530.

Rural development, class structure, and labor force participation: the reproduction of labor power in El Salvador.
See item no. 553.

Situación demográfica, social, económica y educativa de El Salvador. (Demographic, social, economic and educational situation of El Salvador.)
See item no. 558.

Social problems

285 **Report of a medical fact-finding mission to El Salvador, 11-15 January 1983.**
American Association for the Advancement of Science. Washington, DC: AAAS, 1983. 16p.

A team of US doctors went to El Salvador to investigate the whereabouts and legal status of 16 'disappeared' health professionals, to examine the treatment of political prisoners, to determine the status of university and medical education in El Salvador and to assess the effects of political violence and violations of human rights.

286 **Tercer censo nacional de vivienda, 1971.** (Third national census of housing, 1971.)
El Salvador. Dirección General de Estadística y Censos. San Salvador: Dirección General de Estadística y Censos, 1974. 464p.

This volume contains detailed statistical information on housing in El Salvador in 1971.

287 **Diagnóstico social: situación actual de las necesidades básicas en El Salvador.** (Social diagnosis: the present situation regarding basic necessities in El Salvador.)
FUSADES. San Salvador: Departamento de Estudios Económicos y Sociales, Fundación Salvadoreña para el Desarrollo Económico y Social (FUSADES), 1986. 38p.

An overview of El Salvador's very serious social problems and their relation to the economy. The authors consider the characteristics of the population and employment, noting the seriously high unemployment, warning of the repercussions in political instability that this causes. They comment on the need for more education, better housing, nutrition, and health services, with statistical tables. The unequal benefits of the economic growth of the 1970s are noted, but it is argued that the key to improvement in the situation is greater productivity. That will depend, however, the study acknowledges, on improved education, health services, and nutrition. It is acknowledged that solutions are not easy, but the authors call upon all sectors to work toward improvement.

288 **Evaluación nutricional de la población de Centro América y Panamá: El Salvador.** (Nutritional evaluation of the population of Central America and Panama.)
Instituto de Nutrición de Centro América y Panamá. Guatemala: Ministerio de Salubridad Pública, 1969. 142p.

Prepared by an organization (INCAP) of the Central American integration movement, this work provides statistical evidence of serious malnutrition in rural El Salvador.

289 **Condiciones de la mujer en El Salvador**. (Conditions of the woman in
     El Salvador.)
     Lilian Jiménez.   México: Editorial Muñoz, 1962. 76p.

Considers the status of women in El Salvador in terms of their rights in both the
home and the work place, with attention to the careers open to women. See also
Cisneros, *Condición jurídica de la mujer salvadoreña*. (The legal position of the
Salvadoran woman).

290 **El terremoto de octubre de 1986 en San Salvador y la situación
     habitacional de los sectores populares**. (The October 1986 earthquake
     in San Salvador and the housing situation in the populous sectors.)
     Mario Lungo.   Ciudad Universitaria Rodrigo Facio, Costa Rica:
     Confederación Universitaria Centroamericana, 1987. 26p.

A report on the housing problems created in El Salvador by the devastating
earthquake of October 1986.

291 **The ecology of malnutrition in Mexico and Central America: Mexico,
     Guatemala, British Honduras, Honduras, El Salvador, Nicaragua,
     Costa Rica and Panama.**
     Jacques Meyer May, Donna L. MacLellan.   New York: Hafner,
     1972. 408p. maps. bibliog. (Studies in Medical Geography, no. 11).

Detailed demographic, economic, and dietary information relating to nutrition in
each country reflects the serious problem of malnutrition in El Salvador and
emphasizes the need for attention to serious ecological change.

**Some factors in urbanism in a quasi-rural setting: San Salvador and San
José.**
See item no. 39.

To bear a child: meanings and strategies in rural El Salvador.
See item no. 295.

El Salvador 1987: Salvadoreños refugiados en los Estados Unidos. (El
Salvador 1987: Salvadoran refugees in the United States.)
See item no. 314.

The soft war: the uses and abuses of U.S. economic aid in Central America.
See item no. 405.

Social Services, Health, and Welfare

292   **Social welfare programmes in El Salvador, prepared for the Government of El Salvador.**
Maude T. Barrett.   New York: United Nations, 1954. 18p.
This is a reissue of an earlier report of 30 August 1951. Of little use for understanding contemporary Salvadoran welfare programmes, this pamphlet does, however, describe the situation in the early 1950s.

293   **Boletín de Psicología.** (Bulletin of Psychology.)
San Salvador: Universidad Centroamericana José Simeón Cañas, Departamento de Psicología, 1981-. irregular.

294   **Seroepidemiological studies of malaria in pregnant women and newborns from coastal El Salvador.**
Carlos C. Campbell, Juan Miguel Martínez, William E. Colline.
American Journal of Tropical Medicine and Hygiene, vol. 29 (1980), p. 151-57.
A medical study of 113 Salvadoran women during pregnancy and of their newborns to determine the incidence of malaria, and to discover if certain antibodies resulting from antimalarial treatment of the mother could be acquired and retained by the infants during the first 6 months of life.

295   **To bear a child: meanings and strategies in rural El Salvador.**
Polly Fortier Harrison.   PhD Dissertation, The Catholic University of America, 1983. (University Microfilms order no. 8318797).
An analysis of childbearing as a distillation of rural problems and attitudes in El Salvador. The author stresses the roles of modern and traditional medicine within the

psychological framework of women with regard to health care, particularly childbearing.

296 **Salud pública y crecimiento demográfico en Centro América.** (Public health and population growth in Central America.)
Instituto Centroamericano de Población y Familia. Guatemala: Edic ICAPF-IDESAC, 1968. 81p. (Colección Monografías Diagnósticas, no. 1.)

A concise report, principally statistical, of population and health care in each Central American country. Successive sections analyse the population, present indicators of the health situation, and discuss public health resources in Central America.

297 **ISSS. Estadísticas.** (S[alvadoran] I[nstitute of] S[ocial] S[ecurity]. Statistics.)
San Salvador: Instituto Salvadoreño de Seguro Social, 1970-84. annual.

Statistics on Salvadoran social security system and service.

Plantations, population, and poverty: the roots of the demographic crisis in El Salvador.
See item no. 224

Traditional medicine.
See item no. 652.

Bibliografía médica de El Salvador, 1900-1970. (Medical bibliography of El Salvador, 1900-1970.)
See item no. 653.

Human Rights

General

298 **El Salvador: ¿por qué la insurrección?** (El Salvador: why the insurrection?)
Higinio Alas.   San José: Comisión para la Defensa de los Derechos Humanos en Centroamérica, 1982. 293p.

A much illustrated work that surveys the agro-export structure of El Salvador, focusing on exploitation of the peasants, followed by a review of the military governments since 1970 and their violations of human rights. The author blames the selfishness of the Salvadoran élites for the problems and supports the armed rebellion. Additional chapters deal with labour organizations, guerrilla forces, religious involvement in the struggle, and the continued brutality of the military.

299 **Report on human rights in El Salvador.**
Compiled by Americas Watch Committee and the American Civil Liberties Union.   New York: Vintage Books, 1982. 312p.

This report by a committee headed by Roberto Alvarez provided detailed evidence of massive violations of human rights by Salvadoran government forces. It has been supplemented regularly by numerous other Americas Watch reports. See also *The continuing terror* (New York: Americas Watch, 1985) and Jemera Rone, *Settling into routine* (New York: Americas Watch Committee, 1986). A brief summary report on the situation in Central America is *An Americas Watch report. Human rights in Central America: a report on El Salvador, Guatemala, Honduras and Nicaragua* (New York: Americas Watch Committee, 1984). A list of available publications may be obtained from Americas Watch, 36 West 44th Street, New York, NY 10036; telephone (212) 840-9460. Amnesty International also reports regularly on human rights violations in El Salvador.

300 **Boletín. Ante la conciencia nacional** (Bulletin. Before the national
conscience.)
San Salvador: Comisión de Derechos Humanos de El Salvador, 1984-.
irregular

301 **Human rights and El Salvador.**
W. Scott Burke. *Strategic Review*, vol. 11 (spring 1983), p. 62-67.
The US Deputy Assistant Secretary for Human Rights and Humanitarian Affairs
explains US human rights policy in El Salvador. While human rights, he says, must
be an integral and indispensable part of the American consensus on which a
sustainable US foreign policy is based, it must also be applied in concert with other
US interests, rather than 'in an absolute way that ignores local conditions or relative
progress'. He criticizes past human rights policy for its 'single-dimensionality that
obscures the ravages of the conflict, the question of a moral choice between the
combatants, and the issue of the likely consequences of a cessation of US assistance',
and favours amending the certification process 'to avert irremediable damage to US
interests'.

302 **Managing the facts: how the administration deals with reports of
human rights abuses in El Salvador.**
Holly Burkhalter. New York: Americas Watch Committee, 1985.
42p.
A criticism of how the Reagan administration dealt with factual reports of human
rights abuses in El Salvador during 1981-85.

303 **Derechos humanos en El Salvador en 1986.** (Human rights in El
Salvador in 1986.)
Instituto de Derechos Humanos. San Salvador: Universidad
Centroamericana José Simeón Cañas, 1987.

304 **Report on the situation of human rights in El Salvador.**
Inter-American Commission on Human Rights. Washington:
Organization of American States, 1978. 188p.
The formal report of the OAS commission that investigated alleged human rights
violations in January 1978. The report concluded that such violations were
widespread and made recommendations for remedying the situation.

305 **El Salvador under General Romero.**
Latin American Bureau. London: Latin American Bureau, 1979.
254p.
Bitterly critical of human rights violations and repression under the government of
Carlos Humberto Romero, this work contains considerable detail on the politics of
the country and its socio-economic problems from a leftist perspective.

306   **El Salvador: human rights dismissed; a report on 16 unresolved cases.**
      Lawyers Committee for Human Rights.   New York: LCHR, 1986.
      100p.
The most recent of a series of reports, beginning with *Justice in El Salvador: a case study* in 1982, by the Lawyers Committee for Human Rights on human rights abuses in El Salvador. The reports focus on specific cases, and emphasize the failure of the Salvadoran judicial system adequately to pursue these cases.

307   **From the ashes: justice in El Salvador.**
      Lawyers Committee for Human Rights.   New York: LCHR, 1987.
      75p.
Details the collapse of El Salvador's criminal justice system and focuses on US government efforts to improve the country's legal system.

308   **Human rights and United States policy toward Latin America.**
      Lars Schoultz.   Princeton, New Jersey: Princeton University Press,
      1981. 421p. bibliog.
A scholarly study of US policy on human rights with respect to Latin America, with frequent reference to human rights in El Salvador, especially during the Jimmy Carter administration.

309   **The situation in El Salvador.**
      United States. Congress. House Committee on Foreign Affairs,
      Subcommittee on Human Rights and International Organizations.
      Washington: GPO, 1984. 342p.
This volume contains documents, testimony and comment on the human rights situation in El Salvador based on testimony to, and investigation by, the congressional committee.

Update Latin America.
See item no. 28.

Report of a medical fact-finding mission to El Salvador, 11-15 January, 1983.
See item no. 285.

Central America: human rights and U.S. foreign policy.
See item no. 418.

Labor rights in El Salvador.
See item no. 548.

Refugees

310 El Salvador, the other war.
Tom Barry and Deb Preusch.   Albuquerque: Inter Hemispheric
Education Resource Center, 1986. 54p.
The authors emphasize the refugee problem and the complicity of the US Agency for
International Development in the civil war in El Salvador.

311 Forced to move.
Renato Camarda.   San Francisco: Solidarity Publications, 1985. 26p.
Camarda describes the plight of Salvadoran refugees in Honduras, with many
photographs, interviews, individual case descriptions, and testimony of the United
Nations High Commission on Refugees. He is critical of the violation of human rights
involved and of United States policy in the region.

312 The Central American refugees.
Elizabeth G. Ferris.   New York: Praeger, 1987. 159p.
A comprehensive survey of the refugee problem as it relates to the United States.
Topics discussed include: the causes of the exodus from Central America; migration
patterns; conditions in refugee camps in Costa Rica, Honduras, and Mexico; and
United States policies and practice. In this competent study, considerable attention is
devoted to the Salvadoran refugees.

**313 Sanctuary: a resource guide for understanding and participating in the
Central American refugees' struggle.**
Edited by Gary McEoin.   San Francisco: Harper & Row, 1985. 217p.
These papers derived from the Inter-American Symposium on Sanctuary, Tucson,
Arizona, in January 1985, deal with many aspects of the Central American refugee
problem and with the sanctuary movement in the United States.

314 El Salvador 1987: salvadoreños refugiados en los Estados Unidos. (El
Salvador 1987: Salvadoran refugees in the United States.)
Segundo Montes.   San Salvador: Instituto de Investigaciones,
Universidad Centroamericana José Simeón Cañas, 1987. 263p.
bibliog.
A study of Salvadoran emigration to the United States by a leading Salvadoran
sociologist. He concludes that the socio-economic and political situation in El
Salvador has caused permanent damage to the traditional Salvadoran traits of hard
work and enterprise. Thousands of Salvadorans have been turned into parasites by
the repression and civil war, and the longer the war continues the worse the situation
will get, he says. Based on detailed research in El Salvador and the United States,
this is an important contribution to understanding both the migration problem itself
and the effects of the civil disorder on the Salvadoran population.

81

315 **Displaced persons in El Salvador**.
United States. Agency for International Development, Bureau for
Latin America and the Caribbean. Assessment Team. Washington:
Bureau for Latin America and the Caribbean, Agency for
International Development, 1984. 292p.

A detailed US-sponsored investigation on the problem of internal refugees in E
Salvador. This study should be compared with the Salvadoran investigation directec
by Segundo Montes, *Informe preliminar, investigación desplazados y refugiado:
salvadoreños* (Preliminary report: research on Salvadoran displaced persons anc
refugees) (San Salvador: Instituto de Investigaciones de la Universidac
Centroamericana de El Salvador José Simeón Cañas, 1985), which contains vas
amounts of information on the refugee problem and internal migration in 1985; anc
Segundo Montes, *El Salvador 1986: en busca de soluciones para los desplazados* (E
Salvador 1986: in search of solutions for the refugees) (San Salvador: Instituto de
Investigaciones e Instituto de Derechos Humanos de la Universidac
Centroamericana de El Salvador José Simeón Cañas, 1986. 205p.). See also Montes
El Salvador 1987.

Politics

General Central American political characteristics

316 **Central American political parties: a functional approach.**
Charles W. Anderson. *The Western Political Quarterly*, vol. 15 (March 1962), p. 125-39.
A useful overview of Central American political parties, placed in the context of Western political systems and the role of parties in the Central American political process. See also Anderson's 1960 University of Wisconsin PhD dissertation, *Political ideology and the revolution of rising expectations in Central America, 1944-1958* (University Microfilms order no. 603161).

317 **Politics in Central America.**
Thomas Anderson. New York: Praeger, 1988. 256p. map. bibliog. rev. ed.
Descriptive detail is included on the political structures and chronology of each Central American state, including a lengthy section on El Salvador, p. 73-123. See also Anderson's briefer survey of El Salvador in Robert Wesson, ed., *Communism in Central America and the Caribbean* (Stanford, California: Hoover Institution, 1982).

318 **Alrededor del problema unionista de Centro América.** (Regarding the unionist problem of Central America.)
Salvador de Mendieta. Barcelona: Maucci, 1934. 2 vols.
Mendieta considered this work as a part of his *Enfermedad de Centro América* (q.v.). Volume 1 is a somewhat autobiographical account of Mendieta and his struggles for unionism on the isthmus, while volume 2 contains historical data on unionist efforts.

319 **La enfermedad de Centro América.** (The Central American illness.)
Salvador de Mendieta. Barcelona: Maucci, 1934. 3 vols.

Salvador de Mendieta was Nicaragua's great advocate for Central American unity in
the early 20th century and the founder of the Central American Unionist Party. This
work is a stinging condemnation of much that was wrong with Central America as
Mendieta saw it. Volume 1 contains a very detailed description of Central America as
of about 1906-7, volume 2 is a sort of history, and not particularly useful, while
volume 3 contains Mendieta's recommendations as to what should be done.

Centro América 19--, análisis económico y político sobre la región. (Central
America 19--, economic and political analyses of the region.)
See item no. 11.

Middle American governors.
See item no. 144.

La hegemonía del pueblo y la lucha centroamericana. (The hegemony of the
people and the Central American struggle.)
See item no. 209.

Salvadoran political characteristics

320 **They won't take me alive: Salvadorean women in the struggle for
national liberation.**
Claribel Alegría, translated by Amanda Hopkinson. London:
Women's Press, 1987. 145p.

The poignant biography of the FMLN guerrilla commander 'Eugenia'. It traces her
career from university student and Catholic missionary in San Salvador to her activity
as a guerrilla leader, providing insight into the issues and nature of the Salvadoran
civil war. The author, a Nicaraguan by birth, but raised in El Salvador and educated
in the United States, is a noted Central American literary figure.

321 **El Salvador, antecedentes de la violencia.** (El Salvador, origins of the
violence.)
Pablo Mauricio Alvergue. San Salvador: ISEP, 1982. 104p.
(Colección Autores Salvadoreños).

A collection of short, provocative essays on various aspects of the background and
foreground of the current crisis in El Salvador, examining Marxism, militarism, the
economic crisis, and liberation theology.

322 **Anatomy of resistance in El Salvador: who are the rebels and what do they want?**
Worldview, vol. 26 (June 1983), p. 5-9.

Describes the various revolutionary groups, noting 'the varieties of Marxist-leftism', but making the charge that the US does not distinguish among them in its 'backyard'. By ignoring this distinction and by its wholesale opposition to the entire Central American left, US policy pushes the non-aligned left into the arms of those who are pro-Soviet.

323 **El Salvador: the face of revolution.**
Robert Armstrong, Janet Shenk. Boston: South End Press, 1982. 285p.

The authors, who are members of the staff of the North American Congress on Latin America, examine the Salvadoran civil war from a leftist perspective, evaluating the role of the Catholic church, various political parties, and grassroots organizations. They also document the role of the US in the conflict.

324 **El Salvador in transition.**
Enrique Baloyra. Chapel Hill, North Carolina: University of North Carolina Press, 1982. 270p. map. bibliog.

Baloyra describes how the Salvadoran oligarchy and conservative element in the Salvadoran armed forces dominate the country in their own interests. He also describes middle sector political organization and argues that a reconciliation between the Christian Democrats and Social Democrats could put an end to the armed conflict. Scholarly and judicious, this is one of the more useful studies of the Salvadoran political scene published during the current decade.

325 **Reactionary despotism in Central America.**
Enrique A. Baloyra-Herp. *Journal of Latin American Studies*, vol. 15 (Nov. 1983), p. 295-319.

This article explains the development of authoritarianism, especially in El Salvador and Guatemala, and is excellent for understanding the development of the Salvadoran oligarchy and its attitude toward other segments of the society. Another article by Baloyra, making much the same point, is 'The model of reactionary despotism in Central America'. It appeared in *Trouble in our back yard*, edited by Martin Diskin (New York: Pantheon, 1984), p. 102-23.

326 **El Salvador entre el terror y la esperanza: los sucesos de 1979 y su impacto en el drama salvadoreño de los años siguientes**. (El Salvador between terror and hope: the events of 1979 and their impact on the Salvadoran drama of the following years.)
Edited by Rodolfo R. Campos. San Salvador: UCA Editores, 1982. 788p.

This publication of the broadcasts from the Archdiocese of San Salvador radio station, YSAX, reports in detail on the tumultuous events of 1979 and reflects the growing rift during that year between Archbishop Oscar Romero and the Salvadoran military. A valuable document of this period.

327 **El Salvador: una democracia cafetalera**. (El Salvador: a coffee democracy.)
Abel Cuenca. México: ARR-Centro Editorial, 1962. 175p.

A bitter criticism of the socio-economic and political structure of El Salvador by one of the leading revolutionary figures of mid-20th century Central America. It is especially critical of the Common Market as a scheme by foreign capitalists and the local élite to enrich themselves without providing for more general improvement of standards of living. The author attacks especially the coffee planter élite as obstructing more progressive and democratic development and industrialization. Cuenca, a Salvadoran exile, participated in many revolutionary movements in Central America.

328 **Why the Christian Democrats of El Salvador abandoned the government and their party**.
Héctor Dada Hirezi. Washington: EPICA, 1981. 23p.

A presentation given by one of the leading Salvadoran Christian Democrats to the Permanent People's Tribunal in Mexico City on 10 February 1981.

329 **Revolution and intervention in Central America**.
Edited by Marlene Dixon, Susanne Jonas. San Francisco: Synthesis Publications, 1983. 344p.

Documents on the conflicts in El Salvador, Guatemala, and Nicaragua, and commentary in opposition to US counter-revolutionary strategy.

330 **Duarte: my story**.
José Napoleón Duarte. New York: Putnam, 1986. 284p.

Autobiography of El Salvador's Christian Democratic leader and president.

331 **The decision-making process in El Salvador.**
Roland Ebel. In: *Latin American urban research*, edited by Francine F. Rabinowitz, Felicity M. Trueblood, vol. 1, p. 189-213. Beverly Hills, California: Sage, 1971. bibliog.

Based on analysis of 16 issues facing the government of San Salvador between 1964 and 1967, Ebel draws conclusions about municipal government in El Salvador and the manner in which decisions are made there. This is an important piece of research which reveals much about the nature of municipal government in El Salvador.

332 **Governing the city-state: notes on the politics of the small Latin American countries.**
Roland Ebel. *Journal of Inter-American Studies and World Affairs*, vol. 14 no. 3 (1972), p. 325-46.
Considerable attention is given to El Salvador in this theoretical article on the nature of the Central American political systems.

333 **El golpe de estado en El Salvador: ¿un camino hacía la democratización?** (The Salvadoran coup d'état: a path toward democratization?)
Fernando Flores Pinel. *Revista Mexicana de Sociología*, vol. 42 (1980), p. 669-94.
An evaluation of the reforms instituted by the military junta after the overthrow of General Humberto Romero. The author maintains that the junta's success depended on its ability to re-establish electoral procedures, neutralize extremist activities, and provide social and economic reform profound enough to undermine the Left but sufficiently moderate to contain the reaction of the Right.

334 **The case for power-sharing in El Salvador.**
Piero Gleijeses. *Foreign Affairs*, vol. 61, no. 5 (summer, 1983), p. 1048-63.
A sharp criticism of Reagan's El Salvador policy, offering a good review of the conflicts and issues in El Salvador and the problems connected with US support of the Salvadoran military. Recommends a negotiated peace with the FMLN and formation of a government that would include representatives of the left.

335 **Guazapa.**
San Salvador: Centro de Ediciones Guazapa, 1984-. irregular.
Contains articles on political analysis and Salvadoran political issues.

336 **Demonstration elections: U.S.-staged elections in the Dominican Republic, Vietnam, and El Salvador.**
Edward S. Herman, Frank Brodhead. Boston: South End Press, 1984. 285p. bibliog.
Focusing on the use of 'free elections' as a tool of public relations, this book compares US involvement in the 1982 El Salvador election, with those of the Dominican Republic in 1966 and in Vietnam in 1967. It argues that the mass media are used in these elections to aid in the military pacification of Third World countries. It also suggests that the 1984 El Salvador election was a similar instance of such policy.

337 **El Salvador, acumulación de capital y proceso revolucionario, (1932-1981).** (Capital accumulation and the revolutionary process in El Salvador (1932-1981).)
Ana Evelyn Jacir Simon. *Investigación Económica* [Mexico], vol. 40 (1982), p. 293-309.

A Marxist interpretation of recent Salvadoran economic history. The author sees 1932 as a watershed, with the expansion of banking and the introduction of cotton as a new export of great importance after that date. She believes that the government's promotion of industrialization put private profit above social gain and failed to solve the structural problems of the country. Middle class alliance with imperialism after the Cuban Revolution is seen as an important contributing factor in the failure of the Central American Common Market.

338 **El Salvador's Marxist revolution.**
Alexander Kruger. *Journal of Social, Political, and Economic Studies*, vol. 6 (1981), p. 119-39.

An analysis of the various Salvadoran guerrilla organizations and their development as splinter groups of the Communist Party. The author concludes that they refuse to participate in elections because they have lost much popular support.

339 **Central America, anatomy of conflict.**
Edited by Robert S. Leiken. New York: Pergamon Press, 1984. 351p. map.

A balanced collection of essays by Leiken and others on the Central American political difficulties, their origins, and their implications for US policy. Among the contributors are Christopher Dickey, Walter LaFeber, Richard Millett, Arturo Cruz Sequeira, Morris Rothenberg, Theodore Moran, Joseph Cirincione and Leslie Hunter, Richard Feinberg, Robert Pastor, Viron Vaky, Howard Wiarda, Tom Farer, Barry Rubin, and I. M. Destler.

340 **Oligarchs and officers: the crisis in El Salvador.**
William M. LeoGrande, Carla Anne Robbins. *Foreign Affairs*, vol. 58 (1980), p. 1084-1103.

A well-reasoned argument that social and economic imbalances in El Salvador after the 1969 Football War increased political tensions because an entrenched oligarchy prevented the military governments of the 1970s from instituting reforms until 1980. The authors maintain that only leftist participation in the government can now halt civil war.

341 **Rasgos sociales y tendencias políticas en El Salvador (1969-1979).** (Social characteristics and political tendencies in El Salvador, 1969-1979.)
Italo López Vallecillos. *Estudios Centroamericanos*, vol. 34 (1979), p. 863-84.

A study of the relationship between a weak social system and the pattern of repression and subversion representative of the confrontation between the dominant and the dominated classes. The author focuses on the military coup of 15 October 1979.

342 **La Unidad Popular y el surgimiento del Frente Democrático Revolucionario.** (Popular Unity and the emergence of the Revolutionary Democratic Front.)
Italo López Vallecillos, Víctor Antonio Orellana. *Estudios Centroamericanos*, vol. 35 (1980), p. 183-206.

During the 1970s several types of popular unity movements emerged in El Salvador against the oligarchy's economic, political, and military dictatorship. These included mass organizations, labour unions, and armed resistance, which have been united in the Revolutionary Democratic Front (FDR). The authors analyse these developments in detail and the role of the FDR in the contemporary Salvadoran crisis.

343 **El Salvador: peaceful revolution or armed struggle?**
Bruce McColm. New York: Freedom House, 1982. 47p.
(Perspectives on Freedom, 1).

McColm reviews Salvadoran politics since 1930 and describes the rise of opposition to military rule. The booklet is more sympathetic to Christian Democrats than to the Marxist-Leninist opposition, warning of communist control of the armed opposition to the government. In commenting on press coverage of El Salvador, it emphasizes the complex nature of the problems in El Salvador and of the positive role of US involvement there.

344 **Electorial behavior and political development in El Salvador.**
Ronald H. McDonald. *Journal of Politics*, vol. 31 (May 1969), p. 397-419.

A useful article on the 1960s, supporting idea that a democratizing tendency was taking place.

345 **The politics of violence: Guatemala and El Salvador.**
Richard L. Millet. *Current History*, vol. 80 (1981), p. 70-74.

An insightful article that attempts to provide some historical perspective to the political violence in El Salvador and Guatemala and evaluates the efforts of governments to alleviate economic and social problems in the 1970s.

346 **Bitter grounds: roots of revolt in El Salvador.**
Liisa North. Westport, Connecticut: Lawrence Hill, 1985. 124p. maps.

A competent historical survey of the conflict in El Salvador, with the focus on the 20th century. Her arguments are summarized in her 'El Salvador: the historical roots of the civil war', *Studies in Political Economy* (summer 1982), p. 59-87.

347 **Promised land: peasant rebellion in Chalatenango, El Salvador**
Jenny Pearce. London: Latin American Bureau, 1986. 324p.

This work charts the growth of the peasant movement in El Salvador, describing the serious hardships the guerrilla war has inflicted on the peasants. The author, who travelled among and talked with many guerrillas and peasants, does not hide her sympathies for them both.

348 **Land reform and democratic development.**
Roy L. Prosterman, Jeffrey M. Riedinger. Baltimore: Johns Hopkins University Press, 1987. 336p. (The Johns Hopkins Studies in Development).

A proposal for a large-scale, non-violent land reform centered on the family farm as a democratic alternative to the repressive status quo and to Marxist revolutionary options in the Third World. It includes a detailed case-study of crisis land reform in El Salvador.

349 **Land reform in El Salvador: the democratic alternative.**
Roy L. Prosterman, Jeffrey M. Riedinger, Mary Temple. *World Affairs*, vol. 144 (1981), p. 36-54.

An optimistic argument that the 1980 agrarian reform policy in El Salvador had increased the chances of moderate democracy.

350 **Revolution in Central America.**
Stanford Central America Action Network. Boulder: Westview Press, 1983. 508p.

A balanced anthology of articles on contemporary Central America, including several on El Salvador by Robert Armstrong, William LeoGrande, Jeff Stein, Susanne Jonas, Edelberto Torres-Rivas, Philip Wheaton, Cynthia Arnson, Plácido Erdozain, T. H. Brewer, Ana G. Martínez, and others.

351 **The new El Salvador: interviews from the zones of popular control.**
Margarita Studemeister. San Francisco: Solidarity Publications, 1986. 40p.

A rare description, through interviews, of the territory in eastern El Salvador under the control of the FMLN, emphasizing popularly based local community governments outside the control of the national government of El Salvador. In these seven interviews, local leaders describe the history, structure, and functioning of the governments and the specific programmes that have been developed by and for the people of the region.

352 **Representational role orientations in a developing country: a preliminary study of the Legislative Assembly of El Salvador.**
Joel G. Verner. *International Review of History and Political Science*, vol. 12, no. 4 (Nov. 1975), p. 29-66.

Verner examines the nature of political representation in the legislative assembly of

El Salvador in this article based on interviews with 50 of the 52 legislators elected in 1972. He concludes that there are significant differences in the political characteristics of these legislators from those in several other Western countries.

353 **The war in El Salvador: current situation and outlook for the future.**
Joaquín Villalobos. San Francisco: Solidarity Publications, 1986. 48p.
An analysis of El Salvador's revolutionary movement and the US-directed counter-insurgency strategy, written by one of the members of the general staff of the FMLN, who outlines the development of the FMLN during 1979 to 1985. He presents the official position of the FMLN and its perspective on the war in El Salvador.

354 **José Napoleón Duarte and the Christian Democratic Party in Salvadoran politics, 1960-1972.**
Stephen Webre. Baton Rouge: Louisiana State University Press, 1979. 246p. bibliog.
Webre describes how Duarte built the Christian Democratic Party in El Salvador. This meticulous study following Duarte's career through his apparent victory as presidential candidate in 1972, when he was denied the office, is a key contribution to understanding the political development of El Salvador in the post World War II period.

355 **Enemy colleagues: a reading of the Salvadoran tragedy.**
Gabriel Zaid. *Dissent*, vol. 29 (1982), p. 13-40.
An excellent analysis of Salvadoran political characteristics, arguing the futility of US military intervention there. Zaid includes a genealogical study of the most powerful Salvadoran families that is unique in the literature on the country.

El Salvador: background to the crisis.
See item no. 7.

El Salvador in crisis.
See item no. 17.

El Salvador: background to the struggle.
See item no. 153.

Gobernantes de El Salvador (biografías). (Governors of El Salvador biographies).)
See item no. 154.

Historia del Ministerio del Interior. (History of the Ministry of the Interior.)
See item no. 156.

Consideraciones sobre el discurso político de la revolución de 1948 en El Salvador. (Thoughts on the political meaning of the revolution of 1948 in El Salvador.)
See item no. 204.

Politics. Salvadoran political characteristics

The long war: dictatorship and revolution in El Salvador.
See item no. 207

Revolution in El Salvador, origins and evolution.
See item no. 211.

Steadfastness of the saints, a journey of peace and war in Central and North America.
See item no. 251.

The religious roots of rebellion: Christians in Central American revolutions.
See item no. 252.

The world remains: a life of Oscar Romero.
See item no. 254.

Salvador witness: the life and calling of Jean Donovan.
See item no. 256.

Archbishop Romero, martyr of Salvador.
See item no. 258.

The church in the Salvadoran revolution.
See item no. 264.

Central America and politicized religion.
See item no. 271.

El compadrazgo, una estructura de poder en El Salvador. (The *compadrazgo*, a power structure in El Salvador.)
See item no. 280.

El Salvador: las fuerzas sociales en la presente coyuntura (enero 1980 a diciembre 1983). (El Salvador: the social forces at the present juncture (January 1980 to December 1983.)
See item no. 281.

El Salvador: ¿por qué la insurrección? (El Salvador: why the insurrection?)
See item no. 298.

El Salvador under General Romero.
See item no. 305.

El Salvador: Central America in the new cold war.
See item no. 387.

Rift and revolution: the Central American imbroglio.
See item no. 430.

The political economy of Central America since 1920.
See item no. 438.

El Salvador land reform 1980-81: impact audit.
See item no. 525.

Así piensan los salvadoreños urbanos (1986-1987). (What urban Salvadorans think (1986-1987).)
See item no. 562.

El Salvador at war: a collage epic.
See item no. 600.

The military

556 **Función política del ejército salvadoreño en el presente siglo.** (Political function of the Salvadoran army in the present century.)
Mariano Castro Morán. San Salvador: UCA Editores, 1984. 455p.
Written by a lieutenant-colonel in the Salvadoran army, this work reviews the 20th-century political history of El Salvador with particular reference to the role of the military, including a detailed look especially at the events of 1979-80 and the outset of the present civil war. The work focuses on coups d'état and argues that successive governments have failed in their promises. It blames the governments rather than the army for these failures, and says that the institutions that army officers helped create, under the liberal, democratic, developmentalist impulse, have degenerated and served interests distinct from those for which they were created. Arguing that the army has been badly used by the government, it concludes that the Salvadoran army in this century has constantly struggled for life, democracy, progress, and the welfare of the population.

557 **El Salvador's divided military: are we supporting murderers or reformers?**
Shirley Christian. *Atlantic Monthly*, vol. 251 (June 1983), p. 50-53, 57-60.
A description of the Salvadoran military, '. . . at war as much with itself as with guerrillas'. The author argues that the United States must play a stronger role in directing them.

558 **Appeal to arms: the army and politics in El Salvador, 1931-1964.**
Robert V. Elam. PhD dissertation, University of New Mexico, Albuquerque, 1968. 217p. (University Microfilms order no. 6813076).
A very useful detailed study of the military in Salvadoran politics during the period indicated.

559 **The United States and militarism in Central America.**
Don L. Etchison. New York: Praeger, 1975. 150p. bibliog.
A scholarly account of the role of the armed forces in contemporary politics in each Central American state, but limited by a failure to consider more fully the history of militarism in these states. Analyses the policies of John Kennedy, Lyndon Johnson

93

and Richard Nixon with respect to the Central American military, but tends to tell us more about US policy than about the Central American military. Statistical appendixes enhance this work.

360 **Crisis política y organización popular en El Salvador.** (Political crisis and peoples' organization in El Salvador.)
Sara Gordon. *Revista Mexicana de Sociología*, vol. 42 (April-June 1980), p. 695-709.

A study in which the author explains the political and military crisis since the 1979 coup as the result of 48 years of military rule. The author claims that the military had blocked the participation of the Salvadoran masses in political activity, thereby creating a profound class polarization.

361 **El ascenso del militarismo en El Salvador.** (The rise of militarism in El Salvador.)
Rafael Guidos Véjar. San Salvador: UCA Editores, 1980. 156p.

An excellent account of the growth of the military in El Salvador following the Great Depression and especially during the early years of the dictatorship of Maximiliano Hernández Martínez.

362 **Realidad dramática de la República: 25 años de traición a la fuerza armada y a la patria.** (The dramatic reality of the Republic: 25 years of treason to the Armed Forces and to the fatherland.)
Roberto López Trejo. San Salvador: Editorial Ahora, 1974. 420p.

A Salvadoran army officer's defence of the Salvadoran military against leftist propaganda efforts to discredit the institution. At the same time, López is critical of all of the Salvadoran governments since 1944 as 'soft' on communism, while he applauds the government of Maximiliano Hernández Martínez (1931-44) for it honesty, public works, and efficiency. The work represents a classic defence of the traditional Salvadoran oligarchy and calls upon the élite and the military to exercise greater responsibility in guiding El Salvador's future.

363 **State terror and popular resistance in El Salvador.**
Michael McClintock. London: Zed, 1985. 387p. bibliog. (Third World Books).

Traces US counter-insurgency efforts in El Salvador since the John Kennedy administration. Based heavily on US government documents, this work looks at the political structure of El Salvador, which has encouraged repression. It is useful for understanding the politics and militarism of El Salvador and the US role in that effort from 1961 to 1980.

364 **El Salvador, un pueblo que se rebelde: conflicto de julio de 1969**. (El Salvador, a people that rebel: the conflict of July 1969.)
Manuel Morales Molina. San Salvador: Tipografía Central, 1973-74. 2 vols. bibliog.

The author, a Salvadoran army officer, argues passionately that the 1969 war with

94

Honduras was a reflection of Salvadoran unity, discipline, and patriotism. The work reflects little understanding of or sympathy with the social problems of the country underlying the conflict, but it is a useful military mirror of the Liberal tradition in El Salvador and reprints a large amount of documentation, as well as Colonel Morales' diary during the war.

365 **The air war and political developments in El Salvador**.
United States. Congress. House Committee on Foreign Affairs, Subcommittee on Western Hemisphere Affairs. Washington: GPO, 1986. 221p.
Documents, testimony and comment regarding the civil war in El Salvador from the congressional committee's investigations.

Vida militar de Centro América. (The military life of Central America.)
See item no. 148.

Historia militar de El Salvador. (Military history of El Salvador.)
See item no. 149.

La Guardia Nacional Salvadoreña, desde su fundación, año 1912, al año 1927. (The Salvadoran National Guard, from its foundation in the year 1912 to the year 1927.)
See item no. 214.

Social classes, accumulation, and the crisis of 'overpopulation' in El Salvador.
See item no. 283.

El golpe de estado en El Salvador: ¿un camino hacía la democratización? (The Salvadoran coup d'état: a path toward democratization?)
See item no. 333.

Oligarchs and officers: the crisis in El Salvador.
See item no. 340.

Low intensity warfare: counterinsurgency, proinsurgency, and antiterrorism in the eighties.
See item no. 420.

Constitution, Laws, and the Judicial System

366 **Constitución de la República de El Salvador, 1983, y reglamento de la Asamblea Legislativa.** (Constitution of the Republic of El Salvador, 1983, and rules of the legislative assembly.)
Asamblea Legislativa. San Salvador: La Asamblea, 1983. 109p.
The current constitution of El Salvador, adopted in 1983.

367 **Condición jurídica de la mujer salvadoreña.** (Legal status of the Salvadoran woman.)
Rosa J. Cisneros A. San Salvador: La Asociación Demográfica Salvadoreña, 1978. 2nd ed. 94p. bibliog.
This discussion of references to women in specific Salvadoran laws includes a substantial section on family law. The author concludes that women are not discriminated against in Salvadoran law, but acknowledges that the country is a male-dominated society. This work extends somewhat the earlier summary of Lilian Jiménez, *Condiciones de la mujer en El Salvador* (q.v.).

368 **Código civil y código de procedimientos civiles (con sus reformas).** (Civil code and code of civil proceedings (with revisions).)
San Salvador: Government of El Salvador, 1984. 384p.

369 **Código penal.** (Penal code.)
San Salvador: Ministerio de Justicia, 1980. 105p.
The 1973 penal code for El Salvador.

96

370 **Constitución política y códigos de la República de El Salvador**.
(Political constitution and codes of the Republic of El Salvador.)
San Salvador: Ministerio de Justicia, 1967. 1304p.

371 **Diario Oficial.** (Official daily.)
San Salvador: Government of El Salvador, 1875-present.

The official publication of laws, decrees, proclamations, etc., of the Salvadoran government. It succeeded the *Boletín Oficial* (Official bulletin) (San Salvador, 1871-75), *El constitucional* (The constitutional) (San Salvador, 1863-71), *Gaceta del Salvador* (Gazette of El Salvador) (Cojutepeque and San Salvador, 1847-63), *El Boletín Oficial* (The official bulletin) (San Salvador, 18-- to 1847), *El Revisor* (183- to 18--), and *Gaceta del Estado de El Salvador* (Gazette of the State of El Salvador) (San Salvador, 1827 to 183-) as the official government newspaper.

372 **Directorio de legislación**. (Directory of legislation.)
San Salvador: CODELSA, 1977-82. 5 vols.

Loose-leaf compilation of Salvadoran law for period 1977-82. Various publications indexed earlier legislation, such as the *Indice de legislación de la República de El Salvador de enero 1937 a diciembre 1963* (Index of legislation of the Republic of El Salvador from January 1937 to December 1963) (San Salvador: Ministerio de Justicia, 1964).

373 **The constitutions of Latin America.**
Gerald E. Fitzgerald.   Chicago: Henry Regnery Company, 1968.
242p.

English translations of the constitutions of Chile, Colombia, Costa Rica, El Salvador, Mexico, and Venezuela with a history and analysis of each. The 1962 constitution of El Salvador, the 11th in its history, is included on p. 105-40. This constitution remained in effect until 1983, although portions of it were frequently suspended.

374 **Cuatro constituciones federales de Centro América y las constituciones políticas de El Salvador**. (Four federal constitutions of Central America and the political constitutions of El Salvador.)
Edited by Miguel Angel Gallardo.   San Salvador: Tipografía La Unión, 1945. 419p.

The texts of the ten Salvadoran constitutions up to 1945, plus four of the national constitutions of the Central American federation, with brief commentary. This volume is largely superseded by Ricardo Gallardo's volume (q.v.).

375 **Las constituciones de El Salvador**. (The constitutions of El Salvador.)
Edited by Ricardo Gallardo.   Madrid: Cultura Hispánica, 1961. 2 vols.

In addition to the texts of the twelve constitutions of El Salvador from 1824 to 1950, including the Central American federal constitutions, this excellent compilation contains a scholarly survey of Salvadoran history integrated with commentary on its constitutions.

Constitution, Laws, and the Judicial System

376 **A statement of the laws of El Salvador in matters affecting business.**
General Legal Division, Department of Legal Affairs, Organization
of American States. Washington: OAS, 1970. 228p.

One of a series on Latin American laws affecting business published by the OAS.
Although now somewhat dated, the volume still provides a useful general guide in
English to Salvadoran business law. Separate sections discuss the constitution (1962),
nationality and immigration, foreigners, investment, merchants, commercial companies, registers, notaries, bankruptcy, contracts, sales, agency, suretyship and
guaranty, mining, petroleum, agrarian legislation, forestry and water, monopolies
and concessions, patents and trademarks, copyright, negotiable instruments,
banking, economic controls, insurance, property rights, mortgages and liens,
bailments, trusts, succession, marriage and divorce, the family, domicile, administration of justice, health and sanitation, nuclear energy, territorial rights and fishing,
economic planning, and the Central American Common Market.

377 **Períodos presidenciales y constituciones federales y políticas de El
Salvador.** (Presidential terms and political and federal constitutions of
El Salvador).
Compiled by María Leistenschneider, Freddy Leistenschneider. San
Salvador: Ministerio de Educación, 1979 [c.1980]. 703p. (Colección
Antropología e Historia, no. 17).

A compilation of all of El Salvador's constitutions with amendments from
independence to 1980. The Central American federal constitution of 1824 is also
included, as well as the proposed Central American constitutions of 1898 and 1921.
Also included is a list of all of the governors of El Salvador from 1821 to 1980.

378 **Recopilación de las leyes del Salvador en Centroamérica.** (Compilation
of the laws of El Salvador in Central America.)
Compiled by Isidro M. Menéndez. San Salvador: Imprenta
Nacional, 1956. 2 vols.

First published in Guatemala in 1855, this is the earliest compilation of Salvadoran
law and covers the period 1821-55. The laws are chronologically arranged within
topical chapters, and there is a useful index. Of related interest may be Jorge Lardé y
Larín's biographical study on the life and work of the compiler, *Isidro Menéndez*
(San Salvador: Ministerio de Cultura, 1958).

379 **Recopilación de leyes.** (Compilation of laws.)
San Salvador: Imprenta Nacional, 1955-77. 5 vols.

A compilation of the laws of El Salvador from 1950 to 1977. An additional volume,
Recopilación de leyes (San Salvador: Corte Suprema de Justicia, 1979), contains the
1962 constitution and the current laws in force on the labour courts, constitutional
procedures, regulations of the legal profession, housing law, misappropriation of
funds by public employees, notarial law, special procedures for traffic accidents, law
regarding dangerous persons, adoption law, rent law, conflict of interests, and
regulations for obtaining a certificate for holding the position of clerk of court.

380   **Historia de las instituciones jurídicas salvadoreñas**. (History of
       Salvadoran juridical institutions.)
       Napoleón Rodríguez Ruiz.   San Salvador: Universitaria, 1959. 2nd
       ed. 199p.
This incomplete legal history of El Salvador was intended as a text. The second
volume was never published. It deals with legal concepts and with law in colonial El
Salvador for the most part, although a final section reviews the various codifications
of the laws of El Salvador from independence through to 1904.

381   **Codificación de leyes patrias de la República de El Salvador, desde la
       independencia hasta el año de 1875.** (Codification of the national laws
       of the Republic of El Salvador from independence to the year 1875.)
       Compiled by Cruz Ulloa.   San Salvador: [n.p.], 1875. 369p.
A compilation of the laws of El Salvador from 1821 to 1875. A subsequent volume
compiled by Francisco Vaquero, *Codificación de las leyes de El Salvador desde 1875
hasta 1889* (Codification of the laws of El Salvador from 1875 to 1889) (San Salvador:
n.p., 1890) continued this codification through to 1889.

From the ashes: justice in El Salvador.
See item no. 307.

Código de trabajo y sus reformas. (Labour code and its revisions.)
See item no. 546.

Administration and Local Government

382 **Código municipal**. (Municipal code.)
  San Salvador: Ediciones ISAM, 1986. 58p.
The municipal code for the city of San Salvador.

383 **Guía de instituciones del estado**. (Guide to institutions of the state.)
  San Salvador: Presidencia de la República, Secretaría de Información, 1975. 72p.
A useful guide to the administrative agencies of Salvadoran government.

384 **Recopilación de leyes relativas a la historia de los municipios de El Salvador.** (Compilation of laws relating to the history of the municipalities of El Salvador.)
  Edited by Jorge Lardé y Larín.   San Salvador: Ministerio de Interior, 1950. 459p.
A compilation of the legislation on the organization and regulation of municipal government in El Salvador from independence to 1950, with brief descriptions of each municipality.

Estudio de vías urbanas, San Salvador. (Study of urban routes in San Salvador.)
See item no. 538.

Foreign Relations

General

385 **Documentos y doctrinas relacionados con el problema de fronteras.**
(Documents and doctrines related to the problem of borders.)
El Salvador. Ministerio de Relaciones Exteriores.   San Salvador:
Editorial Delgado, 1985. 409p.
A collection of official documents and other statements relating to El Salvador's
border disputes, principally with Honduras.

386 **Tratados, convenciones y acuerdos internacionales vigentes en El
Salvador.** (International treaties, conventions, and agreements in
effect in El Salvador.)
El Salvador. Ministerio de Relaciones Exteriores.   San Salvador:
Imprenta Nacional, 1938-72. 8 vols.
The official collection of Salvadoran international treaties and other agreements from
1865 onwards. Additional volumes are published periodically.

387 **El Salvador: Central America in the new cold war**.
Edited by Marvin Gettleman, Patrick Lacefield, Louis Menashe,
David Mermelstein.   New York: Grove Press, 1986. rev. ed. 544p.
An impressive collection of documents and readings on the development of the civil
war in El Salvador within the context of Cold War politics. It includes selections from
a broad spectrum of political and ideological points of view. As such, it is a very
useful volume on the Salvadoran crisis, and especially the Salvadoran role in the
renewed United States-Soviet rivalry. The work overlooks some of the really first
rate writings by Salvadorans, although this edition does include many items not
included in the first edition (1981).

101

388 **Boundaries, possessions, and conflicts in Central and North America and the Caribbean.**
Gordon Ireland. New York: Octagon, 1971. 432p. maps.
The standard reference work for border disputes in the region up to 1940. Originally published in 1941 by Harvard University Press, the work summarizes disputes and treaties related to them.

389 **It's no secret: Israel's military involvement in Central America.**
Milton Jamail, Margo Gutiérrez. Belmont, Massachusetts: Association of Arab-American University Graduates, 1986. 117p. (AAUG Monograph, no. 20).
A documented account of Israel's supplying of weapons, munitions, military technology, and counter-insurgency aid to the Salvadoran and other Central American governments. See also 'The Israeli Connection: Guns and Money in Central America', in *NACLA Report on the Americas*, vol. 21, no. 2 (March/April 1987), p. 13-32; and Cynthia Arson, 'Israel and Central America', *New Outlook*, vol. 27 (March-April 1984), p. 19-22. Also of note is the forthcoming volume by Damián J. Fernández, *Central America and the Middle East: the internationalization of the crisis* (Boulder: Westview Press, 1988), c. 200p.

390 **Canada and the suppression of the Salvadorean revolution of 1932.**
Harvey Levenstein. *Canadian Historical Review*, vol. 62 (1981), p. 451-69.
Well researched in archives in London, Ottawa, and Washington, this study explores the role of Royal Canadian Navy destroyers in intervening in the internal affairs of El Salvador. The author concludes that Canada's present policy of non-intervention stems from its economic and military weakness, not from its diplomatic heritage.

A Palmerstonian diplomat in Central America: Frederick Chatfield, Esq.
See item no. 198.

With other Central American states

391 **The war of the dispossessed: Honduras and El Salvador, 1969.**
Thomas P. Anderson. Lincoln: University of Nebraska, 1981. 203p. maps. bibliog.
An objective, general history of the 1969 'soccer war' with an excellent bibliography of works on the conflict. Anderson's work provides straightforward reporting of the events and an intelligent discussion of the underlying causes of the conflict.

392 **Análisis sobre el conflicto entre Honduras y El Salvador.** (Analysis of
the conflict between Honduras and El Salvador.)
Marco Virgilio Carías.   Tegucigalpa: Universidad Nacional
Autónoma, 1970. 2nd ed. 118p. bibliog.

A worthy attempt to explain the causes of the 1969 football war in terms of class
struggle and economic dependency. Carías blames the conflict on several factors,
including the failure of the Salvadoran élite to solve serious social problems and still
maintain its position, with resulting Salvadoran immigration into Honduras, but also
on Honduran neglect of Salvadoran concerns and the attempts of Salvadoran
businessmen to expand into Honduras, and finally, on North American imperialism
which, the author says, contributes to the continued underdevelopment of both
countries. This work was republished in the *Revista Mexicana de Sociología*, vol. 32
(May-June 1970), p. 549-657, and in Carías, Daniel Slutsky, (et al.), *La guerra inútil:
análisis socio-económico del conflicto entre Honduras y El Salvador* (The useless war:
socio-economic analysis of the conflict between Honduras and El Salvador) (San
José: EDUCA, 1971).

393 **The politics of regional integration: the Central American case.**
James D. Cochrane.   New Orleans: Tulane University, 1969. 232p.
(Tulane Studies in Political Science, vol. 12).

A study of the political aspects of the Central American integration movement,
emphasizing the unique characteristics of the Central American case. Cochrane
warns against trying to impose models from other regions, where the circumstances
are different.

394 **Regional integration in Central America.**
Isaac Cohen Orantes.   Lexington, Massachusetts: D. C. Heath,
1972. 126p. bibliog.

A survey of the Central American integration effort to about 1970, cautioning that
the success during the 1960s was limited and dependent on considerable external
support. The author is pessimistic about political integration of the isthmian states.

395 **The republic of El Salvador against the republic of Nicaragua;
complaint of the republic of El Salvador, with appendices.**
El Salvador, translated by Harry W. Van Dyke.   Washington:
Gibson Brothers, 1917. 85p.

The Salvadoran case against Nicaragua's lease of a naval base on the Gulf of Fonseca
to the United States, as argued before the Central American Court of Justice. See
also Salvador Rodríguez González, *El Golfo de Fonseca y el tratado Bryan-Chamorro
celebrado entre los Estados Unidos de Norte América y Nicaragua: doctrina Meléndez*
(The Gulf of Fonseca and the Bryan-Chamorro treaty between the United States of
America and Nicaragua: the Meléndez doctrine) (San Salvador: Imprenta Nacional,
1917. 458p. map), which is the official statement and protest of the Salvadoran
government against the Bryan-Chamorro treaty published together with substantial
documentary support. President Carlos Meléndez of El Salvador strongly opposed
establishment of a US naval base in the Gulf of Fonseca, arguing that the waters of

that gulf were held jointly by El Salvador, Honduras, and Nicaragua, and that Nicaragua could not unilaterally grant rights to the United States for the use of these waters.

396 **Central American economic integration: the politics of unequal benefits.**
Stuart I. Fagan. Los Angeles and Berkeley: University of California Press, 1970. 95p. bibliog.

A brief analysis of the failures of the Central American Common Market, blaming the inequities in the CACM as a major cause of the 1969 war between El Salvador and Honduras. Agrees with Cochrane (q.v.) about the dangers of imposing a model based on experiences of other regions.

397 **Entre la guerra y la paz: el conflicto Honduro-Salvadoreño, 1969-1979.**
(Between war and peace: the Honduran-Salvadoran conflict, 1969-1979.)
Fernando Flores Pinel. *Estudios Centroamericanos*, vol. 34 (1979), p. 675-98.

An explanation, based mainly on periodical sources, of the reasoning behind the diplomacy of the Football War and its aftermath. Lack of employment is seen as the source of mass emigrations from El Salvador to Honduras.

398 **El Salvador: crisis, intervención norteamericana y relaciones con México, 1978-1986.** (El Salvador: crisis, North American intervention and relations with Mexico, 1978-1986.)
Sara Gordon Rapoport. México: CIDE, 1987. 76p. (Relaciones Centroamérica-México).

Reviews Mexican relations with El Salvador, suggesting major inconsistencies in that policy and advocating a stronger Mexican policy in support of Central American self-determination and against US intervention.

399 **La unión de Centroamérica.** (The Central American union.)
Alberto Herrarte. Guatemala: Centro Editorial José Pineda Ibarra, Ministerio de Educación Pública, 1964. 2nd ed. 428p.

First published in 1955, Herrarte's work remains one of the more important standard works on the efforts of Central Americans to reunify the isthmus politically.

400 **Honduras y El Salvador ante la Corte Internacional de Justicia.**
(Honduras and El Salvador before the International Court of Justice).
H. Roberto Herrera Cáceres. Tegucigalpa: Centro de Documentación de Honduras, 1987. 87p.

The Honduran case in the smouldering dispute with El Salvador stemming from the 1969 war.

401   **Historia de las relaciones interestatuales de Centro América.** (History
       of Central American interstate relations.)
       Laudelino Moreno.   Madrid: Cía. Iberoamericana de Publicaciones,
       1928. 507p. map. bibliog.
A thorough examination of Central American interstate relations up till 1923, with
detailed examination of the pertinent documents, treaties, etc. An important
contribution to the history of Central American union and disunion.

402   **Central American regional integration.**
       Joseph P. Nye.   New York: Carnegie Endowment for International
       Peace, 1967. 66p. (International Conciliation, no. 562).
A good account of the political-bureaucratic aspect of the integration movement. Nye
describes the new class of technocrats in all five Central American states who led the
way in the movement.

403   **Autonomy or dependence as regional integration outcomes: Central
       America.**
       Philippe C. Schmitter.   Berkeley: University of California, Institute
       of International Studies, 1972. 87p. bibliog.
A well-documented, but rather narrowly conceived monograph on the common
market experience, from a dependency point of view. Schmitter blames foreign,
especially United States, interests for the failure of the integration movement in
Central America.

The failure of union: Central America, 1824-1960.
See item no. 141.
**Scarcity and survival in Central America: ecological origins of the Soccer
War.**
See item no. 222.

With the United States

404   **The Martínez era: Salvadoran-American relations, 1931-1944.**
       C. F. E. Astilla.   PhD dissertation, Louisiana State University, 1976.
       249p. bibliog. (University Microfilms order no. 7710354).
A case-study of relations between El Salvador and the United States during the
presidency of Maximiliano Hernández Martínez, 1931-44, documenting the generally
good relations between the two countries. Astilla sees this as exemplary evidence of
the success of Franklin Roosevelt's Good Neighbor Policy in improving US-Latin
American relations.

405 **The soft war: the uses and abuses of U.S. economic aid in Central America.**
Tom Barry, Deb Preusch. New York: Grove Press, 1988. 320p.
The authors criticize US aid programmes in El Salvador and other Central American states, claiming that such programmes are designed to sustain economic élites at the expense of continued poverty in the region.

406 **Confronting revolution: security through diplomacy in Central America.**
Edited by M. J. Blachman, W. M. Leogrande, K. E. Sharpe. New York: Pantheon, 1986. 438p.
This anthology of 15 articles on US policy in Central America, specifically written for this volume by leading specialists, includes a chapter on El Salvador, p. 50-87, by Martin Diskin and Kenneth Sharpe, as well as a chapter on 'The economics of strife', by Richard Newfarmer that pays considerable attention to El Salvador.

407 **The evolution of U.S. policy toward El Salvador: the politics of repression.**
John A. Booth. In: *The Caribbean challenge: U.S. policy in a volatile region.* Edited by H. Michael Erisman. Boulder, Colorado: Westview Press, 1984, p. 117-40.
A particularly careful and thoughtful review of the evolution of US policy in El Salvador.

408 **La primera administración Reagan y El Salvador.** (The first Reagan administration and El Salvador.)
Centro de Estudios Centroamericanos de Relaciones Internacionales. México: CECRI, 1986. 127p.
Examines the Mexican perspectives on US relations with El Salvador during Ronald Reagan's first administration.

409 **Turning the tide: U.S. intervention in Central America and the struggle for peace.**
Noam Chomsky. Boston: South End Press, 1985. 298p.
A critical commentary on US policy in El Salvador and Nicaragua. In reviewing the recent history of US involvement in Central America, Chomsky cites considerable US support of injustice there and calls for a more constructive US policy in support of institutional reform against élite abuses. This is a provocative challenge to North American assumptions in dealing with its Central American client states, calling for more involvement by the public in determining foreign policy.

410 **Help or hindrance? United States economic aid in Central America.**
Kevin Danaher, Philip Berryman, M. Benjamin. New York: Institute for Food and Development Policy, 1987. 105p.
The authors are critical of US aid policy in Central America which has increasingly

focused on security and military aid at the expense of economic development assistance. The book includes a chapter on El Salvador.

411 **The impact of U.S. policy in El Salvador, 1979-1985.**
Martin Diskin.   Berkeley: The Institute of International Studies, University of California, 1986. 67p. bibliog. (Policy Papers in International Affairs, no. 27).

A clearly reasoned essay that challenges US assumptions regarding El Salvador's government. Diskin reviews the policy of the United States there since 1931 and especially since 1979, and argues that Congressional support of Reagan's policy in El Salvador, while it temporarily prevented a leftist victory, also deepened the civil war and ultimately strengthened the left while weakening democratization in the country. He favours a negotiated peace settlement and inclusion of the left in the political process.

412 **The continuing crisis: U.S. policy in Central America and the Caribbean.**
Edited by Mark Falcoff and Robert Royal.   [Washington]: Ethics and Public Policy Center, 1987. 568p. maps. bibliog.

A major collection of speeches, documents, and essays relating to US policy in the Caribbean Basin from several perspectives, although generally representing a conservative focus. Part Three, p. 191-289, is devoted to US policy in El Salvador and includes a chronology of events and selections by John Kurzweil, Julia Preston, Shirley Christian, José Napoleón Romero, and the US State Department.

413 **Central America, international dimensions of the crisis.**
Edited by Richard E. Feinberg.   New York: Holmes & Meier, 1982. 280p. map. bibliog.

A collection of essays on the international aspects of the crisis in Central America, brought on to large measure by the Nicaraguan revolution. Feinberg considers alternatives for US policy, Cold War implications, and the role of the USSR, Cuba, and other Latin American states in the region. There is considerable reference to El Salvador in this volume.

414 **History and motivation of U.S. involvement in the control of the peasant movement in El Salvador: the role of AIFLD in the agrarian reform process, 1970-1980.**
Carolyn Forche.   Washington: EPICA, 1980. 30p.

Reviews the Salvadoran agrarian reform programme of 1980 with particular reference to the role of the American Institute for Free Labor Development, which, this report says, is 'economically sustained by the [US] Agency for International Development'. It further argues that the AIFLD-supported agrarian reform programme is more anti-communist than pro-democratic.

415 **The U.S. and the rise of General Maximíliano Hernández Martínez.**
Kenneth J. Grieb. *Journal of Latin American Studies*, vol. 3
(Nov. 1971), p. 151-72.

Providing evidence of long-term US interest in El Salvador, this scholarly article
details North American involvement in the accession to power of the dictator of El
Salvador from 1931 to 1944.

416 **Central America and the Reagan doctrine.**
Edited by Walter F. Hahn. Boston: Center for International
Relations, Boston University, 1987. 336p.

A compilation of articles originally published in the *Strategic Review* focusing on
Reagan's Central American policy. In general, the volume reflects a strong anti-
Soviet perspective. It is more especially concerned with Nicaragua than El Salvador,
but it includes some attention to the latter, including a chapter by H. Joachim
Maitre, 'The dying war in El Salvador', p. 121-36, that argues that since 1984 the US-
supported government of El Salvador has been winning the civil war.

417 **Crisis in Central America: regional dynamics and U.S. policy in the
1980s.**
Edited by Nora Hamilton, Jeffry A. Frieden, Linda Fuller, Manuel
Pastor, Jr. Boulder, Colorado: Westview Press, 1988. 272p.

Reviews US policy on the isthmus and US efforts to re-establish hegemony by
increased involvement in political conflicts there. Although much of the book is
concerned with the policy debate in the US, the second part of the book analyses the
problems of the Central American states, including the changing balance of forces in
El Salvador.

418 **Central America: human rights and U.S. foreign policy.**
Edited by Dermot Keogh. Cork: Cork University Press, 1985. 168p.
bibliog.

An anthology of essays, critical of US policy in Central America, several of which
focus on El Salvador. About half of the volume is taken up with two essays by
Keogh, which are especially oriented toward US policy in El Salvador. In addition,
there are relevant essays by Tom Quigley, Walter LaFeber, Peter Barry, William
Luers, Bill McSweeney, and Anibal Romero.

419 **The report of the president's National Bipartisan Commission on
Central America.**
Henry A. Kissinger. New York: Macmillan, 1984. 158p.

An overview of Central America's history and socio-economic and political
problems, with a survey of the region's security from a US perspective. It
recommends more US economic and military aid to check Soviet and Cuban
pretensions. The report was the result of an investigation made in 1983 by a
presidential commission headed by Kissinger. The commission also published an 829-
page *Appendix to the report of the National Bipartisan Commission on Central*

America (Washington: GPO, 1984), containing much of the testimony it received in its investigation.

420 **Low intensity warfare: counterinsurgency, proinsurgency, and anti-terrorism in the eighties.**
Edited by Michael Klare, Peter Kornbluh.   New York: Pantheon, 1988. 250p.
A collection of nine reports on US involvement in unconventional conflicts in the Third World, including El Salvador, focusing on the debate over US policy in such conflicts.

421 **Inevitable revolutions: the United States in Central America.**
Walter LaFeber.   London: Norton, 1983. 357p.
An historical review of US policy in Central America by a distinguished US diplomatic historian. LaFeber is highly critical of the US record in Central America and argues persuasively that the US creation of Central America as a dependent region has made inevitable the anti-American insurgency that now exists on the isthmus. There is considerable attention to El Salvador in this provocative volume.

422 **Central America and the polls: a study of U.S. public opinion polls on U.S. foreign policy toward El Salvador and Nicaragua under the Reagan administration.**
William M. LeoGrande.   Washington: Washington Office on Latin America, 1984. 42p.
A special report on US public opinion polls relating to US policy in El Salvador during 1981-84.

423 **A splendid little war: drawing the line in El Salvador.**
William M. LeoGrande.   *International Security*, vol. 6 (1981), p. 27-52.
An examination of the conflict in El Salvador within the context of the Reagan administration's general foreign policy. In contrast to the approach of former President Carter, Reagan has used the Salvadoran situation as an example of his tough stance towards the Soviet Union.

424 **United States efforts to foster peace and stability in Central America: 1923-1954.**
Anne Warrick Lommel.   PhD dissertation, University of Minnesota, 1967. 336p. (University Microfilms order no. 681628).
Lommel traces the failure of US policy to achieve peace and stability in Central America during the indicated period.

425 **Central American paralysis.**
Richard Millett.   *Foreign Policy*, vol. 39 (summer 1980), p. 99-117.
A survey of recent Central American, including Salvadoran, political developments,

stressing the active role the US must play in the development of the region. The author maintains that the unwillingness of the US to do so represents a type of paralysis.

426 **Under the eagle: U.S. intervention in Central America and the Caribbean.**
Jenny Pearce.   London: Latin American Bureau; Boston: South End, 1982. 295p. maps.

A not always objective survey of US policy in Central America from 1823 to the 1980s, especially focusing on trends since the Cuban Revolution. Special attention is paid to the civil war in El Salvador, which the author perceives as part of a large pattern of US military intervention and economic dominance in the Caribbean region.

427 **El Salvador and the crisis in Central America.**
Roger Reed.   Washington: Council for Inter-American Security, 1984. 59p. map.

428 **El Salvador: America's next Vietnam?**
Steffen W. Schmidt.   Salisbury, North Carolina: Documentary Publications, 1983. 224p. map.

A brief, rather simplistic history of El Salvador, followed by a more detailed description of US policy toward El Salvador under the Carter and Reagan administrations. The author warns that the United States is moving in the direction of military intervention and deplores the tradition of violence in El Salvador. This work is not a major contribution to the literature on US policy in the area, but it provides an introductory overview. It includes some photographs.

429 **The morass: United States intervention in Central America.**
Richard Alan White.   New York: Harper & Row, 1984. 319p.

A sharp indictment of US policy in El Salvador, comparing it to earlier US policy in Vietnam. White discusses US interventionism, the 'domino theory', and alarmist military solutions to the problems in Central America; he opposes the trend toward increased US military involvement in Central America.

430 **Rift and revolution: the Central American imbroglio**.
Edited by Howard Wiarda.   Washington: American Enterprise Institute, 1984. 392p.

A collection of essays by Wiarda, Thomas Karnes, Gary Wynia, Roland Ebel, Thomas Anderson, Ronald McDonald, Giri and Virginia Valenta, Jeanne Kirkpatrick, E. J. Williams, Mark Falcoff, and Eusebio Mujal-León, providing background on the crisis in Central America. Although the authors represent a variety of opinions the book tends toward a conservative position on US policy in Central America.

431 **The communist challenge in the Caribbean and Central America.**
Howard J. Wiarda, Mark Falcoff.   Washington: The American
Enterprise Institute, 1987. 264p.

A collection of essays concerned with the Soviet challenge to US hegemony in the
Caribbean Basin. Attention to El Salvador is not extensive, but is present in many of
the essays.

The Central America fact book.
See item no. 2.

Dollars and dictators, a guide to Central America.
See item no. 3.

**Inside Central America: the essential facts past and present on El Salvador,
Nicaragua, Honduras, Guatemala, and Costa Rica**.
See item no. 4.

El Salvador: embassy under attack.
See item no. 92.

**Documentos para la historia de la guerra nacional contra los filibusteros en
Nicaragua**. (Documents for the history of the National War against the
filibusters in Nicaragua.)
See item no. 188.

**The five republics of Central America, their political and economic
development and their relations with the United States**.
See item no. 212.

**Steadfastness of the saints, a journey of peace and war in Central and North
America**.
See item no. 251.

Murdered in Central America: the stories of eleven U.S. missionaries.
See item no. 253.

**The impact of Monsignor Romero on the churches of El Salvador and the
United States**.
See item no. 273.

Human rights and El Salvador.
See item no. 301.

**Managing the facts: how the administration deals with reports of human
rights abuses in El Salvador**.
See item no. 302.

Human rights and United States policy toward Latin America.
See item no. 308.

El Salvador, the other war.
See item no. 310.

Foreign Relations. With the United States

The Central American refugees.
See item no. 312.

El Salvador 1987: Salvadoreños refugiados en los Estados Unidos. (El Salvador 1987: Salvadoran refugees in the United States.)
See item no. 314.

Displaced persons in El Salvador.
See item no. 315.

Anatomy of resistance in El Salvador: who are the rebels and what do they want?
See item no. 322.

El Salvador: the face of revolution.
See item no. 323.

The case for power-sharing in El Salvador.
See item no. 334.

Demonstration elections: U.S.-staged elections in the Dominican Republic, Vietnam, and El Salvador.
See item no. 336.

Enemy colleagues: a reading of the Salvadoran tragedy.
See item no. 355.

The United States and militarism in Central America.
See item no. 359.

State terror and popular resistance in El Salvador.
See item no. 363.

The republic of El Salvador against the republic of Nicaragua; complaint of the republic of El Salvador, with appendices.
See item no. 395.

Development assistance in Central America.
See item no. 449.

Foreign aid to the small farmer: the El Salvador experience.
See item no. 510.

A bibliography of United States-Latin American relations since 1810; a selected list of eleven thousand published references.
See item no. 658.

With the United Nations

432 **Las Naciones Unidas en el ámbito centroamericano; guía de estudio.**
(The United Nations in the Central American environment; a study
guide.)
José Vicente Moreno.   San Salvador: Dirección de Cultura,
Ministerio de Educación, 1970. 206p. (Colección Estudios y
Documentos, no. 31).

A guide to UN activities in Central America.

433 **Yearbook of the United Nations.**
United Nations. Office of Public Information.   New York: United
Nations, 1947-. annual.

This annual publication provides an indexed, concise and accurate record of the
activities of the UN with references to its documents. It is useful for checking on UN
activities related to El Salvador, such as development assistance, social and health
conditions, etc.

Economics

434 **Administración y empresas**. (Administration and enterprises.)
San Salvador: Universidad Centroamericana José Simeón Cañas,
Depto. de Administración de Empresas, 1979-. irregular.

The journal of the University school of business administration.

435 **Productive activities and economic contributions to family income of El Salvador women.**
Revathi Balakrishnan.   PhD dissertation, Ohio State University,
Columbus, 1981. 253p. (University Microfilms order no. 8128958).

Based on research on 1,178 Salvadoran women, the author analyses the differences in the productive activities of female heads of households and female spouses and the effect of these activities on per capita income.

436 **Boletín de Investigación**. (Research Bulletin.)
San Salvador: Instituto de Investigaciones Económicas, Facultad de
Ciencias Económicas, Universidad de El Salvador, 1973-. irregular.

Notes and reports on ongoing research in economics at the University of El Salvador.

437 **Boletín económica y social**. (Economic and Social Bulletin.)
San Salvador: Fundación Salvadoreña para el Desarrollo Económica y
Social (FUSADES), 1984-present. bi-monthly.

FUSADES is a private, non-profit-making foundation dedicated to proposing solutions to El Salvador's enormous economic and social problems. Although recognizing the gravity of the social problems, it tends toward economic solutions, and leans especially toward private sector development with a strongly negative view toward further public sector development. Its regular bulletin contains news of its activities and reports, several of which are listed elsewhere in this bibliography.

438 **The political economy of Central America since 1920.**
Victor Bulwer-Thomas.   Cambridge: Cambridge University Press,
1987. 438p. maps. bibliog.

A major study of the 20th-century economy of Central America, based on previously
unpublished estimates of the national accounts. The author pays considerable
attention to El Salvador, as he examines variations in economic development among
the Central American states. He also relates the economic development to the
political developments of the period. See also his summary article, 'Economic
development over the long run – Central America since 1920', *Journal of Latin
American Studies*, vol. 15 (Nov. 1983), p. 269-94.

439 **Acumulación de capital y empresas transnacionales en Centroamérica.**
(Capital accumulation and transnational companies in Central
America.)
Donald Castillo Rivas.   México: Siglo Veintiuno, 1980. 277p.
bibliog.

A detailed study of the penetration of foreign capital in Central America in the mid-
twentieth century, paying particular attention to the role of the Common Market,
transnational corporations, and agribusiness. It includes a number of useful statistical
appendixes, as well as many tables in the text. While this work does not especially
focus on El Salvador, it is a good analysis of the general question of foreign
investment in Central America, and it includes much data on El Salvador in
comparison with the other Central American states.

440 **El Salvador: crisis económica.** (El Salvador: economic crisis.)
Centro de Investigación y Acción Social.   México: CINAS, 1987.
86p. bibliog. (Cuaderno de Trabajo no. 9).

Two scholarly studies on El Salvador's economic difficulties: 'Factores endógenos del
conflicto centroamericano: crisis económica y desequilibrios sociales' (Internal factors
in the Central American conflict: economic crisis and social disequilibrium), by
Ignacio Ellacuría, Rector of the Universidad Centroamericana José Simeón Cañas,
and 'Crisis económica de El Salvador' (Economic crisis of El Salvador), by Francisco
Lazo M., a former instructor at the same university. Both essays, supported by
numerous statistical tables, seek to explain the economic reorientation toward the
commercial sector that is occurring in El Salvador, doubting that it will work or bring
a peaceful solution to the conflict.

441 **Economic integration in Central America.**
Edited by William R. Cline, Enrique Delgado.   Washington: The
Brookings Institution, 1978. 712p.

Jointly sponsored by the Brookings Institution and by the Secretariat for Economic
Integration in Central America (SIECA), this mammoth study contains a great deal
of information and analysis on the integration movement in the last decade. A basic
source for any study of the Central American Common Market and the integration
movement.

115

442 **La economía de El Salvador y la integración centroamericana, 1954-1960.** (The economy of El Salvador and Central American integration, 1954-1960.)
Héctor Dada Hirezi. San José: EDUCA, 1983. 2nd ed. 133p. bibliog.

A leading Salvadoran Christian Democrat analyses the growth of the Salvadoran economy at the beginning of the Central American integration movement. A valuable contribution to Salvadoran economic history, explaining the attempt to diversify the economy in this period and relating it to the socio-economic class conflict in the country and with the general economic problems of Latin American dependency.

443 **Indicadores económicos y sociales CONAPLAN.** (CONAPLAN economic and social indicators.)
El Salvador. Consejo Nacional de Planificación y Coordinación Económica. San Salvador: CNPCE, 1967-. irregular.

These reports on economic and social indicators contain statistical data on the progress of El Salvador's economy and social development, as viewed by the National Council of Planning and Coordination. Although published somewhat irregularly, the reports are numerous.

444 **Análisis crítico de la política fiscal.** (Critical analysis of fiscal policy.)
FUSADES. San Salvador: Fundación para el Desarrollo Económico y Social, 1986. 72p.

A penetrating review of Salvadoran fiscal policy and its relation to economic development. This report, published in December of 1986, takes a hard and critical look at the role of the government in Salvadoran economic development since 1979 and makes recommendations toward what FUSADES regards as more rational government tax policy. It calls for substantial restructuring of the tax system, one which will provide better incentives for increases in productivity. Consistent with FUSADES commitment basically toward capitalist development, it takes a negative view toward government participation in economic activities and calls for a programme of privatization.

445 **Estrategía ante la crisis: reconstrucción y reactivación.** (A strategy in the face of the crisis: reconstruction and reactivation).
FUSADES. San Salvador: Departamento de Estudios Económicos y Sociales, Fundación Salvadoreña para el Desarrollo Económico y Social (FUSADES), 1986. 15p.

The recommendations of a private, non-profit-making Salvadoran foundation following the devastating earthquake of 10 October 1986. It argues, consistent with other reports of FUSADES, that the key to rapid recovery is increased productivity, and proposes a strategy of reconstruction and revitalization of economic production which it believes will speed the recovery process. This includes strong recommendations for greater private activity and decentralization and deconcentration of the public sector.

446 **La necesidad de un nuevo modelo económico para El Salvador: Lineamientos generales de una estrategía.** (The necessity of a new economic model for El Salvador: General outline of a strategy.) FUSADES. San Salvador: Fundación Salvadoreña para el Desarrollo Económico y Social, 1985. 60p.

The outline of an economic strategy for economic revitalization of El Salvador as seen by a major independent foundation established in El Salvador for Economic and Social Development. Written in 1985, as El Salvador was facing one of the worst economic crises in its history, the proposal emphasizes utilization of El Salvador's human resources to develop new export potential and to reduce the political polarization that plagues Salvadoran development. The proposed model is based on economic diversification and increases in production of exportable products, by which it hopes to promote a better distribution of income and a more efficient and competitive economy. Clearly within a capitalist framework, FUSADES is promoting greater production of goods with which El Salvador can compete in the world market.

447 **Central America: regional integration and economic development.** Roger D. Hansen. Washington: National Planning Association, 1967. 106p. (Studies in Development Progress, no. 1).

A non-technical description of the Central American Common Market with emphasis on the problems facing the integration movement.

448 **Revista de Economía de El Salvador.** (El Salvador economic review.) Instituto de Estudios Económicos, Ministerio de Economía. San Salvador: Ministerio de Economía, 1951-61.

The review publishes articles on a broad range of economic topics.

449 **Development assistance in Central America.** John F. McCamant. New York: Praeger, 1968. 351p.

An excellent description of the multiplicity of foreign and international agencies involved in Central America and the nature of their activities. The work includes a considerable amount of statistical information and is useful for understanding the degree of involvement of the United States in internal Central American development.

450 **The Central American Common Market: economic policies, economic growth, and choices for the future.** Donald H. McClelland. New York: Praeger, 1972. 256p. (Praeger Special Studies in International Economic Development).

A detailed survey of the Central American Common Market, with considerable statistical data on the economic development of each of the states.

451 **Crisis del desarrollismo: caso El Salvador.** (Crisis of developmentalism: the case of El Salvador.)
Rafael Menjívar. San José: EDUCA, 1977. 139p.

An overview of the Salvadoran economy with sharp criticism of the land tenure situation in the country. The author blames the coffee élite for an economic development policy in El Salvador that has emphasized exports for the benefit of that élite and has ignored the social welfare of the majority. This has created a socio-economic crisis in the country which can only be solved, the author believes, by a radical change in the development priorities. See also the author's *El Salvador* (San José: EDUCA, 1980).

452 **Growth and crisis in the Central American economies 1950-1980.**
Hector Pérez Brignoli, Yolanda Baires Martínez. *Journal of Latin American Studies*, vol. 15 (Nov. 1983), p. 365-98.

An excellent overview of Central American economic development from 1950 to 1980, examining the nature of the structural change that occurred as a result of the integration movement and industrialization.

453 **Sistemas tributarios de América Latina: El Salvador.** (Latin American taxation systems: El Salvador.)
Organization of American States, Inter-American Development Bank. Washington: Pan American Union, 1966. 88p.

A clear, concise survey of the tax structure of El Salvador as it existed in the period 1961-64. Separate sections discuss taxes on income, assets, sales, inheritance, consumption, transactions and documents, and overseas trade.

454 **Rapid development in small economies: the example of El Salvador.**
David R. Raynolds. New York: Praeger, 1967. 141p. maps.

An optimistic view of Salvadoran economic development, lauding US aid programmes that have helped El Salvador expand her agricultural and industrial exports. Raynolds thinks El Salvador should be an example to other small, developing nations. He appears to be unconcerned about the serious socio-economic imbalances in the country, to some degree caused by the sort of development he advocates, but the study is useful for its detailed description of the various productive industries and commodities.

455 **Economic development of El Salvador, 1945-1965.**
Daniel K. Royer. PhD dissertation, University of Florida, Gainesville, 1966. 296p. map. bibliog. (University Microfilms order no. 673503).

A detailed survey of the Salvadoran economy during the critical two decades following the fall of the Hernández Martínez régime. The work is based on a broad range of sources and on research in El Salvador. It reflects the considerable economic growth of the period, but also recognizes the serious social inequities that were growing as real income of the poor actually declined during the period. The study emphasizes the importance of industry to El Salvador's future prosperity and forewarns of some of the major economic problems that will occur in the following two decades.

456 **La economía nacional, un año después del 15 de Octubre de 1979.** (The national economy, one year after 15 October 1979.)
Luis de Sebastián. *Estudios Centroamericanos*, vol. 35 (1980), p. 953-70.

An analysis of the Salvadoran economy, based on official statistics, government and private sector publications, and newspapers, in the year following the coup d'état of 15 October 1979. All indicators reflected a general decline and progressive deterioration of economic conditions, which the agrarian, banking, and foreign trade reforms of the past had failed to arrest.

457 **La deuda externa salvadoreña.** (The Salvadoran foreign debt.)
Seminario Permanente de Estudios de El Salvador. San Salvador: Editorial Universitaria, 1987. 118p. (Colección Ensayo, no. 3).

A series of studies on the Salvadoran foreign debt. An historical article by Italo López Vallecillos reviews the history of the country's foreign debt from 1824 to 1940, and Rafael Menjívar Larín continues this discussion through to 1984. Roberto López considers the effect of the foreign debt on political stability. Mario Lungo and Ricardo Sol, in separate chapters, deal with the social effects of the growing foreign debt, and Santiago H. Ruiz Granadino suggests alternatives on payment of the debt.

458 **La concentración económica en El Salvador**. (The concentration of wealth in El Salvador.)
Manuel Sevilla. Managua, Nicaragua: Instituto de Investigaciones Económicas y Sociales, Coordinadora Regional de Investigaciones Económicas y Sociales, 1985. 37p.

Sevilla studies the concentration of wealth and income in El Salvador in the 1970s to show the enormous inequities in the Salvadoran economy, comparing small, medium, and large enterprises. He argues that this concentration of wealth in the hands of a few is inefficient use of capital and is socially unjust, and recommends full implementation of the agrarian reform law of 1980 and political recognition of the FMLN/FDR.

459 **An analysis of the economy of El Salvador.**
George P. Turner. Los Angeles: the author, 1961. 124p. bibliog.

A description of the economy as of about 1960, encouraging more industrial development. The book includes many tables and photographs.

460 **Consideraciones jurídico-políticas sobre la transformación agraria.**
(Political-legal considerations on the agrarian transformation.)
Guillermo Manuel Ungo. *Estudios Centroamericanos*, vol. 31 (1976), p. 451-62.

The leader of the Salvadoran social democratic movement discusses agrarian reform in El Salvador with specific reference to legal considerations. His comments are specifically addressed to the 1975 law creating the Institute of Agrarian Transformation (Instituto de Transformación Agraria). He notes ambiguities in the law that make its value doubtful, for, he says, 'Legal ambiguity is favorable to the dominant class'. The article is a strong argument for more responsible use of private property in the best interests of the whole society, a principle stated in the 1950 and 1962 constitutions, but which Ungo says has been a 'dead letter' for 25 years.

461 **Taxes and tax harmonization in Central America.**
Virginia G. Watkin. Cambridge, Massachusetts: Harvard University Press, 1977. 532p. maps. bibliog.
A detailed study of efforts to develop a uniform tax structure in the Central American states as a part of the Central American economic integration movement. This major work includes detailed information on the tax systems of each of the five states, including El Salvador.

462 **The economies of Central America.**
John Weeks. New York; London: Holmes & Meier, 1985. 209p. bibliog.
An excellent introduction to the Central American economy, with general chapters on various topics relating to the Central American states, including political economy, growth, trade, agriculture, and manufacturing. A final chapter surveys each state in terms of the present economic crisis. It presents a pessimistic view of current economic policy in El Salvador and elsewhere.

463 **Politics and planners; economic development in Central America.**
Gary Wynia. Madison, Wisconsin: University of Wisconsin Press, 1972. 227p. bibliog.
A major study of economic planning in Central America in the 1960s.

Dollars and dictators, a guide to Central America.
See item no. 3.

Centro América 19--, análisis económico y político sobre la región. (Central America 19--, economic and political analyses of the region.)
See item no. 11.

Atlas económico de El Salvador, 1974. (Economic atlas of El Salvador, 1974.)
See item no. 46.

Origen, desarrollo y crisis de las formas de dominación en El Salvador. (The origins, development and crisis of the forms of domination in El Salvador.)
See item no. 152.

Manual de historia económica de El Salvador. (Manual for the economic history of El Salvador.)
See item no. 155.

The five republics of Central America, their political and economic development and their relations with the United States.
See item no. 212.

Human resources of Central America, Panama, and Mexico, 1950-1980, in relation to some aspects of economic development.
See item no. 221.

Fundamentos económicos de la burguesía salvadoreña. (Economic foundations of the Salvadoran bourgeoisie.)
See item no. 279.

Interpretación del desarrollo social centroamericano, procesos y estructuras de una sociedad dependiente. (Interpretation of Central American Social development, processes and structures of a dependent society.)
See item no. 284.

El Salvador, acumulación de capital y proceso revolucionario, (1932-1981). (Capital accumulation and the revolutionary process in El Salvador (1932-1981).)
See item no. 337.

Análisis sobre el conflicto entre Honduras y El Salvador. (Analysis of the conflict between Honduras and El Salvador.)
See item no. 392.

Regional integration in Central America.
See item no. 394.

Central American regional integration.
See item no. 402.

Help or hindrance? United States economic aid in Central America.
See item no. 410.

El Banco Central de Reserva en el desarrollo económico de El Salvador. (The Central Reserve Bank in the economic development of El Salvador.)
See item no. 465.

Opciones para financiar el deficit fiscal de 1987. (Options for financing the fiscal deficit of 1987.)
See item no. 469.

Tax reform in El Salvador.
See item no. 471.

Public finance in a developing country: El Salvador – a case study.
See item no. 476.

El Salvador.
See item no. 479.

Economics

Growth and integration in Central America.
See item no. 480.

Economic integration in Central America, empirical investigations.
See item no. 486.

Central America: regional integration and national political development.
See item no. 487.

El Salvador and economic integration in Central America: an econometric study.
See item no. 488.

Roots of rebellion: land and hunger in Central America.
See item no. 506.

Foreign aid to the small farmer: the El Salvador experience.
See item no. 510.

Programa de reactivación de la caficultura. (Programme for the reactivation of coffee cultivation.)
See item no. 515.

Situación demográfica, social, económica y educativa de El Salvador.
(Demographic, social, economic and educational situation of El Salvador.)
See item no. 558.

Boletín de Ciencias Económicas y Sociales. (Bulletin of Economic and Social Sciences.)
See item no. 629.

Investment, Finance, Banking, and Currency

464 **The coins and paper money of El Salvador.**
Alcedo F. Almanzar, Brian R. Stickney. San Antonio, Texas:
Almanzar's Coins of the World, 1973. 88p.

This publication provides standard data for numismatic reference such as dates of coins, descriptions of obverses and reverses, types of metal, weights, diameters, and valuations in US dollars. With regard to banknotes, it gives detailed descriptions of denomination, physical size, and colour. It includes many illustrative photographs, and covers the period 1789-1970.

465 **El Banco Central de Reserva en el desarrollo económico de El Salvador.** (The Central Reserve Bank in the economic development of El Salvador.)
Stanley Avalos Miranda, Guillermo Hidalgo Qüehl, José Leandro Echeverría. San Salvador: Banco Central de Reserva de El Salvador, 1985. 182p. bibliog.

This useful volume contains two informative studies. Both trace the history of the Central Reserve Bank from its establishment in 1934 through to 1984, relating it to Salvadoran economic development. The first, by Avalos, includes useful appendixes on the public debt during the 1970s and a chronology of events relating to the bank's history, 1934-1984. The second, by Hidalgo and Echeverría, includes statistical appendixes covering the whole 50-year period, emphasizing the monetary function of the bank in promoting the country's economic development. These essays were the 1st and 2nd prize winners in a competition sponsored by the bank to commemorate its 50th anniversary.

466 **The banknotes of the Republic of El Salvador.**
Banco de Fomento Agropecuario. San Salvador: Banco de Fomento
Agropecuario, 1974. 89p.
An illustrated history of the emission of paper currency in El Salvador.

467 **Banco Hipotecario de El Salvador. Revista**. (Mortgage Bank of El
Salvador. Review.)
San Salvador: Banco Hipotecario de El Salvador, 1944-. irregular.
In addition to this journal dealing with banking and other economic issues, the Banco
Hipotecario also published a series of useful reports in its *Cuadernos de divulgación
agropecuario* (San Salvador, 196- to 198-). It also published a *Bibliografía*
(Bibliography) irregularly in the 1960s and various *Memorias* (Reports) in the 1960s
and 1970s.

468 **Business Latin America**.
New York: Business International Corporation, 1966-.
The best weekly report on Latin American business, with well-researched and
objective coverage. Attention to El Salvador is not extensive, but coverage is usually
accurate and careful.

469 **Opciones para financiar el deficit fiscal de 1987.** (Options for financing
the fiscal deficit of 1987.)
FUSADES. San Salvador: Fundación Salvadoreña para el
Desarrollo Económico y Social, 1986. 28p.
Suggestions of many alternatives for funding the 1987 Salvadoran budget, as well as
recommendations for cutting government spending. It leans heavily in favour of the
private sector and reduction of the public sector in the economy.

470 **Investment and industrial development in El Salvador: a report for the
International Cooperation Administration**.
Robert R. Nathan Associates, Inc. Washington: Nathan Associates,
1961. 221p.
A report with many statistical tables prepared by a Washington consulting firm for
the ICA (predecessor to the US Agency for International Development). It suggests
financial policies to promote foreign investment in industry, and other measures to
promote greater economic activity in El Salvador, including a conservation corps.

471 **Tax reform in El Salvador.**
Oliver Oldman. *Inter-American Law Review*, vol. 6 (July 1964),
p. 379-420.
A detailed explanation of the major Salvadoran tax reform decree of 1963.

472 **La moneda, los bancos y el crédito en El Salvador**. (Money, banking and credit in El Salvador.)
Alfonso Rochac. San Salvador: Banco Central de Reserva de El Salvador, 1984. 2 vols.

Volume 1 discusses money and credit in the country, while volume 2 focuses on the creation of the central reserve bank. The work is a useful source for information on the banking history of El Salvador, and on banking and credit legislation.

473 **Catálogo de monedas y medallas de proclama de Centro América y Panamá**. (Catalogue of coins and commemorative medallions of Central America and Panama.)
Felipe Siliézar Ramos. Guatemala: Eros, [n.d.]. 407p. (Distributed in USA by Almanzar's Coins of the World, San Antonio, Texas).

A detailed guide to coins and medals minted in Central America between 1733 and 1976, with photographs. There are sections on Salvadoran silver coins minted in El Salvador between 1828 and 1976 on pages 179-203, and on gold coins for the period 1892-1971, on pages 353-59.

474 **Estudios de moneda y banca de El Salvador**. (Studies on money and banking in El Salvador.)
José Enrique Silva. San Salvador: Banco Agrícola Comercial de El Salvador, 1979. 2 vols. (Colección BAC).

A history of money and banking in El Salvador. Volume 1 covers the period 1821-1934, and volume 2 continues the account through to 1975. Volume 2 also includes a number of chapters that deal with aspects of the 1821-1934 period that were not covered in the first volume.

475 **The determinants of direct foreign investment in the Central American Common Market, 1954-1970.**
Carmine R. Torrisi. PhD dissertation, Syracuse University, 1976. 222p. bibliog. (University Microfilms order no. 7724413).

A useful study of the common market, 1954-1970, and its relation to foreign investment.

476 **Public finance in a developing country: El Salvador – a case study**.
Henry C. Wallich, John H. Adler. New York: Greenwood Press, 1968. 346p.

Originally published in 1951, this is a pioneering effort at describing and analysing public finance in El Salvador. Although its relevance has been greatly diminished by time, it still has both historical and some practical value in understanding Salvadoran economic issues. It was an especially influential study in determining Salvadoran developmentalist policy in the 1950s and 1960s.

477 **Monetary policy, credit institutions, and agricultural credit in El Salvador.**
D. Sykes Wilford, Walton T. Wilford.   El Salvador: Agency for International Development, 1975.

478 **Central American monetary union.**
John P. Young.   Washington: Agency for International Development, 1965. 180p. tables.

An economist with long experience advising on Central American matters offers a plan for a uniform currency as part of the Central American economic integration programme. This report provides considerable economic data on the region, and makes comparisons with the experience of the European Economic Community. Young is best known for his *Central American currency and finance* (Princeton: Princeton University Press, 1925), which is too old to be of great use in terms of contemporary currency and finance, but it does help to explain many Central American financial difficulties of the past.

Dollars and dictators, a guide to Central America.
See item no. 3

Acumulación de capital y empresas transnacionales en Centroamérica. (Capital accumulation and transnational companies in Central America.)
See item no. 439.

La deuda externa salvadoreña. (The Salvadoran foreign debt.)
See item no. 457.

Banco Central de Reserva de El Salvador: anuario estadístico. (Central Reserve Bank of El Salvador: statistical annual.)
See item no. 556.

Transferencia de tecnología, simulación o realidad de la inversión extranjera (caso: El Salvador). (Transfer of technology, apparent or real foreign investment (the case of El Salvador).)
See item no. 583.

Trade

479 **El Salvador.**
British Overseas Trade Board. London: The Board of Trade, 1978.
47p. bibliog.
A useful handbook of hints to the businessman. Updates are issued periodically.

480 **Growth and integration in Central America.**
Carlos M. Castillo. New York: Praeger, 1966. 188p. bibliog.
(Praeger Special Studies in International Economics and
Development).
An important study of the Common Market experience by a leading US-trained
Costa Rican economist. It describes in clear terms the goals and operations of the
CACM up to 1965, and looks optimistically toward economic integration as a means
towards more satisfactory political development in Central America.

481 **Código de comercio de la República de El Salvador.** (Commercial
Code of the Republic of El Salvador.)
San Salvador: Editorial Ahora, 1985. 457p.
The commercial law of El Salvador up to 1985.

482 **Comercio exterior.** (Foreign trade.)
San Salvador: Dirección General de Estadística y Censos, 1950-1960;
Instituto Salvadoreño de Comercio Exterior, 1961-. irregular.
This bulletin on Salvadoran foreign trade has generally appeared annually, but is
often very much in arrears. See also *Estadísticas de comercio exterior de El Salvador*
(Foreign trade statistics of El Salvador) (q.v.).

483 **El Salvador, directorio de oferta exportable – Exportable offer directory.**
San Salvador: Ministerio de Comercio Exterior, 1986. 49p.
A directory of Salvadoran export products.

484 **Estadísticas de comercio exterior de El Salvador.** (Foreign trade statistics of El Salvador.)
San Salvador: Ministerio de Comercio Exterior, 1986. 56p.
Statistical tables, charts and graphs on El Salvador's foreign trade. This was the first year of a projected annual publication, but it may be the continuation of *Comercio exterior* (q.v.).

485 **FAO Trade Yearbook.**
Food and Agriculture Organization of the United Nations. Rome: FAO, 1947-. annual.
Annual statistics on the volume and value of trade in agricultural products, equipment and materials.

486 **Economic integration in Central America, empirical investigations.**
Jeffrey B. Nugent. Baltimore: Johns Hopkins University Press, 1974. 209p. bibliog.
A quantitative study of the Central American Common Market experience. Highly technical, providing a theoretical analysis of customs unions and testing the Central American experience against it. Nugent concludes that the benefits from the CACM have been substantial. The bibliography contains extensive listing of theoretical literature on customs unions.

487 **Central America: regional integration and national political development**.
Royce Q. Shaw. Boulder, Colorado: Westview Press, 1978. 252p. bibliog.
One of the more recent surveys of the Central American Common Market, rejecting leftist and dependency theory as an explanation for its difficulties. Rather, Shaw blames the Central American élites and domestic problems for the problems the CACM encountered.

488 **El Salvador and economic integration in Central America: an econometric study**.
Gabriel Siri. Lexington, Massachusetts: D. C. Heath 1984. 206p.
An econometric analysis of changes in the Salvadoran economy between 1950 and 1977, reflecting the impact of the economic integration movement. It confirms the hypothesis that El Salvador's economy was highly dependent on the external sector and closely linked to the other Central American economies, especially that of Guatemala. Chapter 6 discusses the effects of world coffee prices on El Salvador's economy.

489 **Yearbook of International Trade Statistics.**
United Nations, Department of International Economic and Social
Affairs, Statistical Office. New York: United Nations, 1951-.
annual.
An annual compilation of international trade statistics by countries and by
commodities. It shows what El Salvador imported and exported and to and from
which countries.

490 **Características básicas y evolución reciente del sector externo de El
Salvador.** (Basic characteristics and recent evolution of the external
sector of El Salvador.)
Juan Héctor Vidal Guerra. San Salvador: Fundación para el
Desarrollo Económico y Social, 1986. 47p.
Details the principal characteristics of El Salvador's foreign trade since 1979, but with
considerable statistical data for the period since 1950. This is a concise, but highly
useful overview of Salvador's dependency on foreign trade and the difficulties it has
faced in recent years.

491 **Free trade in manufactures: the Central American experience.**
L. Willmore. *Economic development and cultural change*, vol. 20
(July 1972), p. 659-70.
Willmore demonstrates that most of the inter-regional trade in Central America is
composed of manufactured goods and points to the Common Market's role in
encouraging industry. The article is especially useful for its analysis of Central
American manufacturing as export-oriented industries.

Indigo production and trade in colonial Guatemala.
See item no. 178.

**Central American commerce and maritime activity in the 19th century:
sources for a quantitative approach.**
See item no. 199.

A statement of the laws of El Salvador in matters affecting business.
See item no. 376.

Regional integration in Central America.
See item no. 394.

Central American economic integration: the politics of unequal benefits.
See item no. 396.

Central American regional integration.
See item no. 402.

**Autonomy or dependence as regional integration outcomes: Central
America.**
See item no. 403.

Trade

Economic integration in Central America.
See item no. 441.

Central America: regional integration and economic development.
See item no. 447.

The Central American Common Market: economic policies, economic growth, and choices for the future.
See item no. 450.

Taxes and tax harmonization in Central America.
See item no. 461.

The determinants of direct foreign investment in the Central American Common Market, 1954-1970.
See item no. 475.

Regional industrial development in Central America. A case study of the integration industries scheme.
See item no. 498.

Anuario estadístico centroamericano de comercio exterior. (Central American foreign trade statistical annual.)
See item no. 555.

Industry

492 **Boletín Estadístico Industrial** (Industrial statistical bulletin.)
San Salvador: Dirección General de Estadística y Censos, 1975-.

493 **The textile industry in El Salvador.**
Percy. M. Feltham. New York: United Nations, 1954. 49p.

494 **Industrial development of El Salvador.**
B. F. Hoselitz. New York: United Nations, 1954. 104p.
A descriptive survey of Salvadoran industry, with discussion of future potential. Important as an index at the point where considerable expansion of Salvadoran industry began to occur.

495 **Industria, ASI.** (Industry, ASI.)
San Salvador: Asociación Salvadoreña de Industriales, 1961-.
The newsletter of the Salvadoran Association of Industrialists.

496 **Industrialización y urbanización en El Salvador, 1969-1979.**
(Industrialization and urbanization in El Salvador, 1969-1979.)
Carlos Roberto López Pérez. San Salvador: UCA Editores, 1984. 186p. bibliog.

497 **Economic analysis of the inland fisheries project in El Salvador.**
E. W. McCoy. Auburn, Alabama: International Center for Aquaculture, Auburn University, 1974. 49p.

498 **Regional industrial development in Central America. A case study of the integration industries scheme.**
David E. Ramsett.   New York: Praeger, 1969. 136p.

A pessimistic report on the effectiveness of this programme for stimulating industrial development.

499 **The fisheries industry and El Salvador.**
John Thompson.   *Journal of Inter-American Studies*, vol. 3 (July 1961), p. 437-46. map.

A brief, first-hand survey of the seafood industry in the late 1950s, with attention to both the saltwater and freshwater fisheries, marketing, and prices. Thompson concludes that the shrimp industry is flourishing, but warns against over-expansion for supply is limited.

Investment and industrial development in El Salvador: a report for the International Cooperation Administration.
See item no. 470.

Free trade in manufactures: the Central American experience.
See item no. 491.

Agriculture

500 **Agricultura en El Salvador**. (Agriculture in El Salvador.)
San Salvador: Ministerio de Agricultura y Ganadería, 1960-. irregular.
The official government journal on agriculture.

501 **Agrociencia**. (Agroscience.)
San Salvador: Facultad de Ciencias Agronómicas, Universidad de El
Salvador, 1977-. irregular.
The publication of research results and commentary by the university school of
agronomy.

502 **Anuario de estadísticas agropecuarias**. (Agriculture and livestock
statistical annual.)
San Salvador: Ministerio de Agricultura y Ganadería, 1967-. annual.
The Ministry of Agriculture and Livestock also publishes a wide range of specialized
bulletins on various topics relating to agricultural and livestock raising under the
general title *M.A.G.*

503 **Las perspectivas del desarrollo agropecuario y la tenencia de la tierra.**
(Perspectives on agricultural development and land tenure.)
Salvador Arias Peñate. *Estudios Centroamericanos*, vol. 35 (1980),
p. 445-62.
Based on the author's experience as Under-secretary of Agriculture and Livestock
and on government documents, this article describes the agrarian history of El
Salvador from 1960 to 1978 in terms of production and financing. The dual
characteristics of production for export and subsistence have resulted in over-
exploitation of the soil and malnutrition of the population. Analysis of land tenure
and agricultural development leads to the conclusion that agrarian reform is

necessary, but that the reforms of the present government in agriculture, finance, and foreign trade will not solve El Salvador's agricultural problems.

504 **Legislación salvadoreña del café, 1846-1955.** (Salvadoran coffee legislation, 1846-1955.)
Asociación Salvadoreña del Café. San Salvador: Editorial Ahora, 1956. 706p.

A compilation of the legislation regarding all aspects of coffee production and marketing in El Salvador during the years indicated.

505 **Banco de Fomento Agropecuario: Carta agropecuario.** (Bank of Agricultural and Livestock Development: Agricultural and Livestock Newsletter.)
San Salvador: Banco de Fomento Agropecuario, 1973-1975 (or possibly longer).

A newsletter, directed toward livestock interests, by the bank for agrarian and grazing development. The bank also published a large number of *Informaciones Económicas* (Economic information) in the mid-1970s, and an annual *Memoria* (Report).

506 **Roots of rebellion: land and hunger in Central America.**
Tom Barry. Boston: South End Press, 1987. 220p.

Examines agro-export systems and international market systems in Central America and their effect on the rural population. The book questions the value of traditional solutions, such as food assistance, rural development programmes, and expanded agro-export production.

507 **Agrarian reform in El Salvador.**
David Browning. *Journal of Latin American Studies*, vol. 15 (Nov. 1983), p. 399-426. maps.

An excellent review of the need for agrarian reform in El Salvador, noting the severe pressures on land use especially since 1930. Browning discusses the land reform programmes of both the government and the guerrilla opposition and the political context of reform in El Salvador, concluding that the 1980 agrarian reform law cannot satisfy El Salvador's long-term needs, but admitting that it is the first serious attempt to combat the negative effects of the country's agricultural development. Browning emphasizes the need for changing land use, as opposed to land ownership.

508 **El café de El Salvador.** (The coffee of El Salvador.)
San Salvador: Asociación Cafetalera de El Salvador, 1930-68.

Major publication of the powerful Coffee Growers Association of El Salvador.

509   **Tenencia de la tierra y desarrollo rural en Centroamérica**. (Land
      tenure and rural development in Central America.)
      Comité Interamericana de desarrollo agrícola (CIDA).
      Tegucigalpa: Instituto Nacional Agrario, 1975. 342p.
This report contains many statistical tables and analyses of the landholding systems of
all of the Central American states.

510   **Foreign aid to the small farmer: the El Salvador experience.**
      L. Harlan Davis.   *Inter-American Economic Affairs*, vol. 29 (1975),
       p. 81-91.
Evaluation of the practice of giving foreign aid to small farmers to promote economic
development. Based on the author's personal experience in El Salvador as well as
various primary and secondary sources.

511   **A comparative analysis of agrarian reform in El Salvador and
      Nicaragua, 1979-1981.**
      Carmen Diana Deere.   *Development and Change*, vol. 13 (1982),
       p. 1-41.
An in-depth study of the demand and scope of recent agrarian reform in El Salvador
and Nicaragua, particularly the varying effects of domestic and· international politics
on reform in each nation. Compares and contrasts the policies of the Carter and
Reagan administrations.

512   **Agricultural modernisation in El Salvador, Central America**.
      T. J. Downing.   Cambridge: Centre of Latin American Studies,
      1978. 70p. (Working papers, University of Cambridge, Centre of
      Latin American Studies, no. 32).

513   **Indigenous tropical agriculture in Central America: land use, systems,
      and problems**.
      Craig L. Dozier.   Washington, DC: National Academy of Sciences,
      National Research Council, 1958. 134p. map.
This survey of Central American agriculture and land use is intended only as an
introduction to the subject and it is now dated, but it is still a useful overview.

514   **FAO Production Yearbook.**
      Food and Agriculture Organization of the United Nations.
      Rome: Basic Data Unit, Statistical Division, FAO, 1947-. annual.
Comprises statistics on agricultural and livestock production, land use, population,
means of production and prices. Formerly Part 1 of the *Yearbook of Food and
Agricultural Statistics*.

515 **Programa de reactivación de la caficultura.** (Programme for the
reactivation of coffee cultivation.)
FUSADES.   San Salvador: Fundación para el Desarrollo Económico
y Social, 1985. 38p.

The first of a series of studies by a Salvadoran foundation dedicated to economic an
social vitalization. Since coffee is Salvador's major export, the foundation considers
indispensable to restoring its production. This report reviews the coffee industry in E
Salvador and analyses government policy and the causes of the current crisis, and
finally, proposes a strategy for revitalizing coffee production and exports. It claim
that its implementation would create 50,000 new jobs and an increase in foreig
exchange of nearly US$80 million.

516 **ISIC. Carta Informativa.** (ISIC Newsletter.)
San Salvador: Instituto Salvadoreño de Investigación del Café,
Departamento de Comunicaciones, 1978-.

The newsletter of a private research institute representing the coffee industry. ISI
also publishes a *Boletín Técnico* (1979-) and *Résumes de Investigaciones en Caj*
(1977-).

517 **The communal cooperative experience: an example from El Salvador.**
Donald Ralph Jackson.   PhD dissertation, University of Wisconsin,
Madison, 1980. (University Microfilms order no. 8110084).

An analysis of the effectiveness of agricultural communal cooperatives, stressing lan
tenure, credit, technology, and markets.

518 **Research on agricultural development in Central America.**
Heraclio A. Lombardo.   New York: Agricultural Development
Council, 1969. 71p. bibliog.

Lombardo discusses Central American agricultural problems and makes suggestior
for needed research.

519 **Evaluation of factors limiting bean production in El Salvador.**
Héctor Medrano-Vaquero.   PhD dissertation, University of Florida,
Gainesville, 1982. (University Microfilms order no. 8302270).

A quantitative study which concludes that pests and diseases limit bean productio
more than other factors. The author recommends that research concentrate on th
development of chemical controls.

520 **Formas de tenencia de la tierra y algunos otros aspectos de la actividad
agropecuaria.** (Forms of land tenure and other aspects of agricultural
activity.)
Rafael Menjívar.   San Salvador: Editorial Universitaria, 1962. 86p.
bibliog.

This publication, which describes the land tenure system in El Salvador based on th

950 census, very useful for understanding the nature and characteristics of land enure and land use in the country.

21 **Programs of agricultural colonization and settlement in Central America.**
Clarence W. Minkel. *Revista Geográfica* (Comisión de Geografía, Instituto Panamericano de Geografía e Historia), vol. 66 (June 1967), p. 19-53.

A very brief survey of land use, reform, and resettlement in Central America, ealing specifically with El Salvador on pages 27-31, and emphasizing El Salvador's hortage of land. While Minkel's coverage is not extensive, this is a useful ntroduction to the topic, and it places El Salvador in the context of land tenure in Central America generally.

22 **Man, crops and pests in Central America.**
George Ordish. Oxford, England: Pergamon Press; New York: Macmillan, 1964. 128p. (The commonwealth and international library. Biology division: biology in action series, vol. 3).

A handbook of agriculture in Central America, with particular reference to pests, iseases and their control. A chapter on pesticides is included.

23 **Cotton and cattle in the Pacific lowlands of Central America.**
J.J. Parsons. *Journal of Inter-American Studies*, vol. 7, no. 2 (1964), p. 149-59.

'his report documents the rapid growth of cotton and beef production along the acific coast of El Salvador in the 1950s and 160s. It is optimistic about the economic enefits of this development.

24 **Modernización agrícola en El Salvador.** (Agricultural modernization in El Salvador.)
Santiago Ruiz Granadino. *Estudios Sociales Centroamericanos*, vol. 8 (1979), p. 71-100.

An informative article, based on printed primary and secondary sources, that laments lat the modernization of Salvadoran agriculture has not been by means of lachinery, but rather by monopoly of land and credit, exclusive production for xport, and payment of low wages.

25 **El Salvador land reform 1980-81: impact audit.**
Laurence R. Simon, James C. Stephens, Jr. Boston: Oxfam America, 1982. 2nd ed. 61p.

his careful study of the Salvadoran agrarian reform programme differs from the first dition (1981) by the addition of a '1982 Supplement' by Martin Diskin. It examines le need for reform and its relation to Salvadoran politics, and describes the structure f the 1980 Agrarian Reform Law and its effects. While sympathetic to the rogramme's original goals, the report is pessimistic about its implementation.

Appendixes provide the principal documents of the programme and its implementation, as well as statistics on political assassinations in El Salvador in 1981.

526 **Effect of increased water supply on net returns to dairy farms in Sonsonate, El Salvador.**
Utah State University of Agriculture and Applied Science, Department of Economics. Logan, Utah: Council of United States Universities for Soil and Water Development in Arid and Sub-humid Areas, 1973. 96p.

A detailed case-study of an important aspect of agrarian development, reflecting the effort to develop commercial dairy farming on the Pacific coast of El Salvador.

527 **Decision making by farmers and by the National Agricultural Research Program on the adoption and development of maize varieties in El Salvador.**
Steven Thomas Walker. PhD dissertation, Stanford University, 1980. (University Microfilms order no. 8103572).

An exploration of the reasons for the stagnating productivity of the staple food crop of El Salvador, maize, and an analysis of the research priorities among the varieties of maize.

528 **Dictionary of tropical American crops and their diseases.**
Frederick Lovejoy Wellman. Metuchen, New Jersey: Scarecrow Press, 1977. 495p.

An useful reference work.

529 **Agrarian reform in El Salvador: a program of rural pacification.**
Philip Wheaton. Washington: EPICA Task Force, 1980. 21p.

Critical comment on the agrarian reform plan of 1980, arguing that it is really more of a programme to assist the counter-insurgency effort than the much-needed reform of land tenure and land use in the country. This report is strongly critical of the US role in El Salvador.

530 **Export agriculture and the crisis in Central America.**
Robert G. Williams. Chapel Hill: University of North Carolina Press, 1986. 257p. maps. bibliog.

A serious, scholarly, and well-written study of the cotton and beef industries in Central America since World War II and their impact on the social and political development of each state, with considerable attention to El Salvador. This excellent interdisciplinary study helps to explain the underlying causes of the social and political unrest in El Salvador especially well.

531 **The economic potential for increasing vegetable production in the Zapotitán District, El Salvador.**
David J. Zimet. Gainesville: Food and Resource Economics Department, Agricultural Experiment Stations, Institute of Food and Agricultural Sciences, University of Florida, 1975. 63p.

An informative report on a specific area, suggesting possibilities for increased food production in a country that suffers severe malnutrition.

La hacienda colonial en El Salvador: sus orígenes. (The colonial hacienda in El Salvador: its origins.)
See item no. 167.

El añil en El Salvador. (Indigo in El Salvador.)
See item no. 173.

Indigo production and trade in colonial Guatemala.
See item no. 178.

Promised land: peasant rebellion in Chalatenango, El Salvador.
See item no. 347.

Land reform and democratic development.
See item no. 348.

Land reform in El Salvador: the democratic alternative.
See item no. 349.

History and motivation of U.S. involvement in the control of the peasant movement in El Salvador: the role of AIFLD in the agrarian reform process, 1970-1980.
See item no. 414.

Crisis del desarrollismo: caso El Salvador. (Crisis of developmentalism: the case of El Salvador.)
See item no. 451.

Consideraciones jurídico-políticas sobre la transformación agraria. (Political-legal considerations on the agrarian transformation.)
See item no. 460.

FAO trade yearbook.
See item no. 485.

Economía agraria y movimiento obrero en Centroamérica (1850-1933). (The agrarian economy and the labour movement in Central America (1850-1933).)
See item no. 551.

¿Movimiento campesino o lucha del proletariado rural en El Salvador? (Peasant movement or proletarian struggle in El Salvador?)
See item no. 552.

Agriculture

Revista Pecuario. (Livestock Review.)
See item no. 632.

Bibliografías agrícolas de América Central: El Salvador. (Agricultural bibliographies of Central America: El Salvador.)
See item no. 649.

Transport
and Communications

532 **Boletín Estadístico de Telecomunicaciones.** (Statistical bulletin of
telecommunications.)
San Salvador: Administración Nacional de Telecomunicaciones,
1974-.
This publication was formerly *Anuario Estadística de Telecomunicaciones* (1959-74).

533 **Road user charges in Central America.**
Anthony Churchill (et al.).   Baltimore: Johns Hopkins University
Press, for the International Bank for Reconstruction and
Development, 1972. 188p. maps. bibliog. (World Bank Staff
Occasional Papers no. 15).
A thorough study of road financing and road use in the Central American states, with
proposals for means of financing more rural highway construction to encourage more
economic development.

534 **Inland transport in El Salvador.**
John H. T. Clarke.   New York: United Nations, 1954. 88p. map.
A report prepared in 1952 for the government of El Salvador, covering highways and
railway transportation.

535 **Comunicaciones.** (Communications.)
San Salvador: Instituto Tropical de Investigaciones Científicas,
Universidad Nacional de El Salvador, 1954-78. irregular.

536   **Railways of Central America and the West Indies**.
William Rodney Long.   Washington: GPO, 1925. 2 vols.
(Department of Commerce, Trade promotion series, no. 5).
Although this detailed guide is now very old, the railroads were largely completed in
Central America by 1925. Service has deteriorated considerably since that time and
there is no modern guide to the railways of El Salvador.

537   **Telecommunications in El Salvador**.
John E. Lundell.   New York: United Nations, 1954. 78p.
A report prepared for the government of El Salvador in 1952.

538   **Estudio de vías urbanas, San Salvador.** (Study of urban routes in San
Salvador.)
Prepared by Napoleón Morúa C. for CONAPLAN, Ministerio de
Obras Públicas y Banco Interamericana de Desarrollo.   San
Salvador: CONAPLAN, 1975. 2 vols.
A detailed description of the street plans of San Salvador.

539   **The harbor system of El Salvador**.
Ricardo M. Ortiz.   New York: United Nations, 1954. 140p. maps.
A report prepared for the government of El Salvador in 1952.

540   **Central American transportation study, 1964-1965. Report prepared
for the Central American Bank for Economic Integration.**
Transportation Consultants, Inc., Wilbur Smith & Associates,
Consultécnica, Ltda.   Washington: T. S. C. Consortium, [c.1965].
2 vols. maps.
This major, detailed report on Central American transport facilities describes the
highways, railways, ports and navigable waterways, and air transport facilities of all
the Central American states. Photographs and drawings enhance the descriptions. It
also includes a transportation plan for development and a discussion of rates, costs,
laws and regulations. The text is contained in vol. 1 (656p.), with vol. 2 containing
statistical appendices. A more recent report by the Central American Bank for
Economic Integration, *Estudio centroamericano de transporte (1974-76) (Central
American transportation study, 1974-76)*, 8 vols., is available only in Spanish.

The Pan American highway from the Río Grande to the Canal Zone.
See item no. 81.

Employment
and Manpower

541 **Encuesta sobre salarios ocupacionales, demanda de mano de obra y formación profesional.** (Survey of occupational salaries, labour demand, and professional training.)
El Salvador. Ministerio de Trabajo y Previsión Social.   San Salvador: Ministerio de Trabajo y Previsión Social, Departamento de Planificación, 1979. 169p.

542 **Salarios mínimos decretados en El Salvador, 1965-1986.**
(Minimum wages decreed in El Salvador, 1965-1986.)
El Salvador. Ministerio de Trabajo y Previsión Social, Departamento de Planificación.   San Salvador: Ministerio de Trabajo y Previsión Social, 1986. 43p.
A guide to legal minimum wages in El Salvador during the period indicated.

543 **Estadísticas de Trabajo.** (Labour statistics.)
San Salvador: Ministerio de Trabajo y Previsión Social, 1955-. annual.
(Title varies slightly).
An annual statistical report on labour and employment.

544 **Migration and the urban labor market: the case of San Salvador.**
Peter Peek, Pedro Antolinez.   *World Development*, vol. 5 (April 1977), p. 291-302.
An examination of employment and wage levels of rural migrants to San Salvador. It tries to determine the amount of discrimination experienced by those rural migrants *vis-à-vis* urban natives in the job market.

545 **Situación y perspectivas del empleo en El Salvador**. (Situation and perspectives of employment in El Salvador.) Regional Employment Program for Latin America and the Caribbean. Santiago, Chile: PRELAC, 1977. 453p.

A detailed report on the labour force of El Salvador and the situation regarding employment and unemployment in the country by an international agency. The study covers the period 1961-73 and emphasizes the fact that population growth was exceeding the development of new jobs. A separate, less detailed report, *La situación ocupacional en El Salvador, 1975* (The occupational situation in El Salvador, 1975) (Santiago, Chile: PRELAC, 1976) preceded this publication.

La hacienda colonial en El Salvador: sus orígenes. (The colonial hacienda in El Salvador: its origins.)
See item no. 167.

Human resources of Central America, Panama, and Mexico, 1950-1980, in relation to some aspects of economic development.
See item no. 221.

El Salvador, estudios de población. (El Salvador, population studies.)
See item no. 228.

Productive activities and economic contributions to family income of El Salvador women.
See item no. 435.

Labour Movement and Trade Unions

546 **Código de trabajo y sus reformas.** (Labour code and its revisions.)
San Salvador: Banco Hipotecario de El Salvador, 1977. 255p.
El Salvador's labour law: for earlier labour and social security legislation, see
Recopilación de leyes y reglamentos sobre trabajo y seguridad social (San Salvador:
Imprenta Nacional, 1951, 2nd ed., 1960).

547 **Cooperativismo en El Salvador: legislación y doctrina.** (Cooperativism
in El Salvador: legislation and doctrine.)
Cooperativa de Abogados de El Salvador. San Salvador:
Cooperativa de Abogados de El Salvador, 1971. 200p.
A history of cooperatives in El Salvador, with special attention to the lawyers'
cooperative.

548 **Labor rights in El Salvador.**
[James Goldston, Holly Burkhalter]. New York: Americas Watch
Committee, 1988. 117p. map.
A very useful survey of labour rights problems in El Salvador. The study includes a
chronology of labour rights violations, and sections on agricultural and non-
agricultural workers, public employees, prospects for reform, and US policy, with
appendixes of key legislation and a glossary of worker associations. The work is
based primarily on research conducted by James Goldston at the Human Rights
Institute of the Universidad Centroamericana José Simeón Cañas in San Salvador
from September to December 1987.

549 **Historia del movimiento obrero en América Latina.** (History of the labour movement in Latin America.)
Edited by Pablo González Casanova. México: Siglo Veintiuno Editores and Instituto de Investigaciones Sociales de la UNAM, 1984-1985. 4 vols. bibliog.

This fine collaborative history of the labour movement in 20th-century Latin America contains an excellent chapter on El Salvador by Rafael Menjívar Larín.

550 **Voluntary association in a climate of repression: union activities in El Salvador.**
Abraham Makofsky. *Human Organization*, vol. 37 (spring 1978), p. 57-63.

A study based on observations and interviews with Salvadoran labour leaders, concentrating on the workings of unions under political pressure. The unions are viewed as conflict groups that affect union leadership in a repressive political climate, especially with reference to the growth of class consciousness.

551 **Economía agraria y movimiento obrero en Centroamérica (1850-1933).** (The agrarian economy and the labour movement in Central America (1850-1933).)
Antonio Murga Frassinetti. México: Universidad Autónoma Metropolitana, Iztapalapa, División de Ciencias Sociales y Humanidades, Departamento de Sociología, 1984. 151p. (Cuadernos Universitarios, 18).

This work surveys labour movements in each Central American country and documents what the author perceives as the emergence of an agricultural proletariat in each state after 1890. It includes specific case discussions of El Salvador.

552 **¿Movimiento campesino o lucha del proletariado rural en El Salvador?** (Peasant movement or proletarian struggle in El Salvador?)
Carlos Samaniego. *Revista Mexicana de Sociología*, vol. 42 (1980), p. 651-67.

Since 1950 the intrusion of a capitalist mode of production on agriculture has transformed peasants into a kind of rural proletariat that shares a common cause with rural workers and is organized into the militant Federación Cristiana de Campesinos Salvadoreños. The author explores the implications of that transformation and the reaction of the government.

553 **Rural development, class structure, and labor force participation: the reproduction of labor power in El Salvador.**
Linda Kay Wright-Romero. PhD dissertation, Ohio State University, 1982. 368p. (University Microfilms order no. 8300382).

Class analysis of the participation and utilization of labour power which shows that the formation of class positions is tied to the process of organizing people within the system production.

La Unidad Popular y el surgimiento del Frente Democrático Revolucionario.
(Popular Unity and the emergence of the Revolutionary Democratic
Front.)
See item no. 342.

Promised land: peasant rebellion in Chalatenango, El Salvador.
See item no. 347.

**History and motivation of U.S. involvement in the control of the peasant
movement in El Salvador: the role of AIFLD in the agrarian reform process,
1970-1980**.
See item no. 414.

Statistics

554 **Anuario Estadístico.** (Statistical annual.)
San Salvador: Ministerio de Economía, Dirección General de
Estadística y Censos, 1956-. annual.
Annual compilation of statistical information compiled by the government of El
Salvador. It was formerly known as *Boletín Estadístico* (1951-55).

555 **Anuario Estadístico Centroamericano de Comercio Exterior.** (Central
American foreign trade statistical annual.)
Guatemala: Secretaría Permanente del Tratado General de
Integración Económica Centroamericana (SIECA), 1967-1978.
This annual presents detailed statistical data on the trade of the five Central
American states, but publication of this useful work has been increasingly in arrears,
and the last volume published (1978) covers 1972-73, a reflection of the decline of
SIECA. This publication was preceded by *Compendio estadístico centroamericano*
(q.v.).

556 **Banco Central de Reserva de El Salvador: Anuario Estadístico.**
(Central Reserve Bank of El Salvador: statistical annual.)
San Salvador: Banco Central de Reserva de El Salvador, 1983-.
annual.
The annual statistical report of the central reserve bank of El Salvador. Formerly
Estadísticas (1966-82), *Memoria* (1959-78),and *Revista Mensual* (1951-65).

557 **Compendio estadístico centroamericano.** (Central American statistical compendium.)
México: United Nations, 1957; New York: United Nations, 1962; Guatemala: Secretaria Permanente del Tratado General de Integración (SIECA), 1963-67. 5 vols.

A compilation of statistics on the Central American common market states. Emphasis is on trade statistics, although other topics are included in the five volumes published between 1957 and 1963. This series was continued by the *Anuario Estadística Centroamericano de Comercio Exterior* (q.v.).

558 **Situación demográfica, social, económica y educativa de El Salvador.** (Demographic, social, economic and educational situation of El Salvador.)
El Salvador: Ministerio de Educación. San Salvador: Ministerio de Educación, 1963. 131p.

Prepared for a conference on education and economic and social development in Latin America in 1962, this useful report contains a great deal of statistical data on El Salvador's population, economy, social development, and education.

559 **Estadística Eléctrica.** (Electrical statistics.)
San Salvador: Inspección General de Empresas y Servicios Eléctricos, Ministerio de Economía, 1976-.

From 1971 to 1975, this publication was known as *Estadísticas de las Empresas Eléctricas de Servicio Público y Privado de la República de El Salvador* (Statistics of the public and private electric service companies of the Republic of El Salvador).

560 **The Caribbean Basin to the year 2000: demographic, economic, and resource use trends in seventeen countries: a compendium of statistics and projections.**
Norman A. Graham, Keith L. Edwards. Boulder, Colorado: Westview Press, 1984. 166p.

A handy compilation of statistical tables on the area. In addition to a number of regional tables that include data on El Salvador, there is a section specifically on that country on pages 54-58.

561 **Indice de precios al consumidor.** (Consumer price index.)
San Salvador: Ministerio de Economía, Dirección General de Estadística y Censos, 1980-.

This publication was formerly called *Indice de precios al consumidor obrero* (Worker consumer price index) (1968-79). See also *Indice de precios al consumidor obrero en San Salvador, Mejicanos y Delgado, 1960-1969* (Worker consumer price index in San Salvador, Mejicanos and Delgado, 1960-1969) (San Salvador: [Government of El Salvador], 1970), for detailed comparison of price indices in three communities.

562 **Así piensan los salvadoreños urbanos (1986-1987)**. (What urban
Salvadorans think (1986-1987).)
Ignacio Martín-Baró.   San Salvador: UCA Editores, 1987. 132p.
(Colección estructuras y procesos, serie menor, vol. 18).
These public opinion graphs are based on a questionnaire survey.

563 **Statistical Yearbook.**
United Nations. Department of Economic and Social Affairs.
Statistical Office.   New York: United Nations, 1948-. annual.
This annual yearbook contains an enormous variety of statistical information on
population, manpower, agricultural and industrial production, mining, manufacturing, construction, energy, trade, transport, communications, consumption, national
accounts, finance, development assistance, housing, health, education, science and
technology, and culture. It is published in English and French. The UN *Statistical
Yearbook* succeeds the *Statistical Year-book of the League of Nations* (title varies)
(Geneva: League of Nations, Economic and Financial Section, 1927-44, annually),
but the amount of information on Central America in the League of Nations volumes
is disappointing in most categories.   .

564 **Statistical Yearbook for Latin America and the Caribbean, 1986.**
United Nations, Economic Commission for Latin America and the
Caribbean.   Santiago de Chile: United Nations, 1987. 782p. bibliog.
Official UN statistical tables on Latin America on a broad range of topics, including
social development and welfare, economic growth, domestic prices, capital formation
and financing, balance of trade, external debt, external trade and finance,
population, national accounts, production, infrastructure, employment, and social
conditions. This edition has a total of 377 tables.

565 **Statistical Abstract of Latin America, vol. 25.**
Edited by James W. Wilkie, David Lorey.   Los Angeles: UCLA
Latin American Center Publications, 1987. 934p. maps.
Issued more or less annually since 1955, this statistical compendium has become a
major reference work for Latin American studies. This latest edition contains 1,063
statistical tables, showing social, economic and political trends and data. In addition
to the *Statistical Abstract*, the UCLA Latin American Center periodically issues
various topical supplements.

The Central America fact book.
See item no. 2.

El Salvador, a country study.
See item no. 5.

Centro América 19--, análisis económico y político sobre la región. (Central
America 19--, economic and political analyses of the region.)
See item no. 11.

Atlas económico de El Salvador, 1974. (Economic atlas of El Salvador, 1974).
See item no. 46.

Human resources of Central America, Panama, and Mexico, 1950-1980, in relation to some aspects of economic development.
See item no. 221.

Demographic Yearbook.
See item no. 227.

El Salvador, estudios de población. (El Salvador, population studies.)
See item no. 228.

Tercer censo nacional de vivienda, 1971. (Third national census of housing, 1971.)
See item no. 286.

Diagnóstico social: situación actual de las necesidades básicas en El Salvador. (Social diagnosis: the present situation regarding basic necessities in El Salvador.)
See item no. 287.

ISSS. Estadísticas. (S[alvadoran] I[nstitute of] S[ocial] S[ecurity]. Statistics.)
See item no. 297.

Economic integration in Central America.
See item no. 441.

Indicadores económicos y sociales CONAPLAN. (CONAPLAN economic and social indicators.)
See item no. 443.

Estadísticas de Comercio Exterior de El Salvador. (Foreign trade statistics of El Salvador.)
See item no. 484.

FAO Trade Yearbook.
See item no. 485.

Yearbook of International Trade Statistics.
See item no. 489.

Boletín Estadístico Industrial. (Industrial statistical bulletin.)
See item no. 492.

Anuario de Estadísticas Agropecuarias. (Agriculture and livestock statistical annual.)
See item no. 502.

Statistics

FAO Production Yearbook.
See item no. 514.

Boletín Estadístico de Telecomunicaciones. (Statistical bulletin of telecommunications.)
See item no. 532.

Environment

566 **Ecodevelopment and international cooperation, potential applications in El Salvador.**
Howard E. Daugherty, Charles A. Jeanneret-Grosjean, H. F. Fletcher. Ottawa: Environment Canada, 1979. 148p.
A report on a joint project on environment and development in El Salvador prepared for the Policy Board of the Canadian International Development Agency and the Advanced Concepts Centre, Department of the Environment. See also Daughtery's *Man-induced ecologic change in El Salvador*, PhD dissertation, University of California, Los Angeles, 1969.

567 **Planos urbanos.** (Urban maps.)
Pablo Arnoldo Guzmán. San Salvador: Instituto Geográfico Nacional, 1984-1986. 3 vols.
Consists primarily of maps of Salvadoran urban areas.

568 **El Salvador y su desarrollo urbano en el contexto centroamericano.** (El Salvador and its urban development in the Central America context.)
Gonzalo Yañes Díaz. San Salvador: Ministerio de Educación, 1976. 103p. maps.
Surveys urban trends in El Salvador, criticizing the domination of the capital city. Argues for autonomous urban centres not dependent on the capital city. Written by one of El Salvador's leading architects, this important study includes some excellent urban maps.

Scarcity and survival in Central America: ecological origins of the Soccer War.
See item no. 222.

153

Environment

Ecología humana en Centroamérica: un ensayo sobre la regionalización como instrumento de desarrollo. (Human ecology in Central America: an essay on regionalization as an instrument of development.)
See item no. 226.

Estudio de vías urbanas, San Salvador. (Study of urban routes in San Salvador.)
See item no. 538.

Education

569 **An experiment in regionalism: the Central American textbook project.**
Manuel A. Arce, Donald A. Lemke.   Milwaukee: University of
Wisconsin, 1970. 43p.
Describes an effort to develop common grade-school textbooks throughout the
Central American states, involving teachers from each state. The problems the
project encountered are discussed and recommendations for similar future projects
are put forward.

570 **Historia de la Universidad de El Salvador, 1841-1930.** (History of the
University of El Salvador, 1841-1930.)
Miguel Angel Durán.   San Salvador: Talleres Gráficos Ariel, 1941.
236p.
A narrative history of the national university, with many long excerpts from key
documents. Durán examines the connection between the university's development
and the country's political history. Of related interest for the subsequent history of
the institution is the Universidad de El Salvador's *Guión histórico de la Universidad
Autónoma de El Salvador* (Historical guide to the Autonomous University of El
Salvador) (San Salvador: Editorial Ahora, 1949), an illustrated synthesis, with
considerable attention to the 1940s.

571 **Education in El Salvador.**
Cameron D. Ebaugh.   Washington: GPO, 1947. 87p. bibliog.
An overview of the educational system in El Salvador as it existed at the end of
World War II, with a description of plans for educational improvements.

572 **Diagnóstico estadístico y proyecciones de la educación primaria en El Salvador.** (Statistical diagnosis and projections on elementary education in El Salvador.)

El Salvador. Ministerio de Educación.   San Salvador: Ministerio de Educación, 1970. 106p.

A statistical analysis of primary education during the period 1968-1972 is presented. The report recommends reducing the high level of drop-outs observed during these years of climbing enrolments by increasing the number of rural schools and by lightening the academic load for first-graders since most of the drop outs have occurred at that level.

573 **La reforma educativa salvadoreña.** (Salvadoran educational reform.)

Manuel Luis Escamilla.   San Salvador: Ministerio de Educación, 1975. 204p.

An extended essay, addressing the basic ideas and issues behind a national educational reform. Stresses the need for El Salvador to plan its educational system around broader goals of socio-economic development.

574 **Nuestros maestros: notas para una historia de la pedagogía nacional.** (Our teachers: notes for a history of the national pedagogy.)

Saúl Flores.   San Salvador: Editorial Ahora, 1963. 635p.

This work comprises brief biographical sketches of Salvadoran teachers, mostly in the 20th century, but including a few from the 19th century. Detail on careers of the biographees is uneven, and criteria for selection is unclear, but the volume is a useful window on the teaching profession in El Salvador.

575 **Historia de la Universidad de El Salvador.** (History of the University of El Salvador.)

Mario Flores Macal.   *Revista del Pensamiento Centroamericano*, vol. 32 (1977), p. 17-50.

Relates the history of the University of El Salvador from efforts to establish an institution of higher learning in San Salvador at the close of the colonial period and the establishment of a university in 1841, through to the takeover and closing of the university by the government of Arturo Molina in 1972.

576 **La educación comercial en Centro América.** (Business education in Central America.)

Peter G. Haines.   Guatemala: Universidad de San Carlos, 1964. 126p.

A description of commercial education in each of the five Central American states, the result of a project by a Michigan State University professor. In general, the report reflects a low quality of business education in the region and calls for improvement as one means of fostering greater economic development.

577 **Educational reform with television: the El Salvador experience**.
John K. Mayo, Robert C. Hornik, Emile G. McAnany. Palo Alto,
California: Stanford University Press, 1976. 227p.

A detailed, readable account of one of the first large-scale applications of television
to formal education in the world. A well-documented study of the history and
development of instructional TV in El Salvador.

578 **La universidad para el cambio social**. (The university for social
change.)
Román Mayorga Quiros. San Salvador: UCA Editores, 1977. 224p.

The rector of the Universidad Centroamericana José Simeón Cañas, proposes that
his university should be more than simply a place to prepare professionals. It should
play an active role in bringing about social change. This work reflects not only the
history of the UCA, but also the increasing academic involvement in the social and
economic changes being demanded in El Salvador. Mayorga was also a civilian
member of the ruling junta formed following the October 1979 revolt.

579 **Historia de la educación general y de El Salvador**. (Historia of
education in general and in El Salvador.)
Carmen de Novoa. San Salvador: the author, 1967. 111p. bibliog.
mimeo.

A superficial introduction to the history of education in El Salvador. The first part of
the book is a general history of the education, highlighting main ideas and
developments in Europe and the United States. The second part is a narrative of
educational developments in El Salvador since the colonial period.

580 **La educación en Centroamérica**. (Education in Central America.)
Ovidio Soto Blanco. San Salvador: Secretaría General de la
Organización de Estados Centroamericanos, 1968. 148p. bibliog.
(Monografías técnicas, 2).

A comparative analysis of the Central American and Panamanian educational
systems based on a 1966 study. The objective is to facilitate future programming for
the integration of Central American educational systems. The work contains a
number of detailed charts and statistical tables.

581 **Fundamentos sociopolíticas y fines de la reforma educativa.** (Socio-
political fundamentals and the goals of educational reform).
Guillermo Manuel Ungo, Luis Fernando Valero Iglesias. *Estudios
Centroamericanos*, vol. 33 (1978), p. 569-78.

A critique of educational reforms made through international aid programmes. The
authors maintain that changes in school texts, programmes, and teacher education
were motivated by political desires to encourage capitalism. They see the influence of
the United States as overwhelming, and seek to bring education under more local or
national control.

582 **Education in Central America.**
George R. Waggoner, Barbara Ashton Waggoner.
Lawrence, Kansas: University Press of Kansas, 1971. 180p. bibliog.
A survey of educational facilities on the isthmus, emphasizing cooperation among the six countries. The work includes a chapter on El Salvador.

Encuesta sobre salarios ocupacionales, demanda de mano de obra y formación profesional. (Survey of occupational salaries, labour demand, and professional training.)
See item no. 541.

Situación demográfica, social, económica y educativa de El Salvador. (Demographic, social, economic and educational situation of El Salvador.)
See item no. 558.

American dissertations on foreign education: a bibliography with abstracts. Volume 10, Central America, West Indies, Caribbean and Latin America (general).
See item no. 657.

Science and technology

583 **Transferencia de tecnología, simulación o realidad de la inversión extranjera (caso: El Salvador).** (Transfer of technology, apparent or real foreign investment (the case of El Salvador).)
Miguel Angel Gómez. San Salvador: Impresos Asociados, 1985. 172p.
A preliminary look at Salvadoran capability in scientific and technological subjects and the problem of financing research and development in a poor, dependent, underdeveloped country. It explains many of the difficulties in transferring technology to underdeveloped countries, and points to Costa Rica as a model to follow.

584 **Tecnología y ciencia.** (Technology and science.)
San Salvador: Universidad Centroamericana José Simeón Cañas, Departamento de Ingeniería y Ciencias Naturales, 1979-.

Bibliografía médica de El Salvador, 1900-1970. (Medical bibliography of El Salvador, 1900-1970.)
See item no. 653.

Literature

585 **Abra, Revista del Departamento de Letras de lad Universidad Centroamericana José Simeón Cañas.** Open, Review of the Department of Letters of the Central American University José Simeón Cañas.)
San Salvador: Universidad Centroamericana José Simeón Cañas, 1974-. irregular.

586 **Cultura.** (Culture.)
San Salvador: Ministerio de Cultura and Ministerio de Educación, 1955-80. bimonthly

Publication of Salvadoran literature, prose and poetry, including many short stories and essays on history, philosophy, and literary criticism, as well as book reviews.

587 **Guión literario.** (Literary guidon.)
San Salvador: Ministerio de Cultura, 1956-60; Ministerio de Educación, 1961-69. monthly.

This publication contains reviews and comment on cultural events, books, poetry, etc., including both Salvadoran and foreign publications.

588 **Panorama de la literatura salvadoreña.** (Panorama of Salvadoran literature.)
Luís Gallegos Valdés. San Salvador: Ministerio de Educación, 1962. 238p. bibliog.

Gallegos surveys Salvadoran literature, with essays emphasizing generational changes. He includes biographical sketches on major writers and bibliographies of their works.

589 **Magnificencia espiritual de Francisco Gavidia**. (The spiritual magnificence of Francisco Gavidia.)
José Mata Gavidia.   San Salvador: Ministerio de Educación, 1968. 268p. bibliog.

A scholarly treatment of a leading Salvadoran literary figure and historian. The work is both a biography and an analytical study of Gavidia's work.

590 **Semblanzas salvadoreñas**. (Salvadoran biographical sketches.)
José Gómez Campos.   San Salvador: Talleres Gráficos Cisneros, 1930. 131p.

Comprises satirical and humorous caricatures of Salvadoran literary figures of the period.

591 **Gavidia: poesía, literatura, humanismo**. (Gavidia: poetry, literature, humanism.)
Mario Hernández Aguirre.   San Salvador: Ministerio de Educación, 1968. 498p. bibliog.

This monograph on one of El Salvador's most prolific writers, poet-essayist-historian-dramatist Francisco Gavidia, relates Gavidia's work to major 20th-century literary schools and trends. See also Juan Felipe Toruño's sympathetic biography, *Gavidia entre raras fuerzas étnicas: de su obra y de su vida* (Gavidia between rare ethnic forces: his life and work) (San Salvador: Ministerio de Educación, 1969).

592 **Estudios literarios: capítulos de literatura centroamericana**. (Literary studies: chapters on Central American literature).
Alfonso M. Landarech.   San Salvador: Ministerio de Cultura, 1959. 282p.

A series of essays on Central American literary figures, especially from El Salvador, where the author, a Spanish Jesuit, worked for many years. Organized topically, the work includes a short history of Salvadoran journalism as well as critical essays on individual writers. Although this is not a comprehensive study of Salvadoran literature, it is a valuable contribution to its history.

593 **Obras completas**. (Complete works.)
Alberto Masferrer.   San Salvador: Tipografía La Unión, 1935-45. 2 vols.

Masferrer (1868-1932) was El Salvador's leading thinker of the early twentieth century and founder of the Labour Party in 1930. He challenged the social and political structure of the country, and was strongly influential in stimulating a spirit of revolt among Salvadoran students and the middle class. Many of his most influential essays appeared first in newspapers and magazines. These volumes, individually titled *El rosal deshojado* (The rose bush stripped of leaves) and *La misión de América* (The mission of America), contain these essays, but do not contain most of Masferrer's major works, thus the general title, *Obras completas*, is a misnomer. Several major works are included in his *Cuadernos masferianos* (San Salvador: Dirección de Cultura, 1968, 7 vols.): 1. *El dinero maldito*; 2. *¿Que debemos saber?*; 3. *La religión*

161

Literature

universal; 4. *El mínimum vital*; 5. *Niñerías*; 6. *Prosas escogidas*; and 7. *Leer y escribir*. Among his other more important works were *Elogio del silencio*, *Ensayo sobre el destino*, *Estudios y figuraciones sobre la vida de Jesús*, *Helios*, and *El libro de la vida*.

594 **Obras escogidas**. (Selected works.)
Alberto Masferrer, edited by Matilde Elena López. San Salvador: Editorial Universitaria, 1971. 527p.

Masferrer was El Salvador's leading intellectual of the 1920s and stimulated the beginnings of revolt against the Liberal oligarchy. A sympathetic biography of Masferrer by Matilde Elena López accompanies this edition of some of Masferrer's more important writings. See also López' 'Masferrer, ¿socialista utópico, reformista o revolucionario?' ('Masferrer, utopian socialist, reformist, or revolutionary?') *La Universidad* (San Salvador), vol. 93 (Sept.-Oct. 1968), p. 101-8, in which she portrays him as a precursor to the 1932 peasant revolt; *Masferrer: alto pensador de Centroamérica* (Masferrer: eminent thinker of Central America) (Guatemala: Ministerio de Educación Pública, 1954); and her *Pensamiento social de Masferrer* (The social thought of Masferrer) (San Salvador: Imprenta Nacional, [1984]).

595 **Biografía del escritor Alberto Masferrer**. (Biography of the writer Alberto Masferrer.)
Manuel Masferrer C. San Salvador: Tipografía Canpress, 1957. 164p.

The materials collected by the leading Salvadoran thinker's brother include assorted letters and essays, with a biographical sketch and commentary by several of Masferrer's contemporaries.

596 **Obras escogidas**. (Selected works.)
Salvador Salazar Arrué. San Salvador: Editorial Universitaria, 1969-70. 2 vols.

These are selections from the influential Salvadoran novelist and short story writer who wrote under the pseudonym 'Salarrué'. Salarrué's work focused on rural life in El Salvador and especially on Indian customs and mythology, often emphasizing the clash of culture in Salvadoran society.

597 **Desarrollo literario de El Salvador: ensayo cronológico de generaciones y etapas de las letras salvadoreñas**. (The literary development of El Salvador: a chronological essay of generations and stages in Salvadoran letters.)
Juan Felipe Toruño. San Salvador: Ministerio de Cultura, 1958. 440p. bibliog.

An excellent introduction to Salvadoran literary trends from the Spanish conquest to the mid-twentieth century. Toruño highlights the principal authors, with bio-bibliographical sketches that focus on generational changes and influences, and with brief sample selections of their work.

162

598 **Panorama de la literatura salvadoreña.** (Panorama of Salvadoran
literature.)
Luis Gallegos Valdés. In: *Panorama das literaturas das Américas (de
1900 a la actualidade)*, edited by Joaquím de Montezuma de
Carvalho. Nova Lisboa, Angola: Edicão do Município de Nova
Lisboa, 1958-63. 4 vols., vol. 2, p. 497-588.

Despite its unlikely place of publication, this is a useful overview of Salvadoran
literary currents during the first half of the 20th century. It also includes a very brief
review of earlier writers. A narrative approach describes various schools or
generations represented by Salvadoran writers and then provides brief bio-
bibliographical sketches of significant Salvadoran writers. The discussion includes
journalists, historians, humourists, literary critics, essayists, poets, prose fiction
writers, and playwrights. While the space allotted to most individual writers is small,
the article is useful for the large number of writers it identifies.

599 **Diccionario de la literatura latinoamericana: América Central.**
(Dictionary of Latin American Literature: Central America.)
Pan American Union, Division of Philosophy and Letters.
Washington: Pan American Union, 1963. 2 vols. bibliog.

Volume 1 of this bio-bibliographical reference work includes an ample section on El
Salvador.

600 **El Salvador at war: a collage epic.**
Marc Zimmerman. Minneapolis: MEP Publications, 1988. 306p.
(Studies in Marxism, vol. 23).

This book weaves revolutionary poetry, testimonial, chronology, and analysis to
portray a Marxist view of contemporary El Salvador, emphasizing the struggle of the
Salvadoran people against repression and US interventionism.

The intellectual infrastructure of modernization in El Salvador, 1870-1900.
See item no. 182.

Estampas y música folklórica. (Folkloric impressions and music.)
See item no. 245.

El folklore en la literatura de Centro América.
(Folklore in Central American literature.)
See item no. 249.

El periodismo en El Salvador. (Journalism in El Salvador.)
See item no. 617.

**A tentative bibliography of the belles-lettres of the republics of Central
America.**
See item no. 651.

The Arts

601 **Arte colonial de El Salvador: criterios de valorización estética.**
(Colonial art of El Salvador: criteria for aesthetic value.)
Isabel Casín de Montes. *Estudios Centroamericanos*, vol. 28 (1973),
p. 243-51.
An examination of the aesthetic value of colonial art, particularly that of the
eighteenth century, with stress on the hitherto neglected field of folk art.

602 **De la pintura en El Salvador**. (Of painting in El Salvador.)
José Roberto Cea. San Salvador: Editorial Universitaria,
Universidad de El Salvador, 1986. 289p.
A commentary with illustrations on contemporary painting in El Salvador.

603 **Pintura salvadoreña del presente siglo**. (Salvadoran painting of the
present century.)
Museo Forma. San Salvador: Museo Forma, 1984. 223p.
A collection of Salvadoran 20th-century painters, with many colour plates.

604 **Indian crafts of Guatemala and El Salvador.**
Lilly de Jongh Osborne. Norman: University of Oklahoma Press,
1975. 411p.
The standard popular description of Indian textiles and other crafts of El Salvador.
The book spends considerably more space on Guatemala than El Salvador, but
includes interesting photographs.

605   **Art as a source for the study of Central America, 1945-1975: an exploratory essay.**
      Vera Blimm Reber.   *Latin American Research Review*, vol. 13 (1978), p. 39-64.
An examination of contemporary painting in Costa Rica, El Salvador, Guatemala, and Honduras which attempts to show the development and history of those countries though art.

606   **Fire from the sky: Salvadoran children's drawings.**
      Edited by William Vornberger.   New York: Writers and Readers Publishing Cooperative, 1986. 63p. photos.
A remarkable collection of drawings by Salvadoran children between the ages of 8 and 14, living in Central American refugee camps. It is accompanied by photographs of the children and of the civil war in El Salvador. The drawings and photos are organized around four themes: (1) the massacre, (2) the airwar, (3) the flight, and (4) the refuge.

Estampas y música folklórica. (Folkloric impressions and music.)
See item no. 245.

The art and archaeology of pre-Columbian Middle America: annotated bibliography of works in English.
See item no. 654.

Architecture

607   **Arqitectura**. (Architecture.)
      San Salvador: Colegio de Arquitectos de El Salvador, 1970-.
      irregular.
The journal of the College of Architects of El Salvador.

608   **Historia de la arquitectura contemporánea en El Salvador.** (History of
      contemporary architecture in El Salvador.)
      Oscar M. Monedero.   San Salvador: Editorial Universitaria, 1970.
      157p. bibliog.
Monedero describes architectural characteristics in El Salvador in the twentieth
century, especially focusing on churches and public buildings.

609   **Iglesias coloniales en El Salvador**. (Colonial churches in El Salvador.)
      Gonzalo Yañes Díaz.   San Salvador: Editorial Universitaria, 1970.
      45p. bibliog.
A collection of photographs of colonial churches.

Sports and Recreation

610   **El Mundo Deportivo.** (The sporting world.)
  San Salvador: El Mundo, 1941-present. Afternoon daily.
Although all major Salvadoran newspapers provide sports coverage, *El Mundo*'s sports supplement is clearly the best.

Libraries, Museums and Archives

611 **Anales del Museo Nacional 'David J. Guzmán'**. (Annals of the David J. Guzmán National Museum.)
San Salvador: Museo Nacional David J. Guzmán, 1903-.

The exact title of this journal of the national museum has varied slightly over the years, but it is known generally as the *Anales*. The museum is also one of the best libraries in El Salvador and this journal frequently describes sections of it. A bibliography of articles published between 1903 and 1977 appeared in no. 51 of the *Anales* (1977), arranged by subject.

612 **Anaqueles, Revista de la Biblioteca Nacional**. (Shelves, Journal of the National Library.)
San Salvador: Biblioteca Nacional de El Salvador, c. 1945-1980.

Contains articles on libraries and acquisitions of the National Library of El Salvador. Of special interest was the 1970 Número Extraordinario on the centennial of the national library, 1870-1970. Since 1937, the National Library has also occasionally published a *Boletín de la Biblioteca Nacional*.

613 **CIDAI. Colección indices: documentos**. (CIDAI. Indices collection: Documents.)
San Salvador: Centro de Información, Documentación y Apoyo a la Investigación, Universidad Centroamericana José Simeón Cañas, 1982-.

The index to manuscript collections at the Universidad Centroamericana, San Salvador.

168

614   **CIDAI. Colección indices: tesario**. (CIDAI. Indices collection:
       Theses.)
       San Salvador: Centro de Información, Documentación y Apoyo a la
       Investigación, Universidad Centroamericana José Simeón Cañas, 1982
An index to theses at the Universidad Centroamericana, San Salvador

615   **Research guide to Central America and the Caribbean**.
       Edited by Kenneth Grieb.   Madison, Wisconsin: University of
       Wisconsin Press, 1985. 446p. bibliog.
A work promoted by the Caribe-Centroamérica Committee of the Conference on
Latin American History, the Central American section, p. 3-193, is edited by
R. L. Woodward, Jr., and consists of two parts: (1) a series of articles by researchers
on Central America history discussing research needs for the region, including an
article on modern El Salvador by Derek Kerr, articles on the colonial period by
Murdo MacLeod and Mario Rodriguez, and topical articles by Neill Macaulay
(military history and guerrilla warfare), Miles Wortman (quantitative history), and
Kenneth Grieb (international relations); and (2) descriptive articles on specific
archives and libraries holding Central American materials in Central America,
Mexico, the United States, Great Britain, and Europe. The description of El
Salvador's archives and libraries was written by Woodward from data compiled by
Italo López Vallecillos and Thomas Schoonover. This volume is intended primarily
for historians but will have utility for other social scientists.

616   **Guide to libraries and archives in Central America and the West
       Indies, Panama, Bermuda, and British Guiana, supplemented with
       information on private libraries, bookbinding, bookselling, and
       printing**.
       Compiled by Arthur E. Gropp.   New Orleans, Louisiana: Middle
       American Research Institute, Tulane University, 1941. 721p. (MARI
       Publication no. 10).
El Salvador is dealt with on pages 559-602. Although much of the information
provided is now outdated, some of it is still applicable and is not easily obtained
elsewhere.

Journalism and Publishing

617 **El periodismo en El Salvador: bosquejo histórico-documental, precedido de apuntes sobre la prensa colonial hispanoamericana**. (Journalism in El Salvador: historical and documentary sketch, preceded by notes on the Spanish-American colonial press.)
Italo López Vallecillos.   San Salvador: UCA Editores, 1987. 478p.
(Colección Estructuras y procesos, vol. 15).
An informative history of journalism in the country with facsimiles of many articles.
Provides detailed information on each newspaper and on many editors and reporters.

La libertad de imprenta en El Salvador. (Freedom of the press in El Salvador.)
See item no. 623.

Mass Media

618 **Ateneo.** (Athenaeum.)
San Salvador: Revista del Ateneo de El Salvador, 1912-1975.

A literary/cultural journal, official organ of the Ateneo de El Salvador, containing articles and speeches that shed light on intellectual trends and upper-class attitudes toward certain social and economic issues. Illustrates the Salvadoran élite's attempt to forge a national culture based on the Western liberal model.

619 **Diario Latino.** (Latin daily.)
San Salvador: Miguel Angel Pinto, (et al.), 1890-present. afternoon daily.

The oldest Salvadoran daily, edited by Waldo Chávez Velasco, *Diario Latino* has a distinguished history, but has been less successful in recent years in competing with newer dailies, and boasting a circulation of only 41,000. Politically it reflects the Christian Democratic Party on most issues and usually supports the government's position, although it cannot be said to be strictly a government organ.

620 **El Diario de Hoy.** (Today's daily.)
San Salvador: Enrique Altamirano Madriz, 1936-present. morning daily.

Principal morning competition to *Prensa Gráfica*, with circulation of 77,000, *El Diario de Hoy* has long been published by the Altamirano family. Its present editor, Enrique Altamirano Madriz, operates it from exile. The paper is strongly right-wing and frequently critical of the Christian Democratic government. Said to be the voice of the right-wing ARENA political party and the Coffee Growers, Association.

621 **El Diario del Occidente.** (Daily of the West.)
Santa Ana, 1910-present. daily.

The leading Salvadoran daily outside of San Salvador.

171

622 **La Crónica del Pueblo.** (The people's chronicle.)
San Salvador, 1968-1981. daily.

Only newspaper in recent Salvadoran history that represented leftist points of view, and was often regarded as a front for the armed left. It suffered serious interference from successive Salvadoran government and right-wing terrorists and finally closed in 1981 after several bombings.

623 **La libertad de imprenta en El Salvador.** (Freedom of the press in El Salvador.)
José F. Figeac.   San Salvador: Universidad Autónoma de El Salvador, 1947. rev. ed. 592p.

Figeac reviews the history of the press in El Salvador and the regulations governing it since national independence, government by government to 1947, often quoting long passages from pertinent documentation. While coverage of any single period is not extensive, the volume is especially useful as a reference work for it includes a list the newspapers published in El Salvador, along with their editors.

624 **El Mundo.** (The world.)
San Salvador: the Borja family, 1941-present. afternoon daily.

With a circulation of about 60,000, *El Mundo* is not the largest of Salvadoran newspapers, but is noted for the best news reporting in the country. It also carries more news than the other papers. While it is said to represent the traditional coffee élite, it tends to avoid political commentary. At the same time, it often accepts paid political announcements from the Salvadoran left, thereby giving the left some voice in the Salvadoran press.

625 **La Noticia.** (The news.)
San Salvador: Dutriz Hermanos, 1986-present. afternoon daily.

Represents same political view as *La Prensa Gráfica* (q.v.) in an effort to meet the challenge of competing afternoon dailies. Most modern of Salvadoran dailies, with tabloid format and lots of colour photographs, it is aimed at a large mass audience, but current circulation is only about 25,000.

626 **Orientación.** (Orientation.)
San Salvador: Archdiocese of San Salvador, Office of Communications, 198- to. weekly.

Edited by Father Amilcar Toruella, this weekly carries both ecclesiastical news and news of a more political nature. This influential paper tries to identify problems in El Salvador, wherever it sees them. It is critical of both the extreme left and extreme right, but is not always sympathetic to the government. It represents the views of the highly independent Salvadoran Catholic hierarchy.

627 **La Prensa Gráfica.** (The graphic press.)
San Salvador: Dutriz Hermanos, 1915-present. morning daily.

The largest and most serious daily in San Salvador, published by the Dutriz family, and currently edited by Rodolfo Dutriz. Circulation is 105,000. Although sometimes critical of the government, *La Prensa* is generally centrist in its political outlook and represents the mainstream in Salvadoran news coverage. Also controls the new afternoon daily, *La Noticia* (q.v.).

628 El Salvador News-Gazette
San Salvador: Mario Rosenthal, 1978-present. weekly.

Mario Rosenthal converted this formerly English-language weekly to a bi-lingual paper in 1985. It grew out of two earlier English-language papers in San Salvador, the *Gringo Gazette* and the El Salvador *News*. With a circulation of 5,000, the *News-Gazette* claims to be the only bi-lingual weekly in the hemisphere. It carries both local and international news, although the emphasis is on the United States and its relations with Central America, as a service to the American community in El Salvador. Politically, the paper reflects the rather strong conservative views of the publisher and editor, often accusing the government of being on a socialist course.

Diario oficial. (Official daily.)
See item no. 371.

Professional Periodicals

629   **Boletín de Ciencias Económicas y Sociales**. (Bulletin of Economic and Social Sciences.)
San Salvador: Universidad Centroamericano José Simeón Cañas, 1978-.

This periodical contains useful analyses of contemporary Salvadoran economic and social problems.

630   **Estudios Centroamericanos**. (Central American Studies.)
San Salvador: Universidad Centroamericano José Simeón Cañas, 1945-. bi-monthly.

The most important scholarly and academic journal in El Salvador, *ECA* reflects considerable sympathy for the radical left and provides an excellent chronicle of Salvadoran political, social, and economic development from a leftist perspective.

631   **Estudios Sociales Centroamericanos**. (Central American Social Studies.)
San José, Costa Rica: Consejo Superior Universitario de Centroamérica, 1971-. quarterly.

A major academic journal, containing articles on a broad range of social science topics by both Central American and foreign academics. It frequently publishes articles on El Salvador and by Salvadoran authors.

632   **Revista Pecuario**. (Livestock Review.)
San Salvador: Ministerio de Agricultura y Ganadería: Centro de Desarrollo Ganadero Técnico Pecuario, 1984-.

This journal, dedicated to cattle raising, is published by the government.

174

633 **Proceso. Informativo Semanal del Centro de Documentación e Información.** (Process. Weekly newsletter of the Center for Documentation and Information.)
   San Salvador: Universidad Centroamericano José Simeón Cañas, 1980-. weekly.

Proceso represents radical Catholic position on political issues and is generally highly critical of the Salvadoran government and US policy in El Salvador.

634 **Revista de la Universidad.** (Review of the University.)
   San Salvador: Universidad de El Salvador, 1876-present. quarterly.

This academic journal is of uneven quality, but contains many articles on a wide range of subjects relating to Salvadoran humanities and social sciences.

Arqitectura. (Architecture.)
See item no. 607.

Encyclopaedias and Directories

635 **Directorio Comercial e Industrial de El Salvador, 1986.** (Commercial and industrial directory of El Salvador, 1986.)
San Salvador: Cámara de Comercio e Industria de El Salvador, 1986. annual. 366p.

An alphabetical listing of Salvadoran business establishments. It was issued under the title *Directorio Industrial de la República de El Salvador* (Industrial directory of the Republic of El Salvador) prior to 1975. For an earlier period see *Directorio Nacional de Establecimientos Industriales y Comerciales 1950* (National directory of industrial and commercial establishments, 1950) (San Salvador: Dirección General de Estadística, 1952). Similar guides were published for most years since about 1890 under a variety of titles, e.g. *Directorio General de la República de El Salvador, 1920* (General directory of the Republic of El Salvador, 1920) (San Salvador: Impr. Diario del Salvador, 1920) and *Directorio General de Centro América. General Directory of Central America. Annuaire Général de 'Amérique Centrale. General Verzeigniss von Central Amerika. 1888/89* (San Salvador, 1889).

636 **Diccionario histórico enciclopédico de la República de El Salvador.**
(Encyclopaedic historical dictionary of the Republic of El Salvador.)
Miguel Angel García.   San Salvador: Tipografía del Diario Latino, Imprenta Salvadoreña, Imprenta Nacional, 1927-50.

Although this collection of volumes does not follow a consistent organizational pattern, nor are they even numbered consecutively, they nevertheless contain an enormous amount of information on Salvadoran and Central American history. In part organized alphabetically, from *A* to *Col*, other volumes deal with specific themes, and García died before completing the series. They include essays, biographical sketches, documents, and other historical materials. Lacking an index, they are difficult to use efficiently, but can prove rewarding when used with patience and perseverance. Included within the series, are massive collections of documents on José Matías Delgado (2 vols., 1933-39) and on the history of the national university (2 vols., 1941). The title varies at different times.

637 **Directorio de El Salvador, Centro América; comercio, industrias, agricultura, y datos geográficos del país . . . .** (Directory of El Salvador, Central America; commerce, industries, agriculture, and geographic information on the country. . . .)
Edited by D. S. Meléndez.   San Salvador, 1924. 736p.

The directory contains valuable social, economic, and geographical data on the 14 departments, including lists of local plantations and their owners, major businesses, local government officials, and general description of each town within departmental jurisdiction. It also has information on climate, area, population, ethnic composition of inhabitants, common diseases, major products, etc. Apparently based on a study conducted under government auspices in 1922. Some photographs are included.

638 **Diccionario biográfico de El Salvador.** (Biographical dictionary of El Salvador.)
Edited by Braulio Pérez Marchant.   San Salvador: Dutriz Hermanos, 1942. 230p.

A who's who of prominent Salvadorans and foreign residents in El Salvador, with a paragraph on each describing their careers.

639 **Socios de la Cámara de Comercio e Industria de El Salvador, agrupado según sus actividades predominantes.** (Members of the Chamber of Commerce and Industry of El Salvador, grouped according to their principal activities.)
San Salvador: Cámara de Comercio e Industria, San Salvador, 1958. 15p.

Published in both Spanish and English.

'Libro azul' de El Salvador/'Blue Book' of Salvador.
See item no. 216.

Guía de instituciones del estado. (Guide to institutions of the state).
See item no. 383.

Nuestros maestros: notas para una historia de la pedagogía nacional. (Our teachers: notes for a history of the national pedagogy.)
See item no. 574.

Bibliographies

General

640 **Latin America and the Caribbean, a bibliographical guide to works in English.**
S. A. Bayitch.   Coral Gables, Florida: University of Miami Press, 1967. 943p.
An extensive bibliography on the region, with topical listings. El Salvador is covered on pages 542-49. Largest number of entries are under economy, labour, and taxation.

641 **Central America in the nineteenth and twentieth centuries: an annotated bibliography.**
Kenneth J. Grieb.   Boston: G. K. Hall, 1988. 573p. (Reference publications in Latin American studies).
An excellent compilation with detailed annotations of books dealing with Central America during the past two centuries. It includes works from many disciplines – history, literature, sociology, political science, economics, etc. There is a general Central American section, with 1,019 entries plus a chapter on each country, with 414 entries on El Salvador. This fine compilation also indicates the location of works, making it an especially valuable research tool.

642 **A bibliography of Latin American bibliographies.**
Compiled by Arthur E. Gropp.   Metuchen, New Jersey: Scarecrow Press, for Pan American Union, 1968. 515p.
This edition extends to 1964 the original edition of 1942 prepared by G. K. Jones and J. A. Granier. About 4,000 additional references have been added to the 1942 edition. The bibliography is arranged by 70 subject divisions, with country subdivisions.

643 **Handbook of Latin American studies.**
Cambridge, Massachusetts: Harvard University Press, 1935-51;
Gainesville, Florida: University of Florida Press, 1952-78; Austin:
University of Texas Press, 1979-present.
The most important single source for current bibliography in Latin American studies,
the *Handbook* is issued annually (since 1965, with alternate years devoted
respectively to the humanities and the social sciences). Annotated entries are
organized by regions within disciplines. Author and subject indexes allow the
researcher to locate quickly entries dealing with El Salvador. The *Handbook* is not
completely comprehensive, but it attempts to include significant books and articles
published throughout the world. Each section is edited by a leading scholar in the
subject and area for which he is responsible.

644 **Inter-American Review of Bibliography.**
Washington: Organization of American States, 1951-. quarterly.
Articles on Latin American bibliography and letters, with an extensive book review
section.

645 **El Salvador: bibliography and research guide.**
David S. Krusé, Richard Swedberg. Cambridge, Massachusetts:
Central American Information Office (CAMINO), 1982. 233p.
An extensive bibliography, focusing on the contemporary crisis and containing 2,000
entries drawn from scholarly literature in English and Spanish, as well as official US
and Salvadoran government sources. A great many periodical articles are included.
The entries are not annotated, but each section includes introductory comment on
the most important items in the section. Topical headings include general works on
history and background, US policy toward El Salvador, agrarian reform, right-wing
policy advocates in the US, opposition to US policy, media coverage, economy,
social structure, politics, Salvadoran opposition forces, military, the church, human
rights, refugees, women, culture, and resources for further study and action.

646 **Central America: A bibliography.**
Latin American Studies Center, California State University, Los
Angeles. Los Angeles: California State University, 1976. 52p.
An extensive bibliography which concentrates on publications in the fields of history,
politics, economics, and development. Entries are arranged by country and further
divided into separate sections for books and articles, but they are not annotated.

647 **A list of books, magazine articles and maps relating to Central
America, including the republics of Costa Rica, Guatemala, Honduras,
Nicaragua and Salvador, 1800-1900.**
P. Lee Phillips, International Bureau of the American Republics.
Washington: GPO, 1902. 109p.
An excellent bibliography for 19th-century materials.

648 **Current national bibliographies of Latin America; a state of the art study.**
Irene Zimmerman.   Gainesville: University of Florida Center for Latin American Studies, 1971. 139p.

Includes a short section on El Salvador, p. 76-78, which reports on Salvadoran progress in developing bibliographical reference tools, but this is now nearly twenty years old.

Handbook of Middle American Indians.
See item no. 241.

Topical

649 **Bibliografías agrícolas de América Central: El Salvador.** (Agricultural bibliographies of Central America: El Salvador.)
Edited by Juan J. Aguilar, Judith Lovato.   Turrialba, Costa Rica: Instituto Interamericano de Ciencias Agrícolas, 1974. 147p.

An unannotated, but extensive list of books and articles dealing with agricultural topics.

650 **The memorias of the republics of Central America and of the Antilles**.
James B. Childs.   Washington: GPO, 1932. 170p.

A guide to government publications, indicating which are in the Library of Congress in Washington. Useful especially for late 19th- and early 20th-century study.

651 **A tentative bibliography of the belles-lettres of the republics of Central America**.
Henry Grattan Doyle.   Cambridge, Massachusetts: Harvard University Press, 1935. 136p.

This work is valuable for 19th- and early 20th century works, but unfortunately there is no more recent work of this type. It includes all of the Central American countries, with entries entered alphabetically under each country.

652 **Traditional medicine.**
Ira E. Harrison, Sheila Cosminsky.   New York; London: Garland Publishing, 1976-84. 2 vols.

An annotated bibliography covering Africa, Latin America, and the Caribbean. Works on each of the Central American countries, including El Salvador, can be located through the index. Topics include ethnomedicine, ethnopharmacology, health care delivery systems, maternal and child health, and public health.

653 **Bibliografía médica de El Salvador, 1900-1970.** (Medical bibliography of El Salvador, 1900-1970.)
Salvador Infante Díaz, Mauricio Ernesto Ponce.   San Salvador: Ministerio de Educación, 1973. 745p. bibliog.
An unannotated bibliography with 4,950 entries of works published in El Salvador by nationals and foreigners. Monographs, articles, and theses are included. A subject and author index make this a valuable and rare reference work.

654 **The art and archaeology of pre-Columbian Middle America: annotated bibliography of works in English.**
Aubyn Kendall.   Boston: G. K. Hall, 1977. 324p.
Containing 2,147 annotated entries, this compilation represents one of the most important bibliographical tools on pre-Columbian Middle America. The bibliography is organized alphabetically by authors, including both books and periodical articles. An ample subject index reveals many items specifically on El Salvador.

655 **Anthropological bibliography of aboriginal El Salvador.**
Jorge A. Lines (et.al.).   San José: Tropical Science Center, 1965. 114p.
A dated but still useful reference source for the study of Salvadoran anthropology from aboriginal times to the date of publication. Works are classified under the topics of archaeology, ethnology, folklore, linguistics, mythology, and physical anthropology, and then entered alphabetically by author.

656 **Middle American anthropology: directory, bibliography, and guide to the UCLA library collections.**
Eileen A. McGlynn.   Los Angeles: Latin American Center, University of California, 1975. 131p. map.
A guide to the major individuals and institutions which have contributed to Middle American anthropological research. Although specifically designed to assist patrons of the UCLA collections, it may also serve as a general guide to library resources in the field. All Central American countries, including El Salvador, and Mexico, are covered.

657 **American dissertations on foreign education: a bibliography with abstracts. Volume 10, Central America, West Indies, Caribbean and Latin America (general).**
Edited by Franklin D. Parker, Betty June Parker.   Troy, New York: Whitson Publishing, 1979. 620p.
Abstracts of 220 doctoral dissertations on all aspects of education in the region, which includes Mexico. The bibliography is organized alphabetically by author, with a subject and geographical index appended. Only nine dissertations deal directly with El Salvador, while a few others discuss it in connection with broader regional studies.

658 **A bibliography of United States-Latin American relations since 1810; a selected list of eleven thousand published references.**
Compiled and edited by David F. Trask, Michael C. Meyer, Roger R. Trask. Lincoln, Nebraska: University of Nebraska Press, 1968. 441p.

An extensive bibliography, containing more than just relations with the US narrowly defined. See also the *Supplement to a bibliography of United States – Latin American relations since 1810*, compiled and edited by Michael C. Meyer (Lincoln, Nebraska: University of Nebraska Press, 1979), with 3,568 additional entries, partially annotated.

659 **Latin America in the nineteenth century: a selected bibliography of books of travel and description published in English.**
Edited by Curtis A. Wilgus. Metuchen, New Jersey: Scarecrow Press, 1973. 184p.

Bibliography, with brief annotations, of 19th-century travel accounts, including many describing El Salvador.

Guía para investigadores, República de El Salvador. (Guide for researchers, Republic of El Salvador.)
See item no. 34.

Central America early maps up to 1860.
See item no. 48.

A catalogue of Latin American flat maps, 1926-1964.
See item no. 49.

Aquatic biota of Mexico, Central America and the West Indies, being a compilation of Taxonomic bibliographies for the fauna and flora of inland waters of Mesoamerica and the Caribbean region.
See item no. 98.

Mesoamerican archaeology, a guide to the literature and other information sources.
See item no. 123.

The historiography of Central America since 1830.
See item no. 140.

The historiography of modern Central America since 1960.
See item no. 146.

El folklore en la literatura de Centro América. (Folklore in Central American literature.)
See item no. 249.

Panorama de la literatura salvadoreña. (Panorama of Salvadoran literature.)
See item no. 588

Diccionario de la literatura latinoamericana: América Central. (Dictionary
of Latin American literature: Central America.)
See item no. 599.

Index

The index is a single alphabetical sequence of authors (personal and corporate), titles of publications and subjects. Index entries refer both to the main items and to other works mentioned in the notes to each item. Title entries are in italics. Numeration refers to the items as numbered.

A

Abra, Revista del Departamento de Letras 585
Academia Salvadoreña de la Historia 157-158
Academia Salvadoreña de la Lengua 244
Acajutla 233
Account of the conquest of Guatemala in 1524 164
Acumulación de capital y empresas transnacionales en Centroamérica 439
Adams, F. 1
Adams, R. 230-231
Adler, J. 476
Administración y Empresas 434
Administration 434
Adoption law 379
ADS. Carta Informativa 219
Advanced Concepts Centre 566
Aerial photographic maps 50
Agency for International

Development *See* United States, Agency for International Development (AID)
Agrarian legislation 376
Agrarian reform 31, 348-349, 414, 451, 458, 460, 503, 507, 511, 521, 525, 529
Agrarian reform in El Salvador: a program of rural pacification 529
Agricultura en El Salvador 500
Agricultural modernisation in El Salvador, Central America 512
Agriculture 462, 500-531
  bibliography 649
  chemicals 519
  coffee 153, 190, 200, 279, 327, 451, 488, 504, 508, 515
  cooperatives 517
  credit 477, 517, 524
  dairy 526
  diseases 522, 528
  exports 454

flora 101
foreign aid 510
history 31
indigenous 190
maize 527
maps 45
markets 517
modernization 512, 524
pre-Columbian 132
reform 348, 460
research 501, 518
social conditions 277
statistics 502, 514, 563
technology 517, 524
trade 485
tropical 528
vegetables 531
Agrociencia 501
Agro-exports 182, 222, 454, 503, 506, 523-524, 530
  relation to human rights 298
  relation to social structure 278
Aguílar, E. Chinchilla 139
Aguilar, J. 649
Aguirre, M. Hernández 591
AIFLD *See* American Institute for Free Labor Development

Air transport 540
Air war and political developments in El Salvador 365
Alas, H. 298
Alcaldes mayores 175
Alegría, C. 239, 320
Alens, A. 228
Almanzar, A. 464
Alonso, I. 250
Alrededor del problema unionista de Centro América 318
Altamirano Madriz, E. 620
Alvarado, P. de 164
Alvarez, R. 299
Alvergue, P. 321
América Central ante la historia 134
América Indígena 234
América Latina: historia de medio siglo 215
American Anthropologist 230
American Antiquity 117
American Association for the Advancement of Science 285
American Bible Society 78
American Civil Liberties Union 299
American dissertations on foreign education 657
American Institute for Free Labor Development (AIFLD) 414
American Journal of Tropical Medicine and Hygiene 294
Americas 20, 182
Americas Watch Committee 299
Americas Watch report. Human rights in Central America 299
Amnesty International 299

Amphibians 105
Anales del Museo Nacional 'David J. Guzmán' 173, 611
Análisis crítico de la política fiscal 444
Analysis of the economy of El Salvador 459
Análisis sobre el conflicto entre Honduras y El Salvador 392
Anaqueles, Revista de la Biblioteca Nacional 612
Anderson, C. 316
Anderson, T. 202, 317, 391, 430
Andrews, E. 110
Andrews, P. 180
Angulo de Castro, M. 27
Annotated index of aerial photographic coverage and mapping 50
Annotated list of the hesperiidae of El Salvador 107
Annual Review of Anthropology 122
Another world: Central America 90
Anthropological bibliography of aboriginal El Salvador 655
Anthropology 231, 241, 242
bibliography 655, 656
Anti-Americanism 421
Anti-clericalism 255
Anti-communism 414, 416
Anti-terrorism 420
Antolinez, P. 544
Anuario de Estadísticas Agropecuarias 502
Anuario de Estudios Centroamericanos 186, 204
Anuario Estadística de Telecomunicaciones 532

Anuario Estadístico 554
Anuario Estadístico Centroamericano de Comercio Exterior 555
Appeal to arms: the army and politics in El Salvador 358
Appendix to the report of the National Bipartisan Commission 419
Approche d'une analyse des classes sociales au Salvador 279
Apuntamientos de historia patria eclesiástica 255
Aquatic biota of Latin America 98
Aquatic biota of Mexico, Central America and the West Indies 98
Aquino, A. 185
Arbingast, S. 45
Arce, M. A. 569
Arce, M. J. 187
Archaeological bridge 130
Archaeology 61, 76, 97, 110, 112, 115-116, 119, 122, 127, 130, 241
bibliography 123, 654-655
glossary 124
government agencies 123
guide to Maya ruins 121
lower Central America 122
Mayan 116, 128, 132
Mesoamerica 123
regional economics 129
research 123, 129
Archaeology and volcanism in Central America 127
Archaeology of Lower Central America 129

186

Archaeology of Quelapa, El Salvador 110
Archaeology of Santa Leticia and the rise of Maya civilization 116
Archbishop Romero, martyr of Salvador 258
Archbishops of San Salvador 262
Architecture 607-608
20th-century 608
Archives 150, 615-616
ARENA 620
Arias de Blois, J. 218
Arias Gómez, J. 203
Arias Peñate, S. 503
Armas, J. Galdames 161
Armas Molina, M. 111
Armed Forces *See* Military
Armenia 233
Armstrong, R. 323, 350
Army 202, 216, 356, 358
modernization 180
See also Military
Arnson, C. 350, 389
Arqitectura 607
Arrué, S. Salazar 596
Art 235, 605, 606
bibliography 654
contemporary 602
folk 601
Art and archaeology of pre-Columbian Middle America 654
Art history
glossary 124
Arte colonial de El Salvador 601
Artefacts 124
Arts
flora 101
Ascenso del militarismo en El Salvador 361
Así piensan los salvadoreños urbanos (1986-1987) 562
Asociación Cafetalera de El Salvador 508

Asociación Demográfica Salvadoreña 219
Asociación Salvadoreña de Industriales 495
Asociación Salvadoreña del Café 504
Assassinations, political 525
Assemblies, legislative 193, 352, 366
Astaburuaga y Cienfuegos, F. 66
Astilla, C. 404
Ateneo 618
Atlantic Monthly 357
Atlas de El Salvador 47
Atlas económico de El Salvador, 1974 46
Atlas of Central America 45
Atlases, 45-47
archaeology 123
Augelli, J. 36
Authoritarianism 325
Autonomy or dependence as regional integration outcomes 403
Avalos Miranda, S. 465
Aviation facilities 540

B

Baily, J. 63, 170
Baires Martínez, Y. 452
Baker, E. 6
Balakrishnan, R. 435
Baloyra, E. 324
Baloyra-Herp, E. 325
Balsam 64
Banco Central de Reserva de El Salvador: Anuario Estadístico 556
Banco Central de Reserva en el desarrollo económico de El Salvador 465
Banco de Fomento Agropecuario 466, 505

Banco de Fomento Agropecuario: Carta agropecuario 505
Banco Hipotecario de El Salvador 467
Banco Hipotecario de El Salvador. Revista 467
Bancroft, H. 133
Bank notes 464, 466
Banking 337, 465, 467, 472, 474, 505
bibliography 467
law 376
Banknotes of the Republic of El Salvador 466
Bankruptcy 376
Barberena, S. 30, 37-38, 165
Barón Castro, R. 158, 181, 220
Barrett, M. 292
Barrios, G. 191-192
Barry, P. 418
Barry, T. 2-3, 310, 405
Basauri, D. 40
Basic Christian Communities 252, 259, 264, 272
Batres Jáuregui, A. 134
Bats 104
Battles 148-149
Baudez, C. 112
Bay Islands, Honduras 68
Bay of Fonseca 64
Bayitch, S. 640
Beans 519
Beef 523, 530, 632
Belize
19th-century 68
description 87
population density 225
Belot, G. 69
Benjamin, M. 410
Berger, R. 117
Bernal, I. 241
Berrigan, D. 251
Berryman, P. 4, 252, 410
Bible 78
Bibliografía 467

187

*Bibliografía médica de
El Salvador,
1900-1970* 653
*Bibliografías agrícolas de
América Central: El
Salvador* 649
Bibliography 640-659
See also specific topic
*Bibliography of Latin
American
bibliographies* 642
*Bibliography of United
States-Latin
American relations
since 1810* 658
Biblioteca Nacional de
El Salvador 612
Biogeography,
bibliography 98
*Biografía de vicentinos
ilustres* 157
*Biografía del escritor
Alberto Masferrer*
595
Biography 154, 157-159,
161-162, 193-194,
216, 262, 574, 588,
590, 598, 636, 638
*Biologia
centrali-americana,
zoology, botany and
archaeology* 97
Biology 522
Birds 106
Birds of tropical America
106
Birth control 219, 224
Bishopric of San
Salvador 186
Bishops of San Salvador
262
*Bitter grounds: roots of
revolt in El Salvador*
346
Blachman, M. 406
Blois, J. Arias de 218
Blue Book of Salvador
216
Blutstein, H. 5
Boggs, S. 113-114
*Boletín Bibliográfico de
Antropología*

Americana 57
*Boletín de Ciencias
Económicas y
Sociales* 629
Boletín de Investigación
275, 436
*Boletín de la Biblioteca
Nacional* 612
Boletín de Psicología 293
*Boletín Económica y
Social* 437
Boletín Estadístico 554
*Boletín Estadístico de
Telecomunicaciones*
532
*Boletín Estadístico
Industrial* 492
Boletín Oficial 371
Boletín Técnico 516
*Boletín. Ante la
Conciencia Nacional*
300
Bolinas 114
Boomer, J. Van der 228
Booth, J. 407
Border disputes 385, 388
Borders 385, 388
Borja family 624
Botany 97
Boundaries 388
Honduras 385
*Boundaries, possessions,
and conflicts . . .* 388
Bourbon reforms 179
Brazil, martyrs in 266
Brett, D. 253
Brett, E. 253
*Breve historia de
Centroamérica* 143
Brewer, T. 350
Bricker, V. 241
Brignoli, H. Pérez 135,
143, 452
British
diplomats 70, 198
interest in Central
America 70
British Honduras 87
See also Belize
British Overseas Trade
Board 479
Brockman, J. 254

Brodersohn, V. 278
Brodhead, F. 336
Brookings Institution
441
Browning, D. 31, 507
Bryan-Chamorro treaty
395
Buckley, T. 94
Bulwer-Thomas, V. 438
Burke, W. 301
Burkhalter, H. 302, 548
Burns, E. B. 182-183
Business 468
guide 479
law 376
Business administration
434
Business directories
636-637
Business International
Corporation 468
Business Latin America
468
Bustamante Maceo, G.
149
Byam, G. 60

C

Cacao 167
Cáceres Prendes, J. 204
Cáceres, H. Herrera 400
CACM *See* Central
American Common
Market
*Cádiz experiment in
Central America,
1808 to 1826* 197
Café de El Salvador 508
Calderón Chacón, G. 32
Calderón, S. 103
*Calendario de fiestas
religiosas
tradicionales de El
Salvador* 247
Calgary Archaeologist
115
Callejas, J. Melgar 156
Caluco 233
Cámara de Comercio e
Industria de El
Salvador 636, 639

Camarda, R. 311
*Cambridge History of
Latin America* 201
CAMINO 7, 645
Campbell, C. 294
Campos, J. Gómez 590
Campos, R. 326
Campos, T. 269
Canadian policy in El
Salvador 390
*Canadian Historical
Review* 390
Canadian International
Development
Agency 566
Candelaria de la
Frontera 232
Capital accumulation
439
*Características básicas y
evolución reciente
del sector externo*
490
Cardenal, R. 255
Cárdenas, J. 159
Cardona Lazo, A. 38
Cardoso, C. F. S. 135
Cardoso, F. H. 136
Carías, M. 392
*Caribbean Basin to the
year 2000* 560
*Caribbean challenge:
U.S. policy in a
volatile region* 407
Carpenter, A. 6
Carpenter, R. 76
Carrigan, A. 256
Carter, J. 270, 308, 423,
428, 511
Cartography 43
colonial 171
Casanova, P. González
209, 215, 549
Casas y Bolsas, S. A.
205
Casín de Montes, I. 601
Castellanos, P. Zamora
148
Castillo Rivas, D. 439
Castillo, C. 480
Castillo, M. de los
Angeles 245

Castro Morán, M. 356
Castro, Marcel Angulo
de 27
Castro, R. Barón 220
*Catalog of nautical
charts, region 2* 54
*Catálogo de monedas y
medallas de
proclama de Centro
América y Panamá*
473
*Catalogue of admiralty
charts and other
hydrographic
publications* 53
*Catalogue of Latin
American flat maps,
1926-1964* 49
Cattle *See* Livestock
Cea, J. 602
Central America 75
archaeology 130
bibliography 175, 201,
641, 646-647
demography 277
dependency 277
foreign domination of
277
geography 36, 277
historiography 146
history 15, 62,
133-148, 174-179,
184, 196-199, 201,
212
human rights 28
integration *See*
Integration
maps 45, 48
military 277
natural resources 43
politics 277
population 226
sociology 277
union 141, 145, 184,
187, 201, 217, 318,
399
violence 277
Central America 63, 112
*Central America and its
problems* 72
*Central America and the
Caribbean* 137

*Central America and the
Middle East* 389
*Central America and the
polls* 422
*Central America and the
Reagan doctrine* 416
*Central America early
maps up to 1860* 48
*Central America fact
book* 2
*Central America in the
nineteenth and
twentieth centuries*
641
Central America
Information Office
7, 645
Central America report
11, 21
*Central America, a
nation divided* 145,
201
*Central America,
anatomy of conflict*
339
*Central America,
international
dimensions of the
crisis* 413
*Central America: a
bibliography* 646
*Central America: human
rights and U.S.
foreign policy*
418
*Central America:
regional integration
and national
political
development* 487
*Central America: The
real stakes* 12
*Central America: how to
get there and back in
one piece* 91
*Central America:
regional integration
and economic
development* 447
Central American Bank
for Economic
Integration 540

189

Central American
  Common Market
  279, 327, 337, 376,
  393-394, 396, 403,
  439, 441, 447, 450,
  452, 475, 480,
  486-488, 491
  bibliography 486
  comparison with
    European Economic
    Community 478
*Central American
  Common Market:
  economic
  policies . . .* 450
Central American Court
  of Justice 395
*Central American
  currency and finance*
  478
*Central American
  economic integration*
  396
Central American
  Federation 184, 201,
  374, 399
*Central American
  Indians and the
  Bible* 78
Central American jungles
  99
*Central American
  monetary union* 478
*Central American
  refugees* 312
*Central American
  regional integration*
  402
Central American report
  22
Central American
  republics 15
*Central American
  transportation study,
  1964-1965* 540
*Central Americans:
  adventures and
  impressions* 80
Central Reserve Bank of
  El Salvador 465,
  472, 556
  statistics 556

*Centro América 19–,
  análisis económico y
  político sobre la
  región* 11
*Centro América,
  subdesarrollo y
  dependencia* 277
Centro de
  Documentación e
  Información 633
Centro de Información,
  Documentación y
  Apoyo a la
  Investigación
  613-614
Centro de Investigación
  y Acción Social 440
*Centroamérica y la
  economía occidental
  (1520-1930)* 135
Ceramics 126
Cerdas, R. 202
Cerrato reforms 177
Chacón, G. Calderón 32
Chalatenango 347
Chalchuapa 126
Chalcuapa 128, 232
Chamber of Commerce
  and Industry of El
  Salvador 639
Chamberlain, R. 160
Chamorro Zelaya, P. J.
  184
Charts, navigation 53-54
Chatfield, F. 198
Chávez Velasco, W. 619
Chiefs of state 144, 154,
  377
Childbearing 295
Childs, J. 650
Chile, diplomats 66
Chinchilla Aguílar, E.
  139
Chinchilla, N. 13
Chinchilla, N. Stoltz 138
Chomsky, N. 409
Choussy, F. 100
Christian Democratic
  Party 324, 328, 330,
  343, 354, 619-620
Christian, S. 357, 412
Christians in Central

  *American
  revolutions* 252
Church 205, 216, 277,
  608
  bibliography 645
  colonial 609
  relation to poor 269
  Roman Catholic 250,
    264, 267, 269, 274,
    323, 626
  women 239
Church-state relations
  255, 262-263
Churchill, A. 533
*CIDAI. Colección
  indices: documentos*
  613
*CIDAI. Colección
  indices: tesario* 614
Cienfuegos, F. S.
  Astaburuaga y 66
Cihuatán 113, 115
CINAS 440
Cirincione, J. 339
Cisneros, R. 289, 367
City-state 332
Civil code 368
Civil war, 1979- 1, 93,
  207, 211, 251, 256,
  310, 314, 321, 323,
  334, 338, 340, 343,
  346, 353, 356, 365,
  387, 411, 416, 426-
  427, 606
  Roman Catholic
    Church and 264
  women in 239
Clark, M. 253
Clarke, J. 534
Class conflict 13, 138,
  207, 360, 392, 442
Class consciousness 550
Class structure 283, 553
Clements, C. 95
Clergy 250, 265, 271
  political activities 271
  revolutionary activity
    of 264
Climate 62, 65, 637
  maps 47
Cline, H. 241
Cline, W. 441

190

Coastal geography 41
Coatepeque 232
Cochrane, J. 393, 396
Cockburn, J. 59
Codificación de las leyes de El Salvador desde 1875 hasta 1889 381
Codificación de leyes patrias de la República de El Salvador 381
Código civil y código de procedimientos civiles 368
Código de comercio de la República de El Salvador 481
Código de trabajo y sus reformas 546
Código municipal 382
Código penal 369
Coffee 153, 190, 200, 279, 327, 451, 488, 504, 508, 515
Coffee Growers Association 508, 620
Cohen Orantes, I. 394
Coiffures 114
Coins 473
Coins and paper money of El Salvador 464
Cojutepec 64
Cojutepeque 162
Cojutepeque Cushutepec: biografía de un pueblo 162
Cold war 387, 413
Colindres, E. 279
College of Architects 607
Colline, W. 294
Colloquialisms 235, 243, 246
Colonization, agricultural 521
Colorado, University of 127
Colvin, G. 87
Comercio exterior 482
Comercio terrestre de y entre las provincias de Centroamérica 176
Comisión de Derechos Humanos de El Salvador 300
Comisión para la Defensa de los Derechos Humanos en Centroamérica 298
Comité Interamericana de desarrollo agrícola (CIDA) 509
Commemorative medallions 473
Commerce *see* Trade
Commercial Code 481
Commercial law 376, 481
Communal cooperative experience: an example from El Salvador 517
Communications 32, 84, 180, 216, 535, 537
statistics 563
Communism 202, 206, 317, 338, 362, 431
Communism in Central America and the Caribbean 317
Communist challenge in the Caribbean and Central America 431
Communist international in Latin America 202
Communist Party 206, 338
Communist revolt of 1932 202-203
Compadrazgo, una estructura de poder en El Salvador 280
Compañía de Jesús en El Salvador, C. A., desde 1864 a 1872 263
Compendio de la historia de la ciudad de Guatemala 170
Compendio estadístico centroamericano 555, 557
Complejo preclásico del occidente salvadoreño 119
Comunicaciones 535
CONAPLAN 443, 538
Concentración económica en El Salvador 458
Concentration of wealth 458
Concessions 376
Condición jurídica de la mujer salvadoreña 367
Condiciones de la mujer en El Salvador 289
Confronting revolution 406
Conquest, Spanish 164, 170, 177
Consejo Nacional de Planificación y Coordinación 443, 538
Conservatives 134
Constitución de la República de El Salvador, 1983 366
Constitución política y códigos de la República de El Salvador 370
Constitucional 371
Constituciones de El Salvador 375
Constituent assemblies 193
Constitutional conventions 193
Constitutions 373-375, 377, 379
1950 460
1962 370, 460
1983 366
Constitutions of Latin America 373
Construction, statistics 563
Consultécnica, Ltda. 540
Consumer price index 561

Consumption, statistics 563
Continuing crisis: U.S. policy in Central America and the Caribbean 412
Continuing terror 299
Contribución a la mineralogía y geología de El Salvador 40
Cooking 235
Cooperativa de Abogados de El Salvador 547
Cooperatives 517, 547
Cooperativism 547
Cooperativismo en El Salvador: legislación y doctrina 547
Copyright law 376
Corregidores 175
Córtes of Cádiz 197
Cortés Society 164
Cortés y Larraz, P. 166
Cortés, F. 164
Cosminsky, S. 652
Costa de El Salvador 41
Costa Rica 88, 583
19th-century 66, 68
description 87
population density 225
refugees in 312
banization 39
Costumes
Indian 114
Cotton 279, 337, 523, 530
Counter-insurgency 420
Cozean, J. 24
Crafts 247
Creamer, L. 90
Credit 472, 477
Creole mentality 172
Creoles 172, 189
CRIES 458
Crisis del desarrollismo: caso El Salvador 451
Crisis in Central America 417
Crisis of national

integration in El Salvador, 1919-1935 217
Crónica del Pueblo 622
Cruz Sequeira, A. 339
Cuadernos de divulgación agropecuario 467
Cuadernos masferianos 593
Cuatro constituciones federales . . . y . . . de El Salvador 374
Cuba 224, 413
compared to El Salvador 8
Cuenca, A. 327
Cuisnahuat 233
Cultura 586
Cultura pipil de Centro América 111
Cultural characteristics 84
Cultural surveys 231
Culture 586-587, 596, 618
bibliography 645
Indian 241
statistics 563
Cunningham, E. 77
Currency 464, 466, 473-474, 478
exchange rates 18
Current Anthropology 128
Current History 345
Current national bibliographies of Latin America 648

D

Dada Hirezi, H. 328, 442
Dairy farms 526
Dalton, R. 8, 206
Damas, A. Rivera 269
Danaher, K. 410
Dance 245
Daugherty, H. 566
David J. Guzmán

National Museum 235
Davis, L. H. 510
De Zendegui, G. 20
Debt 465, 469
foreign 457
Decision making by farmers and by the National Agricultural Research program on the adoption and development of maize . . . 527
Deere, C. 511
Defense Mapping Agency 54, 56
Deficit financing 469
Delgado 561
Delgado, E. 441
Delgado, J. M. 181, 636
Demarest, A. 116, 117
Democracies and tyrannies of the Caribbean 82
Democracy 348, 349
Democratic Revolutionary Front (FDR) 211, 342, 458
Demographic crisis 224
Demographic indicators 228
Demographic Yearbook 227
Demography 20, 219, 228, 277, 291
statistics 558, 560
Demonstration elections 336
Dependency 135-136, 152, 224, 277, 284, 392, 442
Dependency and development in Latin America 136
Dependency theory 136, 487
Dependent capitalism 204
Derechos humanos en El Salvador en 1986 303

Desarrollo Económico 278
Desarrollo literario de El Salvador 597
Descripción geográfica y estadística de la República de El Salvador 30
Descripción geográfico-moral de la diócesis de Goathemala 166
Destler, I. M. 339
Determinants of direct foreign investment in the Central American Common Market, 1954-1970 475
Deuda externa salvadoreña 457
Development and Change 511
Development assistance in Central America 449
Development of geological resources in El Salvador 44
Devine, F. 92
Diagnóstico estadístico y proyecciones de la educación primaria 572
Diagnóstico social: situación actual de las necesidades básicas 287
Diario de Hoy 620
Diario del Occidente 621
Diario Latino 619
Diario Oficial 371
Díaz, G. Yañes 568, 609
Díaz, S. Infante 653
Diccionario biográfico de El Salvador 638
Diccionario de la literatura latinoamericana: América Central 599
Diccionario geográfico de El Salvador 33

Diccionario histórico enciclopédico de la República de El Salvador 636
Dickey, C. 339
Dictionary, geographical 33
Dictionary of tropical American crops and their diseases 528
Didion, J. 93
Diet 291
Directorio Comercial e Industrial de El Salvador, 1986 635
Directorio de El Salvador, Centro América 637
Directorio de legislación 372
Directorio General de Centro América 635
Directorio General de la República de El Salvador, 1920 635
Directorio Industrial de la República de El Salvador 635
Directorio Nacional de Establecimientos Industriales y Comerciales 1950 635
Diseases 519, 522, 528, 637
Diskin, M. 325, 406, 411, 525
Displaced persons in El Salvador 315
Dissent 355
Divorce 227
law 376
Dixon, M. 329
Documentos para la historia de la guerra nacional 188
Documentos y doctrinas relacionados con el problema de fronteras 385
Dollars and dictators, a guide to Central America 3

Domínguez Sosa, J. 185
Domínguez T., Mauricio T. 186
Dominican Republic 88, 336
Domino theory 429
Donovan, J. 253, 256
Downing, T. 512
Doyle, H. 651
Dozier, C. 513
Drost, T. 257
Duarte, J. 330, 354
Duarte: my story 330
Ducoff, L. 221
Dueñas C., A. 156
Dunkerley, J. 207
Dunlop, R. 62
Dunn, H. 60
Durán, M. A. 570
Durham, W. 222
Dutriz Hermanos 625, 627
Dutriz, R. 627

E

Earthquake
1854 70
1917 205
1986 290, 445
Ebaugh, C. 571
Ebel, R. 331-332, 430
ECA 630
Ecclesiastical power 255
Ecclesiastical structure 250
Echeverría, J. L. 465
Ecodevelopment and international cooperation, potential applications in El Salvador 566
Ecología humana en Centroamérica 226
Ecology 129, 222, 226, 291
maps 47, 50
Ecology of malnutrition in Mexico and Central America 291

Econometrics 488
Economía agraria y movimiento obrero en Centroamérica 551
Economía de El Salvador y la integración centroamericana 442
Economic analysis of the inland fisheries project 497
Economic Commission for Latin America and the Caribbean 564
Economic crisis 440
Economic development 221, 444-447, 449-452, 454-455, 465, 476, 533
  statistics 565
Economic development and cultural change 491
Economic development of El Salvador, 1945-1965 455
Economic indicators 443
Economic integration in Central America 441
Economic integration in Central America, empirical investigation 486
Economic planning 463
Economic policy 462
Economic potential for increasing vegetable production in the Zapotitán District 531
Economics 434-553
  bibliography 641, 646
  research 436
Economies of Central America 462
Economy 11-12, 16-17, 20-22, 32, 73, 75, 434-463, 469, 488, 515, 531, 629
  19th-century 61, 70

bibliography 640, 645
colonial 167
maps 45-47
planning 463
pre-Columbian 132
research 629
statistics 558, 560, 564-565
Edmonson, M. 241
Educación comercial en Centro América 576
Educación en Centroamérica 580
Education 180, 216, 569-582
  art 605
  bibliography 657
  business 576
  commercial 576
  elementary 572
  medical 285
  reform 573, 577, 581
  rural 572
  statistics 558, 563, 572
  university 570, 575, 578
  women 239
Education in Central America 582
Education in El Salvador 571
Educational reform with television: the El Salvador experience 577
Edwards, K. 560
Effect of increased water supply on net returns to dairy farms 526
Ekholm, G. 241
El Congo 232
El Salvador 6, 8, 16, 19, 88, 451
El Salvador 1986: en busca de soluciones para los desplazados 315
El Salvador 1987: salvadoreños refugiados en los Estados Unidos 314

El Salvador, a country study 5
El Salvador: America's next Vietnam? 428
El Salvador and economic integration in Central America 488
El Salvador and the crisis in Central America 427
El Salvador, antecedentes de la violencia 321
El Salvador at war: a collage epic 600
El Salvador: background to the crisis 7
El Salvador: beauty among the ashes 1
El Salvador: bibliography and research guide 645
El Salvador: Central America in the new cold war 387
El Salvador: crisis económica 440
El Salvador: crisis, intervención norteamericana y relaciones con Mexico, 1978-1986 398
El Salvador del siglo veinte 73
El Salvador: embassy under attack 92
El Salvador entre el terror y la esperanza 326
El Salvador, estudios de población 228
El Salvador . . . Exportable offer directory 483
El Salvador: historia de sus pueblos, villas y ciudades 163
El Salvador: human rights dismissed 306
El Salvador in crisis 17

194

El Salvador in pictures
10
El Salvador in revival
257
El Salvador in transition
324
El Salvador land reform
1980-81: impact
audit 525
El Salvador: landscape
and society 31
El Salvador: las fuerzas
sociales en la
presente coyuntura
281
El Salvador – Le
Salvador 14
El Salvador
News-Gazette 628
El Salvador: país de
lagos y volcanos 84
El Salvador: peaceful
revolution or armed
struggle? 343
El Salvador: ¿por qué la
insurrección 298
El Salvador: the face of
revolution 323
El Salvador, the other
war 310
El Salvador: una
democracia
cafetalera 327
El Salvador under
General Romero 305
El Salvador, un pueblo
que se rebelde 364
El Salvador: work of
thirty photographers
9
El Salvador y su
desarrollo urbano en
el contexto
centroamericano 568
Elam, R. 358
Elections
1960s 344
1972 354
1982 336
1984 336
Electric service 559
Élites 153, 182, 210, 217,
298, 325, 327, 355,
362, 392, 405, 409,
451, 487
attitudes toward sex
229
coffee 451, 327, 624
cultural attitudes 618
Ellacuria, I. 269, 440
Embassy, US 92
Employment 541, 543,
545
statistics 563-564
Encuesta sobre salarios
ocupacionales,
demanda de mano
de obra y formación
profesional 541
Energy, statistics 563
Enfermedad de Centro
América 318-319
English-American, his
travail by sea and
land 58
Ensayo histórico sobre
las tribus Nonualcas
y su caudillo 185
Entertainment 235
Environment 566-568
Erdozain, P. 258, 350
Erisman, M. 407
Esbozo biográfico:
Farabundo Martí
203
Escamilla, M. 35, 573
Escoto, J. Vivó 240
Español que hablamos
en El Salvador 243
Especies útiles de la flora
salvadoreña médico-
industrial 101
Espy, H. 90
Estadística Eléctrica 559
Estadísticas 556
Estadísticas de comercio
exterior de El
Salvador 482, 484
Estadísticas de las
Empresas Eléctricas
de Servicio Público
y Privado de la
República de El
Salvador 559
Estadísticas de Trabajo
543
Estado general de la
provincia de San
Salvador (año de
1807) 169, 220
Estampas y música
folklórica 245
Estrategía ante la crisis:
reconstrucción y
reactivación 445
Estudio centroamericano
de transporte (1974-
76) 540
Estudio de vías urbanas,
San Salvador 538
Estudio sobre
estratificación social
en El Salvador 282
Estudios
Centroamericanos
210, 274, 341, 397,
456, 460, 503, 581,
601, 630
Estudios de moneda y
banca de El
Salvador 474
Estudios del Reino de
Guatemala 171
Estudios estadísticos
respecto a las
riquezas naturales,
industriales, y
comercio 30
Estudios literarios:
capítulos de
literatura
centroamericana 592
Estudios sobre los
recursos naturales en
las Américas 43
Estudios Sociales
Centroamericanos
167, 200, 524, 631
Etchison, D. 359
Ethnic composition 637
Ethnography 232-233,
235-236
bibliography 235
glossary 124
Santa Ana 232
Sonsonate 233

195

Ethnohistory 241
Ethnology 241
  bibliography 655
Ethnomedicine
  bibliography 652
Ethnopharmacology
  bibliography 652
Ethnos 118
*Etnografía de El
  Salvador* 235
*Etnohistoria de El
  Salvador: el
  guachival
  centroamericano* 237
*Evaluación nutricional
  de la población de
  . . . El Salvador* 288
*Evaluation of factors
  limiting bean
  production in El
  Salvador* 519
Exchange, currency 18
*Experiment in
  regionalism: the
  Central American
  textbook project* 569
*Exploración etnográfica
  en el Departamento
  de Santa Ana* 232
*Exploración etnográfica:
  Departamento de
  Sonsonate* 233
*Export agriculture and
  the crisis in Central
  America* 530
Exports 483
  directory 483
  See also Trade

F

*Facts and artifacts of
  ancient Middle
  America: a glossary*
  124
Facts on File 23
Fagan, S. 396
*Failure of union: Central
  America, 1824-1960*
  141
Faith of a people 259

Falcoff, M. 412, 430-431
Faletto, Enzo 136
Family law 367, 376
Family planning 224,
  229, 239
Family relations 239
*FAO Production
  Yearbook* 514
FAO Trade Yearbook
  485
Farabundo Martí
  National Liberation
  Front *See* FMLN
Farer, T. 339
Fauna 67, 85, 99,
  104-109
FDR 211, 342, 458
Federación Cristiana de
  Campesinos
  Salvadoreños 552
Feinberg, R. 339, 413
Feldman, L. 171
Feltham, P. 493
Fernández, D. 389
Ferris, E. 312
Festivals, religious 247
Fieldiana: Zoology 105
Figeac, J. F. 150, 623
*Figurillas con ruedas de
  Cihuatán y el oriente
  de El Salvador* 113
Figurines 113, 126
  Olmec 114
Filibusters 188
Finance 478
  institutions 32
  statistics 563-564
Finance ministers 194
*Fire from the sky:
  Salvadoran
  children's drawings*
  606
Fisheries 497, 499
Fishing 43-44, 497, 499
  law 376
Fitzgerald, G. 373
*Five republics of Central
  America* 212
Flamenco, J. Mirando
  173
Flemion, P. 151
Flemion, Philip. 187

Fletcher, H. 566
Flora 67, 85, 99, 100-103
Flora and fauna 96-109,
  216, 241
  bibliography 98
Flora salvadoreña 100
Flora y Fauna 96
Flores Macal, M. 152,
  155, 167, 575
Flores Pinel, F. 333, 397
Floyd, Troy 168
FMLN 29, 211, 320, 334,
  338, 351, 353, 458
Fodor's Central America
  51
Folk culture 245
Folklore 245-246,
  248-249
  bibliography 249, 655
Fonseca, P. 37-38
Food 527
Food and Agriculture
  Organization of the
  United Nations 485,
  514
Football War *See* Soccer
  War
Foote, Mrs H. G. 70
*Forced native labor in
  sixteenth-century
  Central America* 17
Forced to move 311
Forche, C. 9, 414
Ford, I. 253
Foreign Affairs 334, 340
Foreign colonies 216
Foreign debt 457
Foreign Policy 425
Foreign relations
  385-433
Foreign residents 216,
  638
Forest
  maps 50
Forestry
  law 376
*Formas de tenencia de la
  tierra y algunos
  otros aspectos de la
  actividad
  agropecuaria* 520
Fortier Harrison, P. 295

Four keys to El Salvador
86
Fourteen families 153
Fox, R. 223
France
interest in
19th-century
Central America 69
Franck, H. 81
Frente Democrático
Revolucionario
(FDR) 211, 342, 458
Frieden, J. 417
From the ashes: justice in
El Salvador 307
Frontier, Mesoamerica
125
Fuentes y Guzmán, F.
172
Fuller, L. 417
Función política del
ejército salvadoreño
en el presente siglo
356
Functional analysis of
late classic period
Maya settlements
132
Fundación de la
Academia
Salvadoreña de la
Lengua 244
Fundación Salvadoreña
para el Desarrollo
Económico y Social
See FUSADES
Fundamentos
económicos de la
burguesía
salvadoreña 279
FUSADES 287, 437,
444-446, 469, 490,
515

G

Gaceta del Estado de El
Salvador 371
Gaceta del Salvador 371
Gage, T. 58
Galdames Armas, J. 161
Gallardo, M. A. 374

Gallardo, R. 375
Gallegos Valdés, L. 588,
598
Games 246
Gámez, J. D. 192
García Paz, A. 188
García, M. A. 636
Gardiner, C. 208
Gardner, D. 106
Garrido, G. 250
Gavidia entre raras
fuerzas étnicas: de
su obra y de su vida
591
Gavidia, F. 189, 589, 591
Gavidia, J. M. 589
Gavidia: poesía,
literatura,
humanismo 591
General Directory of
Central America 635
Geoffroy Rivas, P. 243
Geografía de El Salvador
35
Geography 20, 30-56,
61, 65, 67, 85, 99,
216, 241, 277
bibliography 34
children's 10, 16
coastal 41
economic 530
glossary 124
historical 31
research 34
Geología general de
Centroamérica y
especial de El
Salvador 42
Geology 35, 40, 43-44,
50, 67
general 42
maps 47
Georgetown University
270
Gerardo Barrios ante la
posteridad 192
Gerardo Barrios y su
tiempo 192
Gettleman, M. 387
Gierloff-Emden, H. 41
Gleijeses, P. 334
Gobernantes de El

Salvador
(biografías) 154
Godfrey, H. 52
Goldston, J. 548
Golfo de Fonseca y el
tratado
Bryan-Chamorro
395
Gómez Campos, J. 590
Gómez, J. Arias 203
Gómez, M. A. 583
González Casanova, P.
209, 215, 549
González, S. Rodríguez
395
Good Neighbor Policy
404
Goodman, F. D. 97
Gordon Rapoport, S.
398
Gordon, S. 360
Government in FMLN-
controlled territory
351
Government and society
in Central America,
1680-1840 147
Government officials 637
Government
publications
bibliography 650
Governors 144, 154, 377
Graham, N. 560
Granier, J. 642
Great Britain
diplomats 70, 198
interest in Central
America 70
Greenbaum, I. 104
Grieb, K. 415, 615, 641
Griffith, W. 140
Gringo Gazette 628
Gropp, A. 616, 642
Growth and integration
in Central America
480
Grubb, K. 260
Guachipilín 232
Guachival 237
Guardia Nacional
Salvadoreña, desde
su fundación . . . 214

Guatemala 139, 329
    19th-century 68
    20th-century 89, 209
    crafts 604
    description 76, 88-89
    missionaries 78
    politics of violence 345
    population density 225
Guazapa 335
Guerra, J. Vidal 490
Guerra inútil 392
Guerrero, R. 57
Guerrillas 95, 298, 320,
    338, 347, 351, 357,
    507
    women 239
    See also FMLN
Guevara, C. de 247
Guevara, Concecpción
    de 232-233, 246
*Guía de instituciones del
    estado* 383
*Guía para
    investigadores,
    República de El
    Salvador* 34
*Guide to ancient Maya
    ruins* 121
*Guide to libraries and
    archives in Central
    America . . .* 616
Guidos Véjar, R. 361
*Guión histórico de la
    Universidad
    Autónoma de El
    Salvador* 570
*Guión histórico del
    poder legislativo de
    El Salvador* 193
Guión literario 587
Gulf of Fonseca 395
Gutiérrez y Ulloa, A.
    169, 220
Gutiérrez, G. Mejía de
    235
Gutiérrez, M. 389
Guzmán, D. 101, 216
Guzmán, F. Fuentes y
    172
Guzmán, P. 567
*Gypsying through
    Central America* 77

H

Haberland, W. 118-119
Habsburg 142
Haefkens, J. 60
Hahn, W. 416
Haines, P. 576
Haiti 88
Hamer, F. 102
Hamilton, N. 417
Hancock, R. 83
*Handbook of Latin
    American studies*
    643
*Handbook of Middle
    American Indians*
    108, 241
Hansen, R. 447
*Harbor system of El
    Salvador* 539
Hardoy, J. 171
Harrison, I. 652
Harrison, M. 241
Harrison, P. 295
Haverstock, N. 10
Hay, C. 120
Health 180, 277, 292,
    295
    law 376
    statistics 563
Health care delivery
    bibliography 652
Health services 287
*Hegemonía del pueblo y
    la lucha
    centroamericana* 209
*Help or hindrance?
    United States
    economic aid in
    Central America* 410
Hemsley, W. 97
Herman, E. 336
Hernández Aguirre, M.
    591
Hernández Martínez, M.
    82, 213, 217,
    361-362, 404, 415
Hernández Pico, J. 272
Herrarte, A. 399
Herrera Cáceres, H. 400
Hesperiidae 107
Hidalgo Qüehl, G. 465

Highways 81, 533-534,
    540
Hirezi, H. Dada 328,
    442
*Hispanic American
    Historical Review*
    140, 146, 160, 168,
    177-178, 187, 236
*Historia de
    Centroamérica* 139
Historia de El Salvador
    165
*Historia de El Salvador,
    anotaciones
    cronológicas* 195
*Historia de la
    arquitectura
    contemporánea en
    El Salvador* 608
*Historia de la educación
    general y de El
    Salvador* 579
*Historia de la Federación
    de la América
    Central, 1823-1840*
    184
*Historia de la
    Universidad de El
    Salvador, 1841-1930*
    570
*Historia de las
    instituciones
    jurídicas
    salvadoreñas* 380
*Historia de las relaciones
    interestatuales de
    Centro América* 401
*Historia del Ministerio
    del Interior* 156
*Historia del movimiento
    obrero en América
    Latina* 549
*Historia militar de El
    Salvador* 149
*Historia moderna de El
    Salvador* 189
*Historical dictionary of
    El Salvador* 151
Historiography 140, 146
History 133-217, 255
    16th-century 57, 135,
    139, 142, 158, 160,

164, 171, 175-177
17th-century 58, 135, 139, 142, 172, 175-176
18th-century 59, 135, 139, 147, 166, 168, 170-172, 175-176, 178-179
19th-century 30, 60, 62, 63, 133-135, 137, 139, 141, 146, 148, 149, 150, 153-155, 158-159, 175, 180-201, 255, 263, 399, 401, 457, 474, 551
20th-century 19, 37-38, 73-74, 76, 135, 137, 143, 146, 153-154, 202-217, 279, 337, 341, 343, 346, 354, 356, 361, 391, 438, 442, 452, 455, 457, 465, 474, 530, 551
agricultural 503
banking 465, 472, 474
bibliography 641, 646
colonial 57-58, 84, 133-135, 142, 147, 150, 155, 158, 160, 164-179, 220, 255, 617
constitutional 375
demographic 220
diplomatic 198, 421, 424, 426
ecclesiastical 255, 262-263, 267
economic 31, 135, 142, 153, 155, 167, 170-171, 173, 176, 178-179, 182, 199, 212, 216-217, 279, 284, 337, 438, 442, 452, 455, 457, 465-466, 472, 474, 530
economic, 20th-century 84
education 570, 574-575, 578-579

foreign debt 457
general 15-17, 20, 31-32, 75, 86, 139, 143, 145, 151, 428, 636
historiography 140
intellectual 182, 597, 617
journalism 592, 617, 623
labour 177, 549, 551
legal 380
literary 597
local 37-38, 157-163, 384
military 148-149
Ministry of the Interior 156
political 216-217
pre-Columbian 84, 139, 165
research 615
San Salvador 158
social 142, 167, 216, 279
socio-economic 142, 145, 152
urban 37, 158-159, 161-163, 171
History and motivation of U.S. involvement in the control of the peasant movement in El Salvador 414
History of Central America 133
Hombres y cosas de Santa Ana: crónicas históricas 161
Honduras
19th century 67-68
description 76, 87-88
population density 225
refugees 311-312
relations with El Salvador 391-392, 400
travel literature 65
Honduras y El Salvador ante la Corte Internacional de Justicia 400

Hopkinson, A. 320
Hornik, R. 577
Hoselitz, B. 494
Hotels 18, 51, 205
Household composition 227
Housing 286-287, 290
law 379
statistics 563
Hoz y el machete: la internacional comunista en América Latina 202
Huguet, J. 223
Human Organization 550
Human Relations Area Files 123
Human resources of Central America, Panama, and Mexico 221
Human rights 28, 93, 239, 261, 285, 298-308, 310-311, 315, 418
bibliography 645
US policy 301
Human rights and United States policy toward Latin America 308
Humour 235
Hunger 506
Hunter, C. 121
Hunter, L. 339
Hunting 43
Hurlbert, S. 98
Hutchinson, M. 51
Hydrography 53-56
Hydrology 43, 47

I

Iglesia en América Central y el Caribe 250
Iglesias coloniales en El Salvador 609
Iglesias de los pobres y organizaciones populares 269

Iglesias, F. Valero 581
Ilopango 127, 132
*Impact of Monsignor
    Romero on the
    churches . . .* 273
*Impact of U.S. policy in
    El Salvador,
    1979-1985* 411
Imperialism 209
    US 392
*Incidents of travel in
    Central America,
    Chiapas and
    Yucatan* 61
Income tax 453
Independence
    movement 181, 189
*Indian crafts of
    Guatemala and El
    Salvador* 604
Indiana 238
Indians 113, 182, 230,
    234, 237-238,
    241-242
    crafts 604
    customs 596
    Maya 131
    mythology 596
    Nahuat 240
    Nonualca 185
    Pipil 111, 238
    population 78
    slavery 177
*Indicadores económicos
    y sociales
    CONAPLAN* 443
Indicators
    economic 443
    social 443
*Indice clasificado de la
    Relación breve y
    verdadera de
    algunas* 57
*Indice de legislación de
    la República de El
    Salvador* 372
*Indice de precios al
    consumidor* 561
*Indice de precios al
    consumidor obrero*
    561
Indice de precios al

*consumidor obrero
    en San Salvador,
    Mejicanos y
    Delgado* 561
*Indice del Diccionario
    geográfico de El
    Salvador* 33
*Indice geográfico de la
    República de El
    Salvador* 33
*Indigenous tropical
    agriculture in
    Central America* 513
Indigo 153, 167-168, 173,
    178, 190
Industria, ASI 495
*Industrial development
    of El Salvador* 494
*Industrialización y
    urbanización en El
    Salvador, 1969-1979*
    496
Industrialization 337,
    452, 496
Industry 16, 216, 277,
    455, 470, 491-499
    coffee 516
    exports 454
    flora 101
    seafood 499
    statistics 492, 563
    textile 493
*Inevitable revolutions:
    the United States in
    Central America* 421
Infante Díaz, S. 653
*Informaciones
    Económicas* 505
*Informe preliminar,
    investigación
    desplazados y
    refugiados* 315
*Inforpress
    Centroamericana* 11,
    22
Infrastructure 226
    statistics 564
*Inland transport in El
    Salvador* 534
*Inside Central America:
    the essential facts
    past and present* 4

Institutions
    government 383
    legal 380
    local 37
Instituto
    Centroamericano de
    Población y Familia
    296
Instituto de Derechos
    Humanos 303
Instituto de Estudios
    Económicos 448
Instituto de
    Investigaciones
    Económicas y
    Sociales 458
Instituto de Nutrición de
    Centro América y
    Panamá (INCAP)
    288
Instituto de
    Transformación
    Agraria 460
Instituto Geográfico
    Nacional 33
Instituto Salvadoreño de
    Investigación del
    Café (ISIC) 516
Instituto Salvadoreño de
    Seguro Social 297
Instituto Tropical de
    Investigaciones 535
Insurance law 376
Integration
    economic 393-394,
    396, 402-403,
    441-442, 447, 450,
    452, 461, 478, 480,
    486-488, 491, 498,
    540
    educational 580
    industry 498
    political 393, 403
    regional 402, 441-442,
    447, 450, 478, 480,
    486-488, 491, 580
    transportation 540
Intellectuals 182, 216,
    618
Intendants 175
Inter-American
    Commission on

Human Rights 304
Inter-American
    Development Bank
    453
Inter-American
    Economic Affairs
    510
Inter-American Law
    Review 471
Inter-American Review
    of Bibliography 644
Inter-American
    Symposium on
    Sanctuary 313
Interaction on the
    southeast
    Mesoamerican
    frontier 125
International agencies
    449
International
    Cooperation
    Administration
    (ICA) 470
International Court of
    Justice 400
International Review of
    History and Political
    Science 352
International Security
    423
Interpretación del
    desarrollo social
    centroamericano 284
Interstate relations 401
Investigación Económica
    337
Investment 376, 468-470
    foreign 2, 279, 439,
    475, 583
    law 376
Investment and industrial
    development in El
    Salvador 470
Ireland, G. 388
Ishuatán 233
ISIC. Carta Informativa
    516
Isidro Menéndez 378
Israel
    military assistance 389
ISSS. Estadísticas 297

It's no secret: Israel's
    military involvement
    in Central America
    389
Izalco 64, 233, 238
Izalco volcano 42

J

Jacir Simon, A. 337
Jackson, D. R. 517
Jamail, M. 389
Japanese 208
Jarves, J. 60
Jáuregui, A. Batres 134
Jeanneret-Grosjean, C.
    566
Jefes políticos 175
Jesuit order 263, 271
Jiménez, L. 289, 367
Jiménez, R. López 262
Johnson, F. 120
hnson, H. 153
Johnson, L. 359
Jonas, S. 329, 350
Jones, G. K. 642
Jones, P. 228
Jordan, W. 78
José Matías Delgado y el
    movimiento
    insurgente de 1811
    181
José Napoleón Duarte
    and the Christian
    Democratic Party
    354
Journal of American
    Folklore 249
Journal of Developing
    Areas 183, 229
Journal of Field
    Archaeology 131
Journal of
    Inter-American
    Studies 499, 523
Journal of
    Inter-American
    Studies and World
    Affairs 145, 208, 332
Journal of International
    Affairs 264

Journal of Latin
    American Studies
    325, 415, 438, 452,
    507
Journal of Politics 344
Journal of Social,
    Political, and
    Economic Studies
    338
Journalism 592, 617, 623
Juarros, D. 170
Juayúa 233
Juridical institutions 380
Justice, criminal 307
Justice in El Salvador: a
    case study 306

K

Kapp, K. 48
Karnes, T. 141, 430
Karush, G. 224
Kazel, D. 253
Kendall, A. 654
Kennedy, J. 359, 363
Kennedy, P. 89
Keogh, D. 261, 418
Kerr, D. 190
Kerr, K. 615
Kinkead, D. 171
Kirkpatrick, J. 430
Kissinger Report 419
Kissinger, H. 419
Klare, M. 420
Koebel, W. 75
Kornbluh, P. 420
Krehm, W. 82
Kruger, A. 338
Krusé, D. 645
Kuhn, G. 191
Kurzweil, J. 412

L

Labor rights in El
    Salvador 548
Labour 277, 281, 524,
    541, 545-553
    agricultural 551

Labour *contd.*
  American Institute for
    Free Labor
    Development
    (AIFLD) 414
  bibliography 640
  law 379
  organizations 2, 298,
    342, 550
  politics 553
  rights 548
  statistics 543
Labour code 546
Labour Party 593
Lacefield, P. 387
LaFeber, W. 339, 418,
  421
Laínez, J. 162
Lakes 84
Land
  reform 348-349
  tenure 31
Land beyond Mexico 76
Land reform *See*
  Agrarian reform
*Land reform and
  democratic
  development* 348
Land tenure 451, 503,
  506-507, 509, 517,
  520-521, 529
Land use 50, 506-507,
  513, 520-521, 529
Landarech, A. 592
*Lands and peoples of
  Central America* 87
Lange, F. 129
Langley, L. 12
Language 243
  Pipil 111
Lanks, H. 81
Lapper, R. 153
Lardé y Larín, J. 163,
  378
Lardé, Jorge 42
Lardé, José 158
Larín, J. Lardé y 378
Larín, R. Menjívar 457,
  549
Larraz, P. Cortés y 166
Latin America 25
Latin America 19– 24

Latin America, 19– 23
*Latin America and the
  Caribbean, a
  bibliographical
  guide to works in
  English* 640
*Latin America Economic
  Report* 25
*Latin America in the
  nineteenth century*
  659
*Latin America Political
  Report* 25
*Latin America Regional
  Reports: Caribbean*
  25
*Latin America Weekly
  Report* 25
Latin American Bureau
  305
Latin American
  Newsletters 25
*Latin American
  perspectives* 13, 138,
  264, 283
*Latin American Research
  Review* 199, 605
*Latin American urban
  research* 331
Law
  commercial 481
  family 367
  labour 546
Laws 378-379, 381
  19th century 381
  municipal 384
Lawyers 379, 547
Lawyers Committee for
  Human Rights
  306-307
Lazo M., F. 440
Lazo, A. Cardona 38
Lefebvre, A. 14
Legal institutions 380
Legal system 307
Legends 246, 248
*Legislación salvadoreña
  del café, 1846-1955*
  504
Legislation 372
  coffee 504
Legislators 352

  attitudes on
    population
    problems 229
Legislatures 193, 352,
  366
Leiken, R. 339
Leistenschneider, F.
  154, 377
Leistenschneider, M.
  154, 377
Lemke, D. 569
Lengua salvadoreña 243
LeoGrande, W. 340,
  350, 406, 422-423
Levenstein, H. 390
Leyendas salvadoreñas
  248
Liberalism 145, 180, 183,
  190-192, 196-197,
  200, 217, 364, 618
Liberal Party 255, 263
Liberation theology 252,
  259, 268, 321
*Libertad de imprenta en
  El Salvador* 623
Libraries 611-613,
  615-616, 656
  research 613-614
*Libro azul de El
  Salvador* 216
Limited democracy 209
Lines, J. 655
Linguistics
  bibliography 655
  glossary 124
  Indian 241
*List of books, magazine
  articles and maps
  relating to Central
  America* 647
*Lista preliminar de las
  plantas de El
  Salvador* 103
Literature 84, 585-600
  20th-century 598
  bibliography 588, 641,
    651
  folklore 249
  glossary 124
  Indian 241
Livestock 505, 523, 632
  statistics 502, 514

Lombardo, H. 518
Lommel, A. 424
Long war: dictatorship and revolution in El Salvador 207
Long, W. 536
López Jiménez, R. 262
López Pérez, C. 496
López Trejo, R. 362
López Vallecillos, I. 192, 210, 341-342, 457, 615, 617
López, M. 594
López, Roberto 457
Lorey, D. 565
Louvain, University of 270
Lovato, J. 649
Low intensity warfare 420
Lower Central America archaeology 122
Luers, W. 418
Luna, D. 155
Lundell, J. 537
Lungo, M. 290, 457

M

M.A.G. 502
Macal, M. Flores 152, 167, 575
Macaulay, N. 615
Maceo, G. Bustamante 149
Machismo 276
Mackie, S. 164
MacLellan, D. 291
MacLeod, M. 142, 615
Madriz, E. Altamirano 620
Maestre, L. Montúfar y Rivera 196
Magee, S. 123
Magnificencia espiritual de Francisco Gavidia 589
Maitre, H. 416
Maize 527
Makofsky, A. 550
Malaina, S. 263
Malaria 294

Malnutrition 288, 291, 503, 531
Man, crops and pests in Central America 522
Man-induced ecologic change in El Salvador 566
Managing the facts 302
Manual de historia económica de El Salvador 155
Manufacturing 462, 491
statistics 563
Maps 45-50
Central America 63
city 51, 54
Marchant, B. Pérez 638
Marihua rojo sobre beige y el problema pipil 118
Mariner's handbook 53
Markets 205, 239
Markman, S. 171
Marmol, M. 206
Márquez, A. de J. 248
Marriage 227, 376
Marroquín, A. 234
Martí Front for National Liberation *See* FMLN 211
Martí, F. 203
Martin, P. 73
Martín-Baró, I. 562
Martínez era: Salvadoran-American relations, 1931-1944 404
Martínez Peláez, S. 172
Martínez, A. 350
Martínez, J. 294
Martínez, M. Hernández 82, 213, 217, 362
Martínez, Y. Baires 452
Martyrs 253, 266
Marxism 321-322, 343
Masahuat 233
Masajuat 232
Masferrer, A. 593-595
Masferrer C. M. 595
Masferrer: alto pensador de Centroamérica 594

Mass media 336
Mass organizations 342
Matanza: El Salvador's communist revolt of 1932 202
Maudslay, A. 97
May, J. 291
Maya
archaeology 121, 128
corn field 131
ruins 121
Maya and their neighbors 120
Mayo, J. 577
Mayorga Quiros, R. 578
McAnany, E. 577
McCamant, J. 449
McClelland, D. 450
McClintock, M. 363
McColm, B. 343
McCoy, E. 497
McDonald, R. 344, 430
McEoin, G. 313
McGlynn, E. 656
McQuown, N. 241
McSweeney, B. 418
Medallions 473
Medals 473
Media, bibliography 645
Medicine 101, 235, 294-295
bibliography 652-653
Medrano-Vaquero, H. 519
Mejía de Gutiérrez, Gloria A. 235
Mejicanos 561
Meléndez doctrine 395
Meléndez, C. 395
Meléndez, D. 637
Melgar Callejas, J. 156
Memoria 505, 556
Memorias 467
Memorias of the republics of Central America and of the Antilles 650
Menashe, L. 387
Mendieta, Salvador de 318-319
Menéndez, I. 378

Menjívar Larín, R. 457, 549
Menjívar, R. 451, 520
Merchants, Guatemalan 168, 178
Mermelstein, D. 387
Mesoamerica 26
Mesoamerican archaeology, a guide to the literature 123
Mestas, A. de 84
Metapán 232
Meteorology 53
Mexico 89, 118
migration to El Salvador 240
refugees 312
relations with El Salvador 398
Meyer, M. 658
Middle America, its lands and peoples 36
Middle American anthropology 656
Middle American governors 144
Middle beat: a correspondent's view . . . 89
Migration 227, 314, 544
Nahuat 240
Pipil 111, 118
Miguel Marmol: los sucesos de 1932 en El Salvador 206
Militarism 204, 321, 359, 361, 363
Military 2, 148-149, 153, 214, 277, 283, 298, 324, 326, 333-334, 340, 342-343, 355-365, 389, 419
bibliography 645
professionalization of 180
Millet, R. 345
Millett, R. 339, 425
Mineralogy 40
Minimum wages 542
Mining law 376
Ministros de hacienda, 1838-1871 194

Ministry of the Interior 156
Minkel, C. 521
Miranda, S. Avalos 465
Mirando Flamenco, J. 173
Misión de América 593
Missionaries
US 78, 253, 256-257, 260
Mitla. A narrative of incidents and personal adventures 64
Mitras salvadoreñas 262
Modernization 182-183, 524
Molina y Molina, R. 193
Molina y Morales, R. 194
Molina, A. 575
Molina, M. Armas 111
Molina, M. Morales 364
Molina, R. 193
Moneda, los bancos y el crédito en El Salvador 472
Monedero, O. 608
Monetary policy, credit institutions, and agricultural credit in El Salvador 477
Money 464, 472-474
Monografía de la República de El Salvador 32
Monografías departamentales 37-38
Monteforte Toledo, M. 277
Monterrey, F. 195
Montes, I. Casín de 601
Montes, Santiago 237
Montes, Segundo 280-282, 314-315
Montgomery, G. 60
Montgomery, T. 211, 264
Montiero, P. 49
Montúfar y Rivera Maestre, L. 196

Monuments 205
Morales Molina, M. 364
Morales, R. Molina y 194
Morán, M. Castro 356
Moran, T. 339
Morass: United States intervention in Central America 429
Moreno, J. V. 432
Moreno, L. 401
Morris, F. 26
Mortgage law 376
Morúa C., Napoleón 538
Moser, D. 99
Moser, R. 14
Mosquito Shore 68
Mujal-León, E. 430
Multinational companies 439
Mundo 624
Mundo Deportivo 610
Municipal code 382
Municipal government 331, 384
Munro, D. 74, 212
Murdered in Central America 253
Murga Frassinetti, A. 551
Murrill, W. 103
Museo Forma 603
Museo Nacional David J. Guzmán 611
Museums 611
Muuser, C. 124
Mythen in der Muttersprache: der Pipil von Izalco in El Salvador 238
Mythology 237
bibliography 655

N

Naciones Unidas en el ámbito centroamericano; guía de estudio 432
Nación internacional, edición centroamericana 27

NACLA Report on the Americas 389
Nahuat migration 240
Nahuizalco 233
Nahulingo 233
Names, geographical 33
Nash, M. 241
Nathan Associates 470
National accounts 438
  statistics 563-564
National Agricultural
  Research Program
  527
National Guard 214, 216
National origins 236
National War
  Salvadoran
  participation in 188
Nationalism 217
Natural disasters 171
Natural resources 32, 40,
  43-44, 50, 65
Naval base 395
Navigation charts 53-54
*Necesidad de un nuevo
  modelo económico
  para El Salvador*
  446
*New El Salvador:
  interviews from the
  zones of popular
  control* 351
New Outlook 389
*New survey of the West
  India's* 58
*New World, A Journal
  of Latin American
  Studies* 136
New York Botanical
  Garden 103
New York Times 137
Newfarmer, R. 406
News 21-24, 26-29
Newspapers 619-625
  history 617
Newton, N. 58
Nicaragua 329
  19th-century 67-68
  20th-century 209
  description 87-88
  population density 225
  relations with El
  Salvador 395
  US public opinion of
  422
Nixon, R. 359
Nonualca 185
*Nonviolent insurrection
  in El Salvador* 213
Noone, J. 265
North American
  Congress on Latin
  America 323
North, L. 346
Notarial law 379
Notaries 376
*Notes on Central
  America* 65
*Notes on neotropical
  nymphalidae and
  hesperiidae* 107
*Noteworthy records of
  bats from El
  Salvador,
  Honduras, and
  Nicaragua* 104
Noticia 625, 627
Novoa, C. de 579
Nuclear energy law 376
*Nuestros maestros: notas
  para una historia de
  la pedagogía
  nacional* 574
Nugent, J. 486
Numismatics 464
Nunley, R. 225
Nutrition 287-288, 291,
  503, 531
Nye, J. 402

O

O'Malley, W. 266
Obras completas
  Lardé, J. 42
  Masferrer, A. 593
Obras escogidas
  Masferrer, A. 594
  Salazar Arrué, S.
  (Salarrué) 596
Obsidian 128
Oceanography 41
Oldman, O. 471
Oligarchy 207, 324-325,
  340, 342, 355, 362,
  594
Olmec 117
*Opciones para financiar
  el déficit fiscal de
  1987* 469
Oral tradition 235
Orantes, I. Cohen 394
Orchideen El Salvador
  102
Orchids 102
Orchids of El Salvador
  102
Ordish, G. 522
Orellana, V. 342
Organization of
  American States 453
  human rights 304
Orientación 626
*Origen, desarrollo y
  crisis de las formas
  de dominación* 152
*Orquídeas de El
  Salvador* 102
Ortiz, R. 539
Osborne, L. de Jongh
  86, 604
Overpopulation 283

P

Pacific coast
  development 523,
  526
*Pacific coasts of Central
  America and United
  States pilot* 55
Packenham, R. 136
Painting 602-603, 605
  20th-century 603, 605
Pajonal 232
Palmer, F. 72
*Palmerstonian diplomat
  in Central America:
  Frederick Chatfield*
  198
*Pan American highway
  from the Río
  Grande to the Canal
  Zone* 81

Panama
  description 87-88
  missionaries 78
*Panorama das literaturas
  das Américas* 598
*Panorama de la literatura
  salvadoreña* 588
Parker, B. 657
Parker, F. 15, 60, 657
Parkman, P. 213
Parsons, J. 523
Parties, political 316
*Paseo de recuerdo: San
  Salvador, 1900-1925*
  205
Pastor, M., Jr. 417
Pastor, R. 339
Patents 376
Patria del criollo 172
Paz, A. García 188
Pearce, J. 347, 426
Peasants 185, 202-203,
  206, 298, 347, 414,
  551-552
Peek, P. 544
Peláez, S. Martínez 172
Penal code 369
Peñate, S. Arias 503
Peninsulares 189
*Pensamiento social de
  Masferrer* 594
Pentecostal missionaries
  257
Pérez Brignoli, H. 135,
  143, 452
Pérez Marchant, B. 638
Pérez, C. López 496
*Periodismo en El
  Salvador* 617
*Períodos presidenciales y
  constituciones
  federales y políticas*
  377
Permanent People's
  Tribunal 328
Pesticides 519, 522
Petroleum law 376
Pharmacy 101
Phillips, P. 648
Photographers 9
Physical anthropology
  241

Pike, F. 267
Pinel, F. Flores 397
Pinto Soria, J. 174
Pinto, M. A. 619
Pintura en El Salvador
  602
*Pintura salvadoreña del
  presente siglo* 603
Pipil 111, 118, 238
  language 238
Place names 33
  Nahuat 240
Planning, regional 226
Planos urbanos 567
Plantations 637
Planters 178
*Población de
  Centroamérica y sus
  perspectivas* 218
*Población de El
  Salvador* 220
*Poblamiento nahuat de
  El Salvador y otros
  paises de
  Centroamérica* 240
*Poder eclesiástico en El
  Salvador, 1871-1931*
  255
Poetry 239, 245-246,
  248, 588-589, 591,
  600
Political economy 438,
  462-463, 530
*Political economy of
  Central America
  since 1920* 438
*Political ideology and the
  revolution of rising
  expectations* 316
Political parties 316
Political science 275
  bibliography 641
Political structure 32,
  281, 317, 363
Politics 11, 21, 277,
  316-365, 387, 411,
  463
  19th-century 61, 65-67
  agrarian policy 525
  bibliography 645-646
  contemporary 94, 207
  current 22, 25-26

  economic policy 444,
    446
  general 16, 20
  leaders 72
  Pipil 111
  statistics 565
*Politics and planners;
  economic
  development in
  Central America* 463
*Politics in Central
  America* 317
*Politics of regional
  integration: the
  Central American
  case* 393
Ponce, A. 57
Ponce, M. E. 653
Pons, G. 226
Population 38, 218-229,
  282-283, 296, 637
  16th-century 142
  17th-century 142
  18th-century 166
  19th-century 65, 169
  colonial 169
  history 142, 220
  Indian 241
  indigenous 234
  maps 45
  overpopulation 13
  prehistoric 132
  statistics 558, 560, 563-
    565
  trends 223, 226, 228
*Population and urban
  trends in Central
  America and
  Panama* 223
Population density 225
Ports 539-540
Porvenir 232
Positivism 190-191
Postclassic Project 127
Pottery 118, 126
Poverty 2, 224, 265, 405
Poverty of progress 183
*Pre-columbian man finds
  Central America* 130
Pregnant women 294
*Prehistory of
  Chalchuapa, El*

206

Salvador 126
Prelates 262
Prensa Gráfica 620, 625, 627
Presidents 377
Preston, J. 412
Preusch, D. 2-3, 310, 405
Prices 561
  statistics 564
Primera administración Reagan y El Salvador 408
Prisoners 285
Privatization 444-445
Proceedings of the XXXII International Congress of Americanists 119
Proceso. Informativo Semanal del Centro de Documentación e Información 633
Production
  19th-century 62, 65
  colonial 169
  statistics 563-564
Productive activities and economic contributions to family income of El Salvador women 435
Programa de reactivación de la caficultura 515
Pro-insurgency 420
Proletarian struggle 552
Promised land: peasant rebellion in Chalatenango, El Salvador 347
Property law 376
Prosterman, R. 348-349
Protestant missions in Central America 260
Proverbs 246
Provincianos 168
Psychology 293, 295
Public buildings 205
Public finance in a developing country: El Salvador 476

Public health 296
  bibliography 652
Public opinion 229, 422, 562
Puerto Rico 88

Q

Quantitative history 199
Qüehl, G. Hidalgo 465
Quelapa 110
Quigley, T. 418
Quiros, R. Mayorga 578

R

Rabinowitz, F. 331
Race and Class 153
Radio station YSAX 326
Raíces históricas del estado en Centroamérica 174
Railways 534, 536, 540
Railways of Central America and the West Indies 536
Rainbow countries of Central America 79
Rainbow republics, Central America 83
Ramos, F. Siliézar 473
Ramsett, D. 498
Rand, S. 105
Rapid development in small economies: the example of El Salvador 454
Rapoport, S. Gordon 398
Raynolds, D. 454
Reactionary despotism 325
Reagan doctrine 416
Reagan, R. 302, 334, 408, 411, 416, 422-423, 428, 511
  policy in Central America 94
Realidad dramática de la República: 25 años de traición . . . 362

Reber, V. Blimm 605
Recollections of Central America and the west coast of Africa 70
Recopilación de las leyes del Salvador en Centroamérica 378
Recopilación de leyes 379
Recopilación de leyes relativas a la historia de los municipios 384
Recopilación de leyes y reglamentos sobre trabajo y seguridad social 546
Recopilación de materiales folklóricos salvadoreños 246
Recordación Florida 172
Recordatorio histórico de la República de El Salvador 150
Red rumba: a journey through the Caribbean and Central America 88
Reed, R. 427
Reforma educativa salvadoreña 573
Refugees 310-315, 606
  bibliography 645
Regalado, T. 180
Regional Employment Program for Latin America and the Caribbean 545
Regional industrial development in Central America 498
Regional integration 393-394, 396, 402-403, 447, 450, 478, 480, 486-487, 491, 580
Regional integration in Central America 394
Relación breve y verdadera de algunas cosas . . . 57

Religion 235, 237, 250-274, 277
  colonial 166
  Pipil 111
Religion in Central America 260
Religious involvement in human rights struggle 298
Religious roots of rebellion 252
Rent law 379
Report of a medical fact-finding mission to El Salvador 285
Report of the president's National Bipartisan Commission 419
Report on human rights in El Salvador 299
Report on the situation of human rights in El Salvador 304
Repression 7, 305, 314, 341
Reptiles 105
Republic of El Salvador against the republic of Nicaragua 395
Repúblicas de Centro América 66
République de Salvador 69
Research 643, 645
  agriculture 501, 518
  anthropology 656
  archaeological 123, 129
  economics 436
  geographical 34
  historical 615
  social science 275
Research guide to Central America and the Caribbean 615
Research on agricultural development in Central America 518
Reseña histórica de Centro-América 196
Reseña histórica de la villa de San

Salvador, desde sus fundación 158
Resources 226
Résumes de Investigaciones en Café 516
Review of Politics 267
Revisor 371
Revista de Economía de El Salvador 448
Revista de la Universidad 634
Revista del Pensamiento Centroamericano 180, 191, 575
Revista Geográfica 225, 521
Revista Latinoamericana de Teología 268
Revista Mensual 556
Revista Mexicana de Sociología 333, 360, 392, 552
Revista Pecuario 632
Revolt
  1932 202-203, 206, 390, 594
  1944 213
  1948 204
  1979 333, 341, 356, 456, 578
  Anastasio Aquino 185
  peasant 185, 347
Revolution 329, 350
  1979 *See* Civil war, 1979-
  20th-century 209
  anti-Americanism 421
  causes 506
  literature 600
  Marxist 338
  poetry 600
  rising expectations 316
Revolution and intervention in Central America 329
Revolution in Central America 350
Revolution in El Salvador, origins and evolution 211
Revolutionary

Democratic Front (FDR) 211, 342, 458
Rhodesia, martyrs 266
Richardson, F. 120
Richer, X. 14
Richmond, D. 91
Richter, E. 13, 283
Riedinger, J. 348-349
Rift and revolution: the Central American imbroglio 430
Rivas, D. Castillo 439
Rivas, E. Torres 284, 350
Rivas, P. Geoffroy 243
Rivera Damas, A. 269
Rivera Maestre, L. Montúfar y 196
Road user charges in Central America 533
Roads 81, 533-534, 540
Robbins, C. 340
Roberts, O. 60
Robinson Wright, M. 71
Robinson, E. 125
Rochac, A. 472
Rodríguez González, S. 395
Rodríguez Ruiz, N. 380
Rodríguez, M. 197-198, 615
Role of the coffee industry in the history of El Salvador 190
Romero, A. 418
Romero, C. 305, 333
Romero, El Salvador's martyr 261
Romero, J. N. 412
Romero, O. 254, 258, 261, 264, 269-270, 273, 326
Romeu, J. 214
Rone, J. 299
Roosevelt, F. 404
Roots of rebellion: land and hunger in Central America 506
Rosal deshojado 593
Rosenthal, M. 628
Rothenberg, M. 339

Royal, R. 412
Royer, D. 455
Rubin, B. 339
Rubio Sánchez, M.
   175-176
Ruhl, A. 80
Ruins, Maya 121
Ruiz Granadino, S. 457,
   524
Ruiz, N. Rodríguez 380
Rural conditions 235,
   295, 506, 509
*Rural development, class
   structure, and labor
   force participation*
   553
Russell, P. 17

S

Sabloff, J. 241
*Sailing directions
   (enroute) for the
   west coast . . .* 56
*Salarios mínimos
   decretados en El
   Salvador, 1965-1986*
   542
Salarrué 596
Salazar Arrué, S. 596
Salazar Valiente, M. 215
Salcoatitán 233
Salitrillo 232
*Salud pública y
   crecimiento
   demográfico en
   Centro América* 296
Salvador 71, 93
*Salvador of the twentieth
   century* 73
*Salvador witness: the life
   and calling of Jean
   Donovan* 256
*Salvadorean indigo and
   the Guatemalan
   merchants* 168
Salvin, O. 97
Samaniego, C. 552
Same fate as the poor 265
San Antonio del Monte
   233

San Antonio Pajonal 232
San José, Costa Rica 39
San Julián 233
San Miguel 64, 159-160,
   175
San Miguel de la
   Frontera 160
*San Miguel y sus
   hombres: apuntes
   biográficos e
   históricos* 159
San Pedro Sula,
   Honduras 59
San Salvador 158, 175,
   382, 538, 561, 568
   18th-century 59
   20th-century 205
   labour 544
   religion 259
   urbanization 39
*San Salvador y sus
   hombres* 158
San Sebastián 232
San Vicente 64, 157, 175
Sánchez, M. Rubio 175
*Sanctuary: a resource
   guide* 313
Sanders, R. 16
Sanitation law 376
Santa Ana 161, 232
Santa Catarina
   Masahuat 233
Santa Isabel Ishuatán
   233
Santa Leticia 116-117
Santa Rosa Guachipilín
   232
Santiago de la Frontera
   232
Santo Domingo de
   Guzmán 233
*Scarcity and survival in
   Central America* 222
Schall, J. 271
Scherzer, C. 67
Schmidt, S. 428
Schmitter, P. 403
School teachers 246
Schoonover, T. 199, 615
Schoultz, L. 308
Schultze-Jena, L. 238
Science 583-584

statistics 563
Sculpture 120
Sebastián, Luis de 456
Secretaría Permanente
   del Tratado General
   de Integración
   Económica
   Centroamericana
   See SIECA
Secretariat for Economic
   Integration in
   Central America
   See SIECA
Semblanzas salvadoreñas
   590
Seminario Permanente
   de Estudios de El
   Salvador 457
*Seroepidemiological
   studies* 294
Settling into routine 299
Sevilla, M. 458
Sharer, R. 126
Sharpe, K. 406
Shaw, R. 487
Sheets, P. 127-129
Shenk, J. 323
Sherman, W. 177
Shrimp 499
SIECA 441, 555, 557
Siliézar Ramos, F. 473
Silva, J. E. 474
Simán, J. 273
Simon, A. E. Jacir 337
Simon, L. 525
Siri, G. 488
*Sistemas tributarios de
   América Latina: El
   Salvador* 453
*Situación demográfica,
   social, económica y
   educativa de El
   Salvador* 558
*Situación ocupacional en
   El Salvador, 1975*
   545
*Situación y perspectivas
   del empleo en El
   Salvador* 545
Situation in El Salvador
   309
Skutch, A. 106

Slavery 177
Slutsky, D. 392
Smith, R. 173, 178
Smith, W. & Associates
    540
Sobrino, J. 269, 272
Soccer War 222, 283,
    340, 364, 391-392,
    396-397, 400
  bibliography 391
Social anthropology 241
Social conditions
    275-297, 506
  statistics 564-565
Social Democrats 324
Social development 558
  statistics 564-565
Social indicators 443
Social organization 237
Social problems 285-291,
    629
Social sciences
  research 275, 629
Social security 546
Social services 292-297
Social structure 210, 224,
    250, 278-284
  19th-century 200
  bibliography 645
Social welfare 292-297,
    451
  statistics 564
*Social welfare
    programmes in El
    Salvador* 292
Sociology 275, 284
  bibliography 641
*Sociology and Social
    Research* 39
*Socios de la Cámara de
    Comercio e
    Industria de El
    Salvador* 639
*Soft war: the uses and
    abuses of U.S.
    economic aid* 405
Soils 35, 43, 50
Sol, R. 457
Solano, F. de 171
Songs 245-246
Sons of the shaking earth
    242

Sonsonate 64, 233, 526
Sonzacate 233
Soria, J. Pinto 174
Sosa, J. A. Domínguez
    185
Soto Blanco, O. 580
*South American
    handbook* 18
Soviet Union 413, 416,
    423, 431
  policy in El Salvador
    387
Spain, diplomats 84
*Spanish Central
    America: a
    socioeconomic
    history, 1520-1720* 142
Spanish, Salvadoran 243
Spores, R. 241
Sports 610
Squier, E. G. 65, 68
Standley, P. 103
Stanford Central
    America Action
    Network 350
Stanger, F. M. 236
State
  formation 200, 210
  historical roots of 174
*State terror and popular
    resistance in El
    Salvador* 363
*Statement of the laws of
    El Salvador in
    matters affecting
    business* 376
States of Central America
    68
States' rights 187
*Statistical Abstract of
    Latin America* 565
*Statistical and
    commercial history
    of the Kingdom of
    Guatemala* 170
*Statistical Year-book of
    the League of
    Nations* 563
Statistical Yearbook 563
*Statistical Yearbook for
    Latin America and
    the Caribbean* 564

Statistics 18, 216,
    554-565
  agriculture 514
  colonial 169
  ecclesiastical 250
  economy 456
  health 297
  historical 30
  labour 543
  military 359
  population 218, 227
  social security 297
  trade 484-485, 489
Steadfastness of the saints
    251
Stein, J. 350
Steinhauser, S. 107
Stephens, J. 61, 525
Stephens, J. L. 60
Stewart, T. D. 241
Stickney, B. 464
Stoltz Chinchilla, N. 138
Stone-cutting industry
    128
Stone, D. 129, 130
Stories 245-246, 248
Strategic Review 301, 416
Street plans 538, 567-568
Strong, D. 120
Stuart, L. 108
Studemeister, M. 351
*Student in Central
    America, 1914-1916*
    74, 212
*Studies in Comparative
    International
    Development* 224
*Studies in Political
    Economy* 346
Sugar 279
*Supplement to a
    bibliography of
    United States-Latin
    American relations
    since 1810* 658
Swedberg, R. 645
Switsur, R. 117

T

Taplin, G. 144
Taxonomy 98

Tax policy 444, 453, 461, 471
Tax reform 471
Taxes 453, 461
  bibliography 640
Taxes and tax harmonization in Central America 461
Teachers 246, 574
Technocrats 402
Technology 583-584
  statistics 563
Tecnología y ciencia 584
Telecommunications 537
  statistics 532
Telecommunications in El Salvador 537
Television 577
Temple, M. 349
Tempsky, G. F. von 64
Tenencia de la tierra y desarrollo rural en Centroamérica 509
Tentative bibliography of the belles-lettres of the republics of Central America 651
Tercer censo nacional de vivienda, 1971 286
Terremoto de octubre de 1986 en San Salvador 290
Territorial rights 376
Territorial waters 35, 53
Terrorism 420
Texistepeque 232
Textbooks 569, 581
Textile industry in El Salvador 493
Textiles 493
  Indian 604
Theology 268
Theology of Christian solidarity 272
Theology of liberation *See* Liberation theology 252
Theses, Universidad Centroamericana 614
They won't take me alive 239, 320

Thomas Gage in Spanish America 58
Thompson, G. 60
Thompson, J. 499
Thompson, W. 79
Thomson, M. 239
Time magazine 82
To bear a child: meanings and strategies in rural El Salvador 295
Toledo, M. Monteforte 277
Topography 50, 65
Torres Rivas, E. 284, 350
Torrisi, C. 475
Toruella, A. 626
Toruño, J. F. 591, 597
Tourism guides 51-52
Tozzer, A. 120
Trade 32, 216, 462, 479-491, 503
  19th-century 62, 65, 199
  agricultural 485
  coffee 488
  colonial 176, 178
  flora 101
  indigo 178
  routes 176
  statistics 482, 484, 489-490, 555, 557, 563-564
Trade unions 549-553
  women 239
Trademarks 376
Traditional medicine 652
Traditions 86
Transferencia de tecnología . . . 583
Transnational companies 439
Transportation 32, 45,. 77, 81, 84, 533-534, 536, 538-540
  statistics 563
Transportation Consultants, Inc. 540
Trask, D. 658
Trask, R. 658

Tratados, convenciones y acuerdos internacionales vigentes 386
Travel accounts 57-95
  bibliography 659
Travellers' guides 18, 51-52
Travels in Central America 62
Travels in Central America, 1821-1840 60
Travels in the free states of Central America 67
Treaties 386, 388, 401
Trejo, R. López 362
Tromp, S. Walle 44
Trouble in our back yard 325
Trueblood, F. 331
Trujillo, H. 200
Turner, G. 459
Turning the tide: U.S. intervention in Central America 409

U

U.S. and the rise of General Maximiliano Hernández Martínez 415
UCLA library 656
Ulloa, A. Gutiérrez y 169, 220
Ulloa, C. 381
Under the eagle: U.S. intervention in Central America and the Caribbean 426
Unemployment 287
Unfortunate Englishman . . . . A journey over land . . . 59
Ungo, G. 460, 581
Unidad Popular 342

211

Union
  Central American 141,
    184, 187, 201, 217,
    318, 394, 399, 401
  disruption of 168
  Unión de Centroamérica
    399
Unionist Party 318-319
United Nations 432-433
  FAO 485, 514
United Nations Fund for
  Population
  Activities 228
United Nations High
  Commission on
  Refugees 311
United Pentecostal
  Church 257
United Provinces of
  Central America 141
United States
  Agency for
    International
    Development
    (AID) 310, 315,
    405, 414, 449, 454,
    470
  anti-communism 423
  Army handbook series
    5
  Central American
    integration 403
  counter-insurgency
    363, 420, 529
  Department of State
    412
  diplomats 61, 65, 68,
    74, 92
  economic assistance
    2-3, 405, 410, 419,
    449, 454, 510
  educational influence
    581
  Good Neighbor Policy
    404
  House Subcommittee
    on Human Rights
    309
  House Subcommittee
    on Western
    Hemisphere Affairs
    365

  human rights 418
  investment 3
  involvement in
    Salvadoran elections
    336
  military assistance 2-3,
    357, 359, 416, 419,
    429
  military intervention
    426
  National Herbarium
    103
  policy in Central
    America 4, 12, 253,
    359, 395, 405-406,
    409-410, 412-413,
    416-419, 421,
    424-426, 429-431,
    449
  policy in El Salvador
    7, 82, 92, 253, 273,
    322, 334, 343, 353,
    357, 387, 395, 398,
    404, 406-409,
    411-416, 418, 420,
    422-423, 427-429,
    511, 633, 645
  policy in Nicaragua
    395, 409, 416, 512
  policy in the
    Caribbean 137, 412,
    426
  policy on human rights
    301, 308, 311-312
  public opinion on
    policy toward El
    Salvador and
    Nicaragua 422
  refugee problem 312-
    314
  relations with Latin
    America,
    bibliography 658
  Soccer War, 1969 392
  *United States and
    militarism in Central
    America* 359
  *United States efforts to
    foster peace and
    stability in Central
    America* 424
  Universidad 594

Universidad
  Centroamericana
  José Simeón Cañas
  264, 578
*Universidad para el
  cambio social* 578
University of El
  Salvador 436, 570,
  575, 636
Update Latin America 28
Urban development 37,
  568
Urban maps 567-568
Urbanization 223, 228,
  384, 496, 538
  San Salvador 39
US Army handbook
  series 5
USSR 413, 416, 423, 431

V

Vaky, V. 339
Valdés, L. Gallegos 588
Valenta, G. 430
Valenta, V. 430
Valero Iglesias, F. 581
Valiente, M. Salazar 215
Valle, R. H. 249
Vallecillos, I. López 192,
  341, 457, 615, 617
Van der Boomer, J. 228
Van Dyke, H. 395
Vaquero, F. 381
Vega, J. 274
Vegetation 43
  maps 50
Véjar, R. Guidos 361
Velasco, W. Chávez 619
Venceremos 29
Verner, J. 229, 352
*Vida militar de Centro
  América* 148
Vidal Guerra, J. 490
Vietnam 336, 429
  compared to El
    Salvador 7
Vilanova, S. 255
Villalobos, J. 353
Villalobos-Figueroa, A.
  98

Violence 251, 277, 285, 321, 345, 428
Violent neighbors 94
Vivó Escoto, J. 240
Vogt, E. 241
Voice of blood: five Christian martyrs of our time 266
Voice of the voiceless 270
Volcán de Izalco 42
Volcanism 127, 129
Volcanoes 44, 84
  Ilopango 127, 132
  Izalco 42
Von Tempsky, G. F. 64
Vornberger, W. 606

W

Wages 524, 541-542
Waggoner, B. 582
Waggoner, G. 582
Walker, S. 527
Walker, William 188
Walle Tromp, S. 44
Wallich, H. 476
Wallström, T. 85
War, 1969, with Honduras *See* Soccer War
War in El Salvador 353
War of the dispossessed: Honduras and El Salvador, 1969 391
Ward, L. 216
Washington Office on Latin America 28
Water law 376
  shortage 44
  supply 526
Watkin, V. 461
Wauchope, R. 241
Wayfarer in Central America 85
Wealth 458
Webre, S. 354
Weeks, J. 462

Welfare 292-297, 451, 564
Wellman, F. 528
Wesson, R. 317
West, R. 36, 241
Western Political Quarterly 316
Wheaton, P. 350
Wheel 113
White, A. 19
White, R. 429
Why the Christian Democrats of El Salvador abandoned . . . 328
Wiarda, H. 339, 430-431
Wilford, D. S. 477
Wilford, W. 477
Wilgus, C. 659
Wilkie, J. 565
Willey, G. 241
Williams, E. 430
Williams, Robert 530
Williamson, R. 39
Willmore, L. 491
Wilson, E. 217
Wilson, J. 60
Witness to war: an American doctor in El Salvador 95
Wolf, E. 242
Wollaston, N. 88
Women 239, 276, 294-295, 435
  bibliography 645
  image 276
  in revolutionary struggle 320
  legal status 367
  rights 289
  social condition 289
Women and war – El Salvador 239
Women of El Salvador: the price of freedom 239
Wood, B. 3
Woodward, R. 145-146,

171, 201, 615
World Affairs 271, 349
World Development 544
World remains: a life of Oscar Romero 254
Worldview 322
Wortman, M. 147, 179, 615
Wright, M. Robinson 71
Wright-Romero, L. 553
Wynia, G. 430, 463

Y

Yañes Díaz, G. 568, 609
Yearbook of Food and Agricultural Statistics 514
Yearbook of International Trade Statistics 489
Yearbook of the United Nations 433
Young, J. 478
Young, T. 60
Your El Salvador guide 52
YSAX 326

Z

Zaid, G. 355
Zamora Castellanos, P. 148
Zapotitán 127, 131-132
Zelaya, P. J. Chamorro 184
Zendegui, G. 20
Zier, J. 132
Zimet, D. 531
Zimmerman, I. 648
Zimmerman, M. 600
Zoo-noticias 109
Zoology 97, 109

Map of El Salvador

This map shows the more important towns and other features.

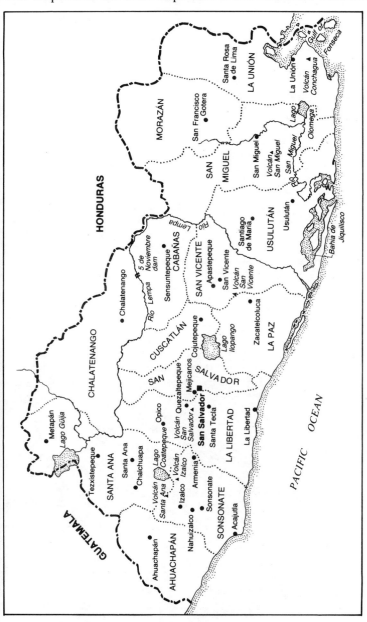